THE APARTMENT COMPLEX

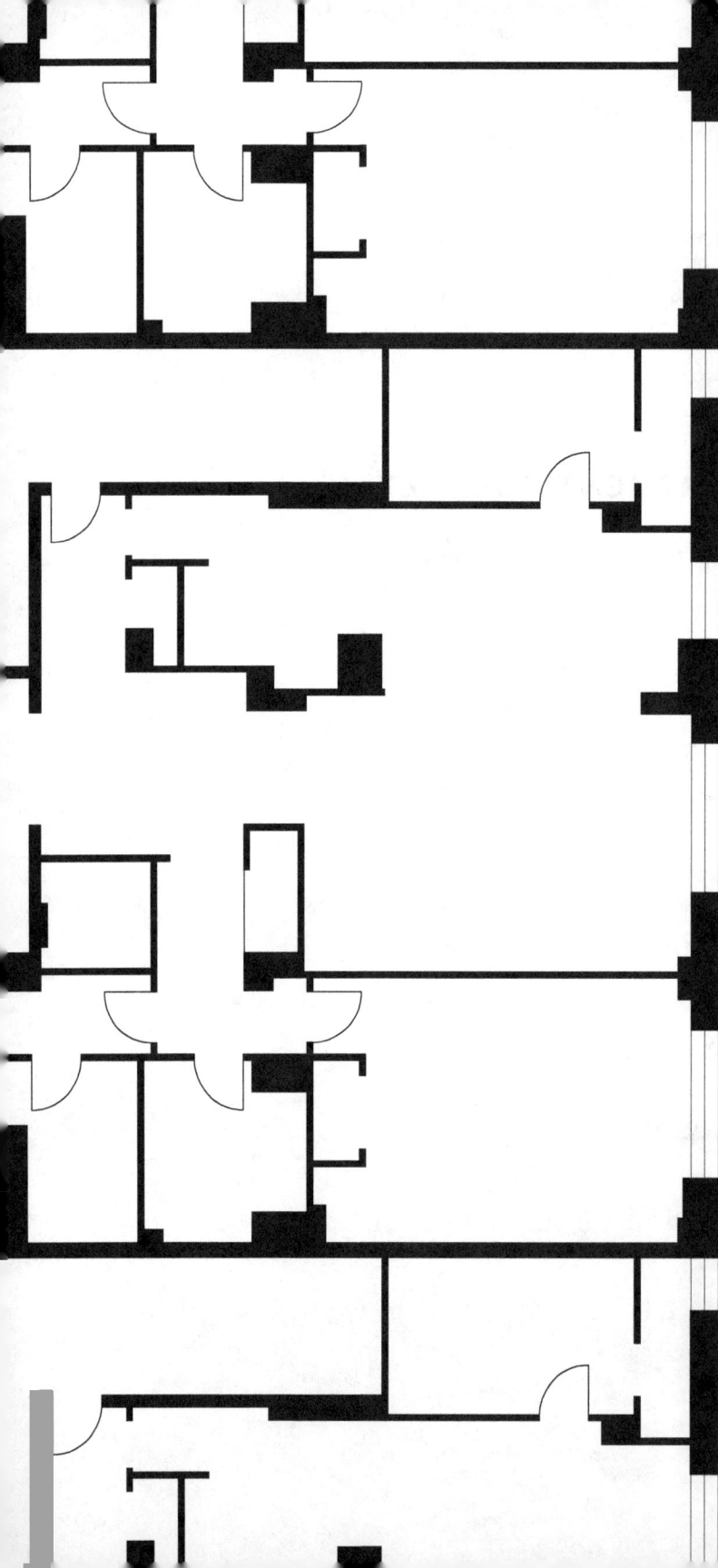

THE APARTMENT COMPLEX

URBAN LIVING
AND GLOBAL
SCREEN CULTURES

Pamela Robertson
Wojcik, editor

DUKE UNIVERSITY PRESS
Durham & London 2018

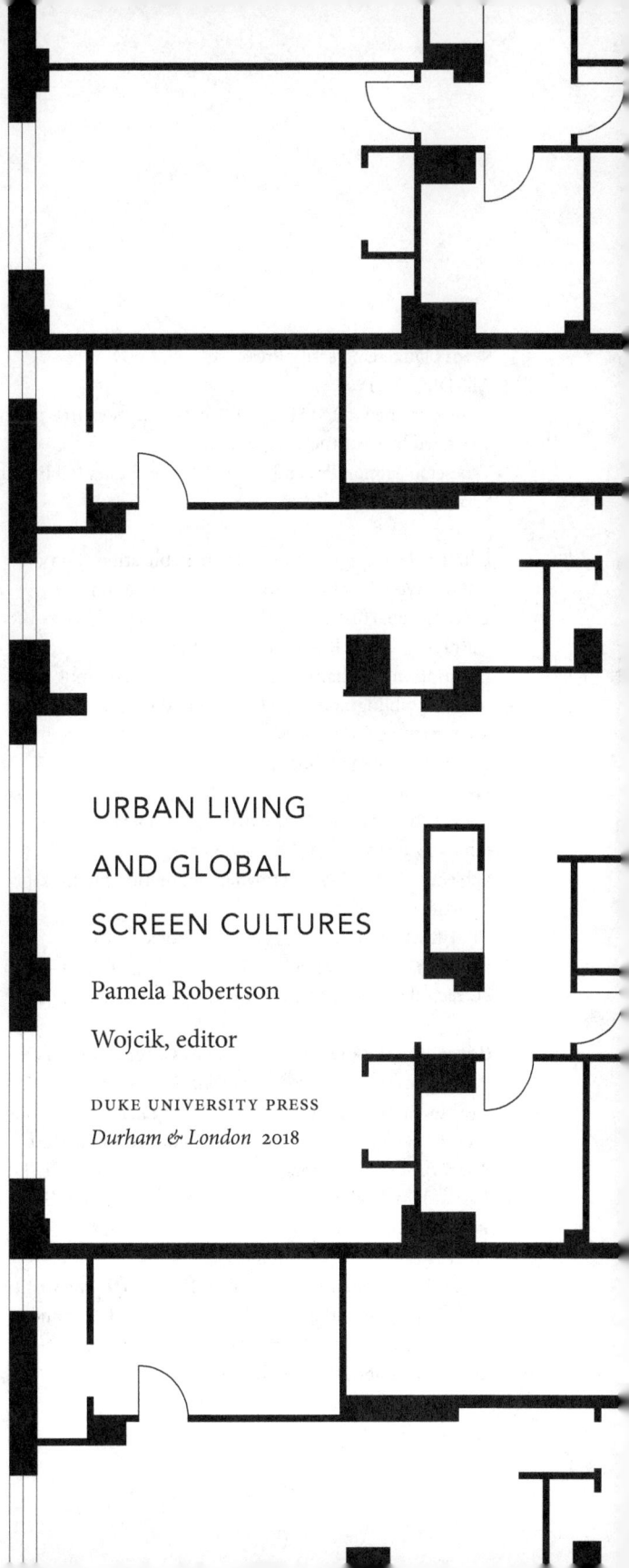

Printed in the United States of America on acid-free paper ∞
Designed by Courtney Leigh Baker
Typeset in Minion Pro and Avenir by Westchester Publishing
Services

Library of Congress Cataloging-in-Publication Data
Names: Wojcik, Pamela Robertson, [date] editor.
Title: The apartment complex : urban living and global screen
cultures / Pamela Robertson Wojcik, editor.
Description: Durham : Duke University Press, 2018. |
Includes bibliographical references and index.
Identifiers: LCCN 2018008256 (print)
LCCN 2018009533 (ebook)
ISBN 9781478002512 (ebook)
ISBN 9781478001089 (hardcover : alk. paper)
ISBN 9781478001423 (pbk. : alk. paper)
Subjects: LCSH: City and town life in motion pictures. |
Apartments in motion pictures.
Classification: LCC PN1995.9.C513 (ebook) | LCC
PN1995.9.C513 A63 2018 (print) | DDC 791.43/621732—dc23
LC record available at https://lccn.loc.gov/2018008256

Cover art: (*clockwise from top right*) *Concussion* (Stacie
Passon, 2013); *The Merchant of Four Seasons* (Rainer Werner
Fassbinder, 1971; Tango Film); *Ali: Fear Eats the Soul* (Rainer
Werner Fassbinder, 1974; Filmverlag der Autoren); *The
Apartment* (Billy Wilder, 1960); *The Wire* (season 3); *The
Easiest Way* (Jack Conway, 1931); *Double Indemnity* (Billy
Wilder, 1944).

Duke University Press gratefully acknowledges the Institute
for Scholarship in the Liberal Arts, College of Arts and
Letters, University of Notre Dame, which provided funds
toward the publication of this book.

This is for students at the
University of Notre Dame and
the School of the Art Institute of Chicago
who have taken
classes on the apartment plot
and enriched and expanded my
understanding of the genre.

CONTENTS

ACKNOWLEDGMENTS

This collection emerged after I saw a scholar give a lecture on recent Latin American cinema using my book *The Apartment Plot: Urban Living in American Film and Popular Culture, 1945 to 1975*. Pleased that someone had taken up the term, I started wondering how other people would talk about the apartment plot and what it would look like in relation to other cinematic and historical contexts. I invited scholars I know and respect to take up the apartment plot, and I encouraged them to engage in a conversation with my book, to trouble the term, to argue with it, and with me. I am indebted to the scholars here, who helped expand my understanding of the apartment plot as well as the canon of what can be called apartment plots. I am also indebted to the contributors for their patience. As collections sometimes do, this one took a while and went through some changes over time. The writers gathered here graciously accepted all delays and all my apologies. Attendees at two panels on the apartment plot at the Society for Cinema and Media Studies provided helpful insights and excellent questions. Patrice Petro, as respondent, offered particularly astute observations and suggestions for the introduction. I am grateful to the anonymous readers whose cogent comments helped us improve the collection, and to our editor at Duke University Press, Courtney Berger, for taking another chance on me. And I am grateful to all potential readers for taking some time to read these essays, and hopefully to watch some apartment plots.

WHAT MAKES THE APARTMENT COMPLEX?

PAMELA ROBERTSON WOJCIK

The Apartment Complex: Urban Living and Global Screen Cultures takes up the category of the apartment plot from my previous book, *The Apartment Plot: Urban Living in American Film and Popular Culture, 1945 to 1975*, to more fully explore the term and, at the same time, put some pressure on the category. This anthology is not intended to be a survey of apartment plots, nor should it be viewed as comprehensive. Instead, this book ruminates upon the following questions: How do different historical contexts modify the ideology of the apartment plot? How do variables of national or transnational context alter the genre? Do analyses of the apartment plot override readings associated with art cinema, auteurism, or traditional genres? Or, vice versa, how does a consideration of the apartment plot as genre make us see films associated with different national cinemas, particular auteurs, or traditional genres differently?

Some of these questions will be answered in the accrual of individual case studies as authors examine a range of films including classical Hollywood films—such as 1950s films by Billy Wilder and 1930s penthouse plots—Taiwanese and French modernist musicals, Fassbinder films, queer British films, indie films, European art cinema, and the American television show *The Wire* (2002). Readers will decide if they find convincing readings of such films as *Weekend* (Andrew Haigh, 2011), *The Hole* (Tsai Ming-liang, 1998), *Why Does Herr R. Run Amok?* (Rainer Werner Fassbinder, 1970), *Repulsion* (Roman Polanski, 1965), or *Jeanne Dielman, 23 Quai du Commerce, 1080 Bruxelles* (Chantal Akerman, 1975) in terms of the apartment plot, or consider the films illuminated by the analysis. By reading about apartment plots across different national and transnational production contexts, readers may find resonances across the diverse selection of films. Many possible apartment plots, nations, subgenres, and auteurs are absent here. My hope is that those who find the concept of the apartment plot useful will discuss apartment plots in other contexts and add to the larger understanding of the genre. My goal here is to map out the parameters of the apartment plot and consider how different historical, national, and generic contexts may alter or expand its definition.

The Apartment Plot as Genre

To begin a consideration of the apartment plot as a genre, at a minimum, we can identify cycles of apartment plots in fiction, film, and television. As Amanda Klein suggests, film cycles "are a series of films associated with each other through shared images, characters, settings, plots or themes."[1] While Klein argues that cycles must be financially viable and have "public discourses circulating around them," which would not be true, as such, of the apartment plot, she also describes cycles as often serving as proto- or pre-genres. In this sense, the apartment plot seems to be a genre that has developed out of a few prominent cycles. In her book *Apartment Stories*, Sharon Marcus identified cycles within the literary genre of apartment plots.[2] In nineteenth-century Paris, as Baron Haussmann's modernization of the city transformed the structure of apartments, Marcus finds a cycle of apartment plots as a subgenre of the realist novel; and in nineteenth-century London, the rise of subdivided homes creates a cycle of supernatural or haunted apartment plots. My book on the apartment plot examined a cycle of American films between 1945 and 1975. Bracketed by the end of World War II, on one end, and New York's municipal and financial crisis in the 1970s, on the other, this cycle emerged as the status of the city was up for grabs due to the rise of suburban domestic ideology and white flight, on the one hand, and, on the other, a massive postwar urban building boom tied to New York's emergence as the cultural capital of the United States.

In television, the apartment plot has been a consistent mode, even a cliché, since *I Love Lucy* (1951), and including *Mr. and Mrs. North* (1952), *My Little Margie* (1952), *My Friend Irma* (1952), *Make Room for Daddy* (1953), *The Honeymooners* (1955), *Love on a Rooftop* (1966), *Occasional Wife* (1966), *Family Affair* (1966), *The Odd Couple* (1970), *The Mary Tyler Moore Show* (1970), *Diana* (1973), *The Jeffersons* (1975), *One Day at a Time* (1975), *Three's Company* (1977), *Seinfeld* (1988), *Melrose Place* (1992), *Friends* (1994), *How I Met Your Mother* (2005), *Rules of Engagement* (2007), *New Girl* (2011), and more. More a consistent subgenre than a single cycle, the apartment plot has been a crucial unacknowledged mainstay of television.

More than merely a cycle, I argue, the apartment plot in film is a genre. At base, apartment plots are narratives in which the apartment figures as a central device. This means that the apartment is more than setting, but motivates or shapes the narrative in some key way. In *The Apartment* (Billy Wilder, 1960), for example, the plot hinges on C. C. Baxter (Jack Lemmon) loaning his apartment to a coterie of married men in hopes of advancement at the office. In *Rosemary's Baby* (Roman Polanski, 1968), when Rosemary (Mia Farrow) and Guy Woodhouse (John Cassavetes) rent an apartment in the chic gothic Bramford apartment building, they come into contact with their neighbors, the Castevets (Sidney Blackmer and Ruth Gordon), who initiate a satanic takeover of Rosemary's body to produce Satan's spawn. Thinking of the apartment as key to the plot eliminates many movies in which the apartment is only setting, such as Woody Allen films. In calling it a plot, I am not suggesting that every apartment plot will follow the same trajectory of events, but that the narrative could not occur without the apartment.

In an apartment plot, not only the space but also the temporality of the apartment structures the events. The temporality of the apartment may relate to the character's being young or single, but, more specifically, in terms of plot, the temporality of the narrative is usually shaped by the temporality of the apartment: beginnings or endings marked by characters moving in or out. Think of the beginnings of *Rosemary's Baby*, *It Should Happen to You* (George Cukor, 1954), *In the Mood for Love* (Wong Kar-wei, 2000), *The Visitor* (Tom McCarthy, 2007), *The Science of Sleep*

(Michel Gondry, 2006), or *The Landlord* (Hal Ashby, 1970), in which the narrative begins with the main character moving into a new apartment. Or consider the endings of *The Apartment, Klute* (Alan J. Pakula, 1971), *Rear Window* (Alfred Hitchcock, 1954), *The Bitter Tears of Petra von Kant* (Rainer Werner Fassbinder, 1972), *Sidewalls* (Gustavo Taretto, 2011), or *Bed and Sofa* (Abram Room, 1927), in which at least one central character exits the apartment, dead or alive, at film's end. *Breakfast at Tiffany's* (Blake Edwards, 1961), *Ali: Fear Eats the Soul* (Rainer Werner Fassbinder, 1974), *Apartment Zero* (Martin Donovan, 1988), *Dark Water* (Hideo Nakata, 2002), and *The Tenant* (Roman Polanski, 1976) are bracketed at the beginning and end by scenes of characters moving in, then out. There is a contradiction between the sense of dwelling—that characters are identified by and with a place of residence—and the sense that one's place is constantly changing, which relates to the sense of transience in the apartment plot.

In addition to having a narrative motivated by the apartment, the apartment plot is an urban genre. In distinction to the other major urban American genre, film noir, the apartment plot accentuates domestic urbanism. Film noir situates action in public spaces—police stations, diners, hotels, bars, phone booths, cars, streets. As Edward Dimendberg notes, much of film noir registers the failure of the protagonist to achieve an ideal of home: "The protagonists in *film noir* appear cursed by an inability to dwell comfortably anywhere."[3] In contrast, the apartment plot situates the urban inside the home, mobilizing urban themes of sophistication, porousness, contact, and encounter within the apartment.

The apartment plot is not only set in the city: it maps the protagonist's identity into his or her spatial location. Apartment plots tend to use aerial shots or other mechanisms to lay out a larger urban space before narrowing to focus on the apartment as a microcosm of the city. In this sense, the apartment plot suggests that each story is one among the millions possible, like the tagline for the TV show *The Naked City* (1958): "There are eight million stories in the naked city. This has been one of them." However, the apartment is never broadly representative of the city, but instead marks class and shows residential differentiation, or the idea that similar people live near one another (so that some people and some neighborhoods are excluded from the apartment plot). In mid-twentieth-century America, the apartment plot told only certain stories about mainly white, middle- to upper-class people living mainly in Manhattan's Upper East Side or West Side or Greenwich Village, rarely Harlem and never Brooklyn or Queens, let alone smaller cities such as St. Louis. Thus the space of the apartment not only motivates action but projects and delimits a character's identity, in terms of gender, race, ethnicity, and class.

Further, the gaze in the apartment plot needs to be understood as an urban gaze. As Marcus suggests, voyeurism is endemic to apartment life: "Apartment houses destroy private life by making each apartment simultaneously function as an observatory, theater, and mirror in which the residents of one apartment spy on those of another, providing unwitting spectacles for each other, and see their own lives reflected or inverted in their neighbors."[4] The apartment engenders passive spying, in which neighbors observe each other's lives with varying degrees of investment or attention. *Rear Window* makes this voyeuristic gaze its plot. *Pillow Talk* (Michael Gordon, 1959) shows the elevator man as an observer who tries to stop maid Alma (Thelma Ritter) from drinking so much. In *Cactus Flower* (Gene Saks, 1969), next-door neighbor Igor (Rick Lenz) witnesses Toni Simmons (Goldie Hawn) attempt suicide through the airshaft window and breaks in to save her. The urban gaze relates to the in-between status of the apartment as neither fully private nor fully public. The public privacy that Jane Jacobs identifies as central to the urban experience balances people's desire for some privacy and anonymity in the city with their desire for contact, enjoyment, or help from people nearby, or contact without entanglement.[5]

Beyond voyeurism, the apartment plot also hinges on eavesdropping. As both a theme and a device, apartment plots emphasize the porousness of urban life and of the apartment itself, in terms of sound as well as vision. Characters can sometimes see but not hear each other, and sometimes hear but not see. This enables mistaken identities, as when the doctor who lives next door to C. C. Baxter in *The Apartment* believes Baxter is a playboy because he hears parties in Baxter's apartment when Baxter's workmates use his apartment for their affairs. The anonymity of urban life is emphasized not only through offscreen sound but also through use of the telephone as a device to create a fissure between sound and body. In *Pillow Talk* and *That Funny Feeling* (Richard Thorpe, 1965), when characters meet who know each other only via the telephone, as disembodied voices, they do not recognize each other, thus enabling a mistaken identity plot.

The porousness of sound is only one form of porousness in the apartment plot. Space is both porous and permeable: doors and windows are less barriers than airlocks, or spaces of transition between places. Thus, the apartment plot often features open doors and windows and shows characters entering apartments unannounced and uninvited. Think of Kramer (Michael Richards) entering Jerry Seinfeld's apartment in *Seinfeld* or Lisa (Grace Kelly) gracefully entering Thorwald's (Raymond Burr) apartment through the front window in *Rear Window*.

In addition, the urban is defined in the apartment plot via simultaneity and synchronicity. Simultaneity allows us to see characters and apartments as separated but also creates the conditions of encounter. Encounter and contact are key to the urban generally, and crucial to the apartment plot. Devices such as crosscutting, widescreen, and split screen serve to show the relationship between apartments and produce the possibility of encounter. In *Pillow Talk*, for example, a split screen links characters played by Doris Day and Rock Hudson as each takes a bath, their toes appearing to touch at the center divide. *Any Wednesday* (Robert Ellis Miller, 1966) shows the triangulated relationship of Jane Fonda's kept woman, her lover, and his wife in split screen. Other films use scenes shot through open doors to show action in two apartments simultaneously. In *The Courtship of Eddie's Father* (Vincente Minnelli, 1963), for example, open doors show widower Tom Corbett (Glenn Ford) in one apartment, on the phone, calling his single neighbor Elizabeth (Shirley Jones) across the hall, for a date, as his son Eddie (Ron Howard) stands between the two open doors, beaming as a proud matchmaker.

Because the possibility of encounter dominates the apartment plot, whether to romantic or dangerous effects, the apartment plot features a lot of improvisation, masquerade, and play. Partly, this has to do with the possibility of encounter, insofar as masquerade enables anonymous encounters; partly with the sense of anonymity afforded by the city, the idea that nobody knows you, so you can be anyone; and partly with a conception of urbanism articulated by Jane Jacobs and Henri Lefebvre that views the city as "replete with improvisation" and "the moment of play and the unpredictable."[6] Numerous plots hinge on a character pretending to be someone else. This dominates variants of the apartment plot linked to romantic comedy, such as *That Funny Feeling*, *Pillow Talk*, *Any Wednesday*, *Lover Come Back* (Delbert Mann, 1961), and *Bells Are Ringing* (Vincente Minnelli, 1960), but also appears in the film noir apartment plot *Scarlet Street* (Fritz Lang, 1945) and the thriller *Wait until Dark* (Terence Young, 1967).

The apartment plot brings together these aspects of setting, theme, and stylistic devices to produce a philosophy of, or reflection upon, urbanism, by exploring urban living's forms and possibilities, and thus produces an imaginary urbanism. As a philosophy of urbanism, the apartment plot not only represents certain cities, such as New York, but also creates an imaginary urbanism, or a fantasy of the urban beyond a particular locale. It maintains and celebrates the urban against forces of suburbanization, sprawl, and the destruction of the city.

The Apartment Plot as Intertext

The apartment plot is not a genre of production or consumption. Directors do not, to my knowledge, describe themselves as making apartment plots, and the apartment plot will not show up as a search term for genre on Netflix or Amazon. Rather, the apartment plot is a critical genre, named after the fact, like film noir. Similar to film noir, it groups together films that were made under different traditional genre categories. Where film noir grouped a relatively small set of genres—detective films, crime films, thrillers—the apartment plot traverses numerous traditional genres, including musicals, romantic comedies, horror films, and film noir itself. Rarely would one characterize a film only as an apartment plot. Often it operates as a genre modifier or hybridizer, to characterize something as an apartment plot musical or apartment plot romantic comedy. For some, this may preclude its being a genre; but as a critical term—as opposed to a production or consumption term—the apartment plot works to open up a film for an alternate critical analysis. To do this does not require that we deny the film's affiliation with another genre, but that we pay attention differently. In an apartment plot musical, for instance, we would not only see the myth of spontaneity, as famously analyzed by Jane Feuer, but would be able to think about how the myth of spontaneity works in terms of encounter and porousness or produces a philosophy of urbanism by imagining the urban itself, and not just certain characters, as available to spontaneity and synchronicity.[7] An apartment plot horror film transforms the taken-for-grantedness of domestic space to remind us of the ghosts and past histories that rental properties carry and of the danger and risk of living in a world of porousness, permeability, and encounter.

As a critical genre, the apartment plot enables us to see affiliations across traditional genres. Moreover, because the apartment plot traverses so many other traditional genres, it invites us to consider how space sets the parameters for plots, themes, and ideologies of both individual films and genres. Rather than think of certain genres such as the western, the road film, and the apartment plot as spatially determined, thinking of space as the primary key to genre in general opens up possibilities to rethink genres in spatial terms, not only to define genre according to setting but perhaps to consider how certain genres use framing or tracking shots, or where certain characters are situated within genres (in public or private space, indoors or out, etc.).

As I have previously argued, space and place are more than just one lexical choice among many; they are imbricated in signifying structures that are historically determined and that carry tremendous connotative and ideological weight related to issues of sex, gender, class, race, the body, individuality, family, community, nation, work, pleasure, capital, and more. If we think of the apartment as motivating action, we can consider not only what the apartment enables that, for example, the home or the road or a ranch or a Broadway stage does not, but also what can't happen in an apartment: What are the limits of an apartment plot? Who can and cannot be represented within an apartment plot? The apartment plot reminds us of the ways in which space shapes our experiences, worldview, and opportunities.

As a critical genre, the apartment plot also shows affiliations across various auteurs. A consideration of the apartment plot reveals a preponderance of apartment plots in such directors as Wilder, Hitchcock, Polanski, Minnelli, Tashlin, Fassbinder, and Akerman, enabling us to deepen our understanding of their authorship, on the one hand, and, on the other, to see affinities among directors that an emphasis on the unique auteur may obscure. At the same time, analyzing films as apartment plots reveals hitherto unnoticed auteurs who work consistently within the apartment plot, such as Richard Quine (director of *Pushover* [1954], *My Sister Eileen* [1955], *Bell, Book and Candle* [1958], and *Sex and the Single Girl* [1964]) or Gene Saks (*Barefoot in the Park* [1967], *The Odd Couple* [1968], and *Cactus Flower*).

Because the apartment plot intersects with other genres and in the oeuvre of auteurs, we can view it as an intertext that creates correspondences among a wide variety of texts. So, as we acknowledge musicals such as *Bells Are Ringing* or *The Hole* as apartment plots, we not only invite consideration of how the musical informs the apartment plot and vice versa, as well as affinities between those musicals and others, but must also consider their relation to films that traditional genre analysis would demarcate as unrelated, such as the horror film *Rosemary's Baby* or the satire on race relations *The Landlord*.

Contextualizing the Apartment Plot

Apartment plots are imbricated by discourses of race, class, sexuality, gender, nation, and religion, and they speak from within systems of power, privilege, and capital. This collection, then, seeks to examine how the philosophy of urbanism shifts from 1930s America to 1950s America, to 1970s Berlin and Brussels, to late twentieth-century Paris, to twenty-first-century London, Taipei, and Baltimore.

Thinking about the apartment plot in a broader time period and more global context, the aspects of the genre—the basic themes and devices of the apartment plot—that I initially identified in *The Apartment Plot* stand. However, when we step outside the cycle of midcentury American films and consider the apartment plot in global context and into the twenty-first century, the philosophy of urbanism will differ because cities will mean different things in different locations and at different historical moments. As in any genre, the framework allows for different emphasis at different moments and in different historical and geographic contexts. (Think of changes in the western's ideology, for example, from the 1930s to the 1950s and in the present, as ideas about race and nation and violence have shifted.) The cycle of apartment plots in American film from 1945 to 1975 emerged because the meaning and status of urban living were undergoing a sea change, related to the rise of suburbanization, white flight, and the postwar building boom in New York. Even within that cycle, however, the subset of African American–centered films within the genre modified the philosophy of urbanism, to remind us that all residences—and their representations—are imbricated by discourses of race and class and speak from within systems of power and privilege. In a different vein, more recent films such as *The Visitor* and *Ghost Town* (David Koepp, 2008) transmute and negotiate issues of trauma, globalization, and immigration related to 9/11, absorbing and reframing themes of porousness, encounter, contingency, density, improvisation, simultaneity, and play in a new global context. Where *The Visitor* shows the utopian promise of contingency, encounter, and multiculturalism in an urban space for its white middle-aged protagonist, it also shows the dark reality of borders and surveillance for the undocumented immigrant couple who share his apartment. *Ghost Town* reworks 9/11 as a literal ghost story to suggest that the work of mourning is ongoing and reminds us to honor the dead by telling their stories, but it also revives the sense of community and empathy engendered by the attacks, thus placing new emphasis on encounter and contingency.[8]

The Apartment Plot considered issues of wealth and poverty as vital to the differentiation of tenants. For example, different economic expectations met white single men versus white single women in midcentury New York representations. Single white women in the apartment plot were most often characterized by a forced bohemianism that made poverty seem cute and that delimited the temporality of women's experience in the city, marking it as a reprieve from the trajectory that would lead them into marriage and suburbia, and away from working and from homosocial friendships. In a different vein, black films transformed the understanding of the suburban option as one that is not rejected in favor of urban living, but as an option that specifically and prohibitively excludes black residents, thus rendering the black apartment more of a space of containment than of encounter or mobility.

Still, *The Apartment Plot* did not, on the whole, consider the issues of austerity and capital as underpinning the apartment plot across the genre. In a genre that offers ways of thinking about cinema and modernity and that is centrally concerned with real estate, capital thoroughly informs and contours the meaning and affect of the apartment plot. Whether dealing with the monetized sexuality of women in *Jeanne Dielman, 23 Quai du Commerce, 1080 Bruxelles* or *Concussion* (Stacie Passon, 2013), issues of poverty and austerity in *Ali: Fear Eats the Soul* and *The Hole*, the role of real estate as aspirational in 1930s penthouse films and the TV show *The Wire* (2002), or gentrification in *Weekend*, the global apartment plot links apartment dwelling to the operations of capital.

Placing the Apartment Plot

Considering the apartment plot in global context, we need to think not only about global production but also about global spectatorship and the kind of border crossing and transnational travel we are invited to do through the apartment plot. As Giuliana Bruno and others have suggested, the experience of travel and the experience of cinema similarly move viewers to other places. At the same time, Bruno suggests that film spectatorship involves a kind of dwelling: "Film spectatorship," she writes, "is thus a *practice* of space that is dwelt in, as the built environment."[9] In Amy Lynn Corbin's provocative analysis, assuming that all films are tourism, in that they place us "there, where I am not," only some films maintain the touristic view by positioning viewers as outsiders, whereas others code the "landscape" as "familiar" and attempt to give viewers a "dwelling experience."[10] While the spectator still, according to Corbin, travels "there, where I am not," she quickly settles into an insider's experience or sense of what Edward Relph calls "vicarious insideness."[11] Of course, one person's exotic is another person's ordinary.[12] But Corbin argues that films position us as outsiders or insiders in ways that exceed or override our familiarity. So, for example, a suburban narrative may work to position the viewer as an insider, familiar with the landscape, taking the setting for granted to focus on something else, such as a child's friendship with an alien in *E.T. the Extra-Terrestrial* (Steven Spielberg, 1982). Alternatively, a film that aims to critique the suburbs may alienate us from our familiar view, as when *Pleasantville* (Gary Ross, 1998) deploys black-and-white cinematography to differentiate the 1950s suburb from the present-tense sensibility of its teen protagonists. In Corbin's analysis, when the film positions us as insiders, space operates as setting; when it makes us outsiders or tourists, space becomes plot.

Within the United States, given the dominance of suburban living, the apartment could be a touristic space for many viewers, and my emphasis on space as plot fits with a touristic positioning. However, for urban American or European viewers, the apartment dominates and would operate as familiar territory. But for spectators of the apartment plot in global context, we could imagine a spectrum of familiarity—so that a native New Yorker would not view *Rear Window* touristically but might view the British council flats in *Weekend* or the crumbling Taipei apartment block in *The Hole* as an outsider; and similarly, twenty-first-century viewers will find the penthouse apartments of *Susan Lenox: Her Fall and Rise* (Robert Z. Leonard, 1931) as potentially strange and distant modes of living.

We can think about how a film situates us, makes us familiar, even if we enter as tourists. The Argentinean film *Sidewalls*, for example, opens with a voice-over narration over a montage of images of residential buildings in Buenos Aires. Discussing the seemingly chaotic growth of Buenos Aires—the incoherence of building styles, the sense of bad planning—the narrator claims that architects are responsible for a host of maladies, including stress, obesity, and anxiety, and he suggests that the chaos reflects the inhabitants' own lack of direction and identity: "We live as if Buenos Aires were a stopover; we've created a culture of tenants." He describes the variety of apartments in the city, ranging from five-room apartments with balconies, playrooms, and servant quarters, to one-room apartments known as "shoeboxes," as a montage shows us examples of each. Acknowledging that "buildings are meant to differentiate between us," the narrator demarcates the hierarchy of front versus back apartments, high versus low, those marked letter A or B, and those marked with letters from the end of the alphabet. In four and a half minutes, he transports us from a touristic position, as outsiders who need to have Buenos Aires explained, to insiders, who can enter his apartment with some understanding that his fourth-floor shoebox, back apartment, in section H signals his low social status.

In the Japanese film *Dark Water*, likewise, we become situated in the apartment complex where single mother Yoshimi (Hitomi Kuroki) moves with her six-year-old daughter Ikuko (Rio Kanno). When Yoshimi and Ikuko are first shown the inexpensive apartment on the outskirts of the city by their real estate agent, Ohta (Yu Tokui), we see the dingy, unkempt building entrance as they do and discover the small vestibule office of the unfriendly apartment manager, Kamiya (Isao Yatsu), seeing the TV that shows him camera shots from around the building. We come to know not only the two-bedroom apartment that Yoshimi and Ikuko take, but the dirty hallways and elevators in their building, and the staircase up to the rooftop water tank that we visit several times over the course of the film. We become familiar with the growing water stain on Yoshimi's bedroom ceiling. Situated, we are not comfortable but conscious of the building's remoteness from the urban center, its shabbiness, and, increasingly, its creepiness as we, along with Yoshimi, become aware of strange occurrences, sounds, and dripping water, all signaling the ghostly presence of a girl who died under mysterious circumstances years before. We become dwellers in the apartment block so that our attention focuses on the supernatural events, not the touristic images.

If we think of dwelling as the place where one lives, then the global apartment plot will be primarily a touristic space for most viewers. However, if we take Edward Casey's notion of dwelling as built on familiarity and repetition—places one frequents as opposed to lives (and including such nonresidential spaces as malls)—then we can think of genre generally and the apartment plot in particular as a kind of dwelling space.[13] As

Casey states, "Dwelling places offer not just bare shelter but the possibilities of sojourns of upbringing, of education, of contemplation and convivial-ity, lingerings of many kinds and durations."[14] If we differentiate between shelter and sojourn, dwelling spaces can be seen as anywhere we hang our hat. In terms of genre, we can think of the way in which certain spaces that we have never visited become familiar to us through our frequent visits. For example, we become familiar with the nineteenth-century American West via the western, and with the beaches of Southern California through nu-merous Hollywood beach movies, starting with *Gidget* (Paul Wendkos, 1959).

Regarding the global apartment plot, even as we see tremendous variance in the kinds of buildings, cities, economics, and cultures, the apartment plot provides a means to connect spaces across the globe. In *Sidewalls*, for example, we discover something about the specificity of apartment life in Buenos Aires when we are shown the practice of tenants illegally creating new windows in their apartments. In an exterior shot, we see Martín (Javier Drolas), the male narrator, standing in his newly cut illegal window, framed by an ad for men's underwear (fig. I.1). An-other shot reveals the female lead, Mariana (Pilar Lòpez de Ayala), at the point of an arrow in her window (fig. I.2). This sequence of events marks specific practices in Buenos Aires that may not exist in other locations, and that suggest both the poverty of living and the anything-goes mode of making space in the city. At the same time, these scenes also work within familiar patterns of the genre of the apartment plot. A shot show-ing the relation of the two lead characters to one another, in facing apart-ments that tower above two smaller buildings, adheres to the apartment plot's generic practice of emphasizing simultaneity and synchronicity, and the promise that the two lonely inhabitants of shoebox apartments will join together (fig. I.3).

Similarly, while *Dark Water* shows specific aspects of Japanese life, in the way characters remove shoes upon entering the apartment, in the food shown when Yoshimi makes Ikuko dinner, in Ikuko's school uniform, and in the use of a futon on the floor for a bed, it nonetheless situates us in fa-miliar generic territory, as we encounter the ghostly presence who haunts the young girl and her mother through her intrusion into the space of their apartment, via the porous sign of water dripping from one apartment to an-other, through the pipes, and eventually in her visible presence in the room.

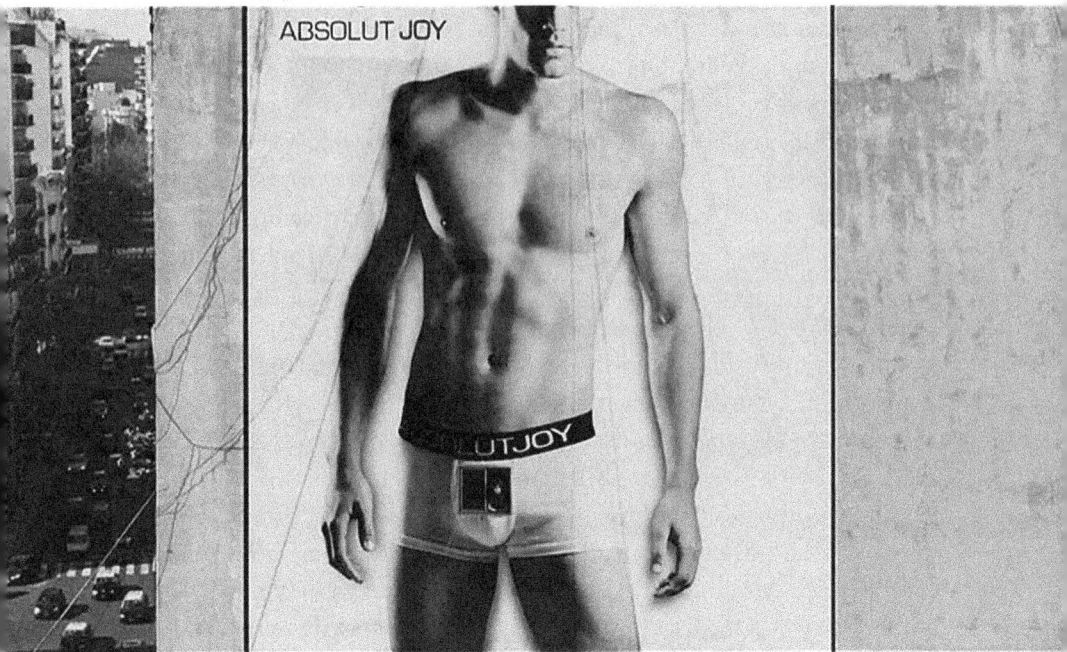

FIG. 1.1. Exterior shot of Martín's illegal window in *Sidewalls*
(Gustavo Taretto, 2011).

FIG. 1.2. Exterior shot of Mariana's illegal window in *Sidewalls*
(Gustavo Taretto, 2011).

FIG. 1.3. Martín's and Mariana's windows communicate with each other in *Sidewalls* (Gustavo Taretto, 2011).

Without losing sight of important differences, we can become vicarious insiders, inhabiting apartments across the globe, if only for a brief time. A consideration of the apartment plot reminds us of the spatiality of spectatorship, our own temporally marked dwelling in a space made familiar that allows us to dwell, if not be at home, across the global apartment complex.

Blueprints

The essays that follow each take up a different case study using the lens of the apartment plot as a critical tool for analysis. In Merrill Schleier's chapter on 1930s penthouse films, she argues that the penthouse is shown as "a sumptuous den of iniquity," peopled with characters who exist outside the traditional nuclear family, living in unorthodox and often immoral arrangements, especially self-indulgent, libertine married men and kept women (chapter 1). Frequently criminal spaces, penthouses are spaces of menace in which unfaithful and often criminal men attempt to control their domains but are punished for their acquisitiveness. In Schleier's reading, the penthouse films mark a shift in views of luxury living, away from the celebration of such spaces in the 1920s as sites of exclusive luxury and display, to a moralistic view in the 1930s, when Depression-era class consciousness rendered the penthouse a sign of overindulgence and moral compromise. Schleier contextualizes her readings of penthouse films using contemporary discourse in architecture, urban planning, shelter magazines, and real estate development.

Steven Cohan's essay retraces my steps in *The Apartment Plot* to consider mid-twentieth-century apartment plots; but his analysis offers a corrective to mine, focusing on the links, rather than the dissimilarities, between film noir and the apartment genre (chapter 2). He discusses the urban habitat of the single man as central to both genres and locates their intersection by looking at the films of Billy Wilder, an auteur associated with both genres. His intertexual analysis argues that Wilder's two noir films, *Sunset Boulevard* (1950) and *Double Indemnity* (1944), originate as incomplete apartment plots arising from intrusions upon a single man's domestic space, just as Wilder's two fully sustained apartment plots, *The Apartment* and *The Seven Year Itch* (1955), generally viewed as sex comedies, view urban bachelorhood from a cynical viewpoint more characteristic of film noir.

Joe McElhaney's chapter assays two modernist apartment plot musicals, the French film *On connaît la chanson* (Alain Resnais, 1997) and the Taiwanese film *The Hole* (chapter 3). McElhaney demonstrates how these two films hearken back to earlier musicals that mobilize the urban world as a hypothetical playground for romance and social success but also shows how the historical context and locale of each film problematize that notion. In the case of *The Hole*, set in a crumbling, dystopic Taipei, suffering a mysterious epidemic, McElhaney characterizes the film's final musical number as a magisterial representation of the musical's utopic impulses, as the Man Upstairs and the Woman Downstairs dance together in his apartment, facing either the end of civilization or their own imminent deaths. *On connaît la chanson*, set in contemporary Paris, does not, according to McElhaney, represent a world facing immediate extinction, but, immersed in a sense of French history, it nevertheless shows that such extinction was (and perhaps still is) immanent.

Michael DeAngelis, Annamarie Jagose, and Veronica Fitzpatrick each examine a European art cinema auteur, focusing on Rainer Werner Fassbinder, Chantal Akerman, and Roman Polanski, respectively. DeAngelis argues that using the lens of the apartment plot "provides keen insight into an elegant, kinetic system that [Fassbinder] devises to demonstrate, through a focus upon movement, a contention that fluidity and permeability in urban domestic spatial relations can never be politically neutral or universally accessible concepts, but rather mechanisms that are always already bound up in a self-perpetuating system of social relations harboring privilege and disadvantage" (chapter 4). In looking at Fassbinder's version of the apartment plot, DeAngelis suggests that we can see a crucial sociopolitical dimension of the apartment plot that deepens and expands upon the themes of the genre. Jagose contextualizes Akerman's film *Jeanne Dielman, 23 Quai du Commerce, 1080 Bruxelles* as not only a feminist film but also, significantly, a film about Brussels (chapter 5). Locating the film in a moment when grassroots protests successfully challenged drastic plans for urban renewal, Jagose argues that "the chronotope of the interwar apartment in a chaotically modernizing Brussels affords a new perspective on an issue that also but differently animates the feminist film reception of *Jeanne Dielman*, namely, how to engage the dense particularities of spatiotemporal experience across historical difference." Veronica Fitzpatrick's essay examines Polanski's *Repulsion* (1965), the first of his "Apartment Trilogy" films, which also include *Rosemary's Baby* and

The Tenant (1976). Fitzpatrick argues that auteurist analyses have largely ignored the generic significance of these films' urban domestic spaces to focus instead on character psychology and art cinema narration. Her analysis finds *Repulsion* at the intersection of Polanski's authorship and two genres—horror and the apartment plot—to produce a form of domestic horror "in which horror within the home works to formally surface an as-yet-submerged encounter with past sexual trauma" (chapter 6).

In her book *Lesbianism, Cinema, Space: The Sexual Life of Apartments*, Lee Wallace situates the apartment as a post-Stonewall chronotope of lesbian spatial identity. In her analysis, the apartment "assists the possibility of an out lesbian life that is not limited to a subcultural or institutional environment"—as are the pre-Stonewall backdrops of bar, prison, schoolroom, and college—"but avails itself of the peculiarly hybridized nature of multiple-dwelling space."[15] In her essay for this volume, she revisits the gay apartment, noting that "many of the coordinates by which we plot lesbian and gay stories have changed, the most significant being the legal recognition of same-sex domestic partnerships and the partial absorption of a sexual subculture into the dominant marriage culture from which it had previously derived its outlaw status" (chapter 7). She argues that *Weekend* and *Concussion* are apartment plots that speak from within the framework of gay marriage but mark the historical shift and changing conceptions of urban gay identity as they do so.

The final essay in the volume examines the TV show *The Wire*. Though *The Wire* is usually viewed as a police procedural or crime drama or located within David Simon's oeuvre, Paula J. Massood links it to both the African American gangster film and the apartment plot (chapter 8). Massood asks, "If the gangster genre is as much about acquiring the American Dream (in the form of social and economic belonging) as it is about criminality, then what happens when that dream is directly connected to real estate?" While some may view the show as primarily about gangs, drugs, and urban poverty, Massood suggests that it is fundamentally about real estate, notably in the figure of Stringer Bell, the gangster who rules the local drug trade but who is also partner in B&B Enterprises, a development company with key holdings in Baltimore's gentrifying downtown area, and a striver whose own apartment marks him as having achieved, briefly, the American Dream at the center of every gangster narrative.

Each of these essays offers insights into both canonical and lesser-known texts. Taken together, they suggest the pliancy of the apartment plot as genre, its ability to hold various kinds of narratives from different subgenres and authors and in different sociohistorical and geographic contexts. They provide a way to rethink the work of auteurs and see anew texts that would otherwise be seen under different generic categories. Most importantly, they show the ways in which the space of the apartment can be mobilized to engage philosophies of urbanism consisting of multiple iterations, revisions, and reframings. We see the meaning and value of porousness, privacy, simultaneity, and encounter shift in different contexts. And we see connections among and between apartment plots that seem far from one another—located in different cities, different times, different genres—that nevertheless speak to each other across the apartment complex.

NOTES

1. Amanda Ann Klein, *American Film Cycles: Reframing Genres, Screening Social Problems, and Defining Subcultures* (Austin: University of Texas Press, 2011), 4.

2. Sharon Marcus, *Apartment Stories: City and Home in Nineteenth-Century Paris and London* (Berkeley: University of California Press, 1999).

3. Edward Dimendberg, *Film Noir and the Spaces of Modernity* (Cambridge, MA: Harvard University Press, 2004), 7.

4. Marcus, *Apartment Stories*, 57.

5. Jane Jacobs, *The Death and Life of Great American Cities* (New York: Random House, 1961), 55–59.

6. Jacobs, *The Death and Life of Great American Cities*, 50; and Henri Lefebvre, "The Right to the City," in *Writings on Cities*, trans. and ed. Eleonore Kofman and Elizabeth Lebas (Oxford: Blackwell, 2003), 129.

7. Jane Feuer, "The Self-Reflective Musical and the Myth of Entertainment," in *Genre: The Musical*, ed. Rick Altman (New York: Routledge and Kegan Paul, 1981), 159–74.

8. These two films are discussed more fully in Pamela Robertson Wojcik, *The Apartment Plot: Urban Living in American Film and Popular Culture, 1945 to 1975* (Durham, NC: Duke University Press, 2010), 272–76.

9. Giuliana Bruno, *Atlas of Emotion: Journeys in Art, Architecture, and Film* (New York: Verso, 2002), 62.

10. Amy Lynn Corbin, *Cinematic Geographies and Multicultural Spectatorship in America* (New York: Palgrave Macmillan, 2015), 7–8.

11. Edward Relph, *Place and Placelessness* (London: Pion, 1976), 51–55.

12. Corbin, *Cinematic Geographies*, 8.

13. Corbin, *Cinematic Geographies*, 9; Edward S. Casey, *Getting Back into Place: Toward a Renewed Understanding of the Place-World* (Bloomington: Indiana University Press, 1993), 114–15.

14. Casey, *Getting Back into Place*, 112.

15. Lee Wallace, *Lesbianism, Cinema, Space: The Sexual Life of Apartments* (London: Routledge, 1990), 11.

1

Penthouses and politicians don't last forever, do they?
—*Susan Lenox: Her Fall and Rise* (Robert Z. Leonard, 1931)

PALACES OF PLEASURE
AND DECEIT AMONG THE CLOUDS

The Depression-Era Cinematic Penthouse Plot

MERRILL SCHLEIER

The last scenes of *Ladies' Man* (Lothar Mendez, 1931) serve as a paradigm of the Depression-era penthouse plot, in which the upscale dwelling drives the spatial and ideological elements of the film. The penthouse is a site of confrontation between its dweller, the effeminate gigolo Jamie Darricott (William Powell), and wealthy banker Horace Fendley (Gilbert Emery), prompted by Darricott's illicit affairs with both Fendley's wife and daughter. Darricott is outfitted in silken attire as the infamous Russian advisor Grigory Potemkin, the lover of Catherine the Great, for a costume party at the Fendley mansion, linking penthouses to the visual spectacle of parties, dissembling, gender dysfunction, and performance. The gun-wielding Fendley has come to Darricott's penthouse to threaten him for the double humiliation he has wrought but is momentarily thwarted. In the darkened confusion, which is a hallmark of cinematic penthouse space and temporality, Darricott wrestles the weapon from him and tosses it away. But Fendley is not dissuaded, taking the physical altercation to the penthouse terrace. Seen in dramatic close-up, Fendley soon gains the upper hand and forces Darricott's head over the ledge, just prior to the latter's plummeting. Such spatial metaphors as ascent and descent are often employed in penthouse plot films as a caveat to the audience that upward class striving in the decade's tarnished or Potemkin architecture will inevitably lead to tragedy.[1]

In such murder mysteries as *The Secret Witness* (Thorton Freeland, 1931), *Penthouse* (W. S. Van Dyke, 1933), *A Shriek in the Night* (Albert Ray, 1933), *Affairs of a Gentleman* (Edwin L. Marin, 1934), *The Ninth Guest* (Roy William Neill, 1934), and *Ellery Queen's Penthouse Mystery* (James P. Hogan, 1941), the action occurs almost exclusively in the penthouse, which structures the plot, the criminal intrigue, and the depiction of spatiality. Melodramas such as *Susan Lenox: Her Fall and Rise*, *The Easiest Way* (Jack Conway, 1931), *Ladies' Man*, *Possessed* (Clarence Brown, 1931), *Skyscraper Souls* (Edgar Selwyn, 1932), and *Baby Face* (Alfred E. Green, 1933) also include the lofty new apartment as a pivotal location that signifies sexual conquest, compromised upward mobility, and dishonestly acquired privilege.[2]

The Depression-era cinematic penthouse is never typical of normative domesticity, a place for the nuclear family or its daily occurrences. Prefiguring the apartment plot in film, especially after World War II, which creates a domestic urbanism composed of playboys, bachelorettes, gays and lesbians, and other nontraditional familial arrangements, the Depression-era cinematic penthouse likewise is a setting filled with nontraditional denizens in unorthodox arrangements. Yet it is often an unsafe recreational location for self-indulgent, libertine married men and bachelorettes, and frequently filled with menace and criminality—a nocturnal space of both possession and confusion in which residents, especially unfaithful men, attempt to control their domains but are punished for their acquisitiveness, in keeping with Depression-era morality tales. I explore how an urban philosophy and a style of life that commenced in the 1920s, which constructed the penthouse as an exclusive, sequestered sphere of designer-made luxury and privilege given over to visual spectacles, both natural and artificial, interior and exterior, circulated through the Depression-era cinematic penthouse plot. These views of the penthouse were promoted by such urban planners as architect and renderer Hugh Ferriss; *New Yorker* magazine columnist Marcia Davenport, who authored "New Apartments" under the pseudonyms "Penthouse" and "Duplex" from 1927 to 1930; articles in architectural periodicals and other shelter magazines that frequently featured the penthouses of various luminaries; and real estate developers who placed regular advertisements in tony magazines such as the *New Yorker* and *Vogue*.[3] However, by the 1930s with its economic debacle, the class-inflected ideas of architectural critic and urban historian Lewis Mumford had gained currency. Mumford viewed the penthouse's spectacular visual delights and putative privileges as irrelevant to the lives of common citizens who could ill afford them, which coincided with the skyscraper's fall from grace in popular culture and cinema.

Penthouses are hybrid spaces or spaces between: both apartments and not apartments, mansion-like domiciles atop skyscrapers that are often multiple stories in height, they conflate the public and the private, the indoor and the outdoor, the urban and the rural, and the everyday and the exotic. Situated in buildings composed of multiple units, they satisfy the wish for a private, sanctuary-like home while appealing to the need for more public services, fulfilling both individual (even mercenary) and collective desires.[4] I consider how filmmakers adopted their architectural structure and space, such as their high ceilings, numerous floors, expansive square footage, often ultramodernist decor, technological conveniences, and isolated locations (many were separate, seemingly free-standing dwellings on building roofs rather than simply upper-story apartments), pointing to the way material culture and its embodied ideology is mediated through set design and cinematography, in this case, to undermine it. In accord with dominant attitudes toward both real and fictional skyscraper space, the cinematic penthouse was viewed as a sumptuous den of iniquity, or what Simon Schama referred to in another context as an "embarrassment of riches," designed to create desire before material acquisition and class rise obtained through moral compromise were renounced.[5]

Air Castles Emerge

Cinematic penthouses were employed in response to the appearance of their real counterparts in the mid-1920s, prompted by a complex interaction of economic, legal, and aesthetic forces, including the post–World War I building boom in New York and the development of midtown around the new Grand Central Terminal, incentives that placed a moratorium on taxes for residential buildings, and new zoning laws, which had an impact on architectural design. In turn, the wealthy sold their stately homes in favor of the new "air castles" or "mansions in the clouds" because of the enormous savings in taxes, heating costs, upkeep, and servant salaries.[6]

Architects such as Emery Roth and Rosario Candela designed these new fifty-story, more dramatic apartment buildings and apartment hotels largely on New York's Park Avenue, which now replaced Fifth Avenue as the prestigious new penthouse address.[7] Roth imbued the penthouse level of his luxury buildings with dramatic architectural crowns; for example, his San Remo (1930) sported ten-story double towers with English baroque penthouse mansions, which were capped by an adaptation of the Choragic Monument of Lysicrates. Monikers such as the San Remo, the Marguery, the Berkshire, the Lombardy, and the Ritz that evoked the royal, far off, and exotic lent these lofty buildings additional publicity value and exclusivity. Hence, penthouses came freighted with an upper-class domestic pedigree normally reserved for mansions, estates, castles, and even historical monuments.

The penthouse was further prompted aesthetically by Hugh Ferriss and Harvey Wiley Corbett's design solution to New York's 1916 zoning ordinance, which limited the height and bulk of buildings. This resulted in the proliferation of a novel architectural idiom: the setback or art deco skyscraper, which sported more tapered upper stories, further differentiating the penthouse accommodations and providing both occupants and pedestrians with an enhanced visual experience. As Ferriss explained in 1929, "The effect of stepping back the building was to draw more attention to the uppermost floor; roof spaces began to be planned on a larger scale as servant's quarters; a few adventurous individuals began to lease some of these floors, throw two or three friends in the diminutive rooms and produce apartments which rather surprised their friends. . . . Realtors appreciated the point—that is to say rents were steeply raised and, at the present moment, the erstwhile janitor's quarters have become the most expensive rentable space in the building."[8] However, as late as the spring of 1926, a *Vogue* editorial claimed that penthouses were still illegal as living quarters in New York.[9]

Ferriss conceived of multileveled skyscraper cities as a solution to urban congestion; such cities would be composed of hundred-story skyscrapers topped by gardens and recreational spaces, with a series of multileveled, horizontal passageways that would accommodate pedestrians and various types of vehicular traffic, including air transport for penthouse dwellers. In Ferriss's richly illustrated book *The Metropolis of Tomorrow*, which represented a decade of work, he rendered penthouses as an integral component of his futuristic urban plan; indeed the city's upper sphere is the site of lofty apartments surrounded by spaces for public outings and entertainments. A penthouse owner himself, and anticipating its dramatic role in cinema, he showed a miniature of himself at an easel, gazing in awe at the metropolitan scene, while categorizing it as a "levitated stage box" where "some gigantic spectacle, some cyclopean drama of forms" of an urban play is about to be revealed.[10]

Havens of Extravagance, Romance, and Crime

Despite the emergence of penthouses by the mid-1920s, it was several years before they fully captured the public imagination, denoting luxury, taste, performance, and erotic play. The most well-known example was publisher Condé Nast's thirty-room duplex extravaganza at 1040 Park Avenue, which contained ten rooms for entertainment alone, including an enormous ballroom connected to a commodious solarium, where politicians and industrialists hobnobbed with famous actors and writers.[11] Nast's abode was so well publicized that it served as the springboard for publisher Van Stanhope's (Clark Gable) penthouse apartment in the film *Wife versus Secretary* (Clarence Brown, 1936).

Although penthouses were inextricably linked with New York modernity, they also made their appearance in Southern California and in Hollywood cinema, beginning with Cedric Gibbon's lavish set designs for the penthouses in *Our Dancing Daughters* (Harry Beaumont, 1928). Writing in the *Los Angeles Times*, R. P. White claimed in a competitive tone that successful civic leader and businessman General Walter P. Story's five-room villa of 1920 on the roof of the older Story Building (1909) was the first such apartment, but that the "penthouse craze" was now concentrated in Hollywood.[12] One of the most prominent downtown abodes in Los Angeles was haberdasher James Oviatt's ten-room penthouse, which he nicknamed his "castle in the air." It was outfitted with a Turkish bath, a gymnasium, a tennis court, a rooftop garden, a pool with sand to make a private beach, and thirty tons of custom-made Lalique glass imported from Paris. Fashion and domestic luxury met in both his clothing shop and his penthouse, which served as a destination for the Hollywood elite, including his friends Cecil B. DeMille, Clark Gable, John Barrymore, and the best-dressed Adolphe Menjou.[13]

Soon penthouse knockoffs of all kinds abounded, such as the glitzy stacked ashtray set christened Penthouse (c. 1935) and designer Norman Bel Geddes's copper penthouse cigarette box (1935), which were both seen as the epitome of sophisticated display. Several songs were even dedicated to penthouses, including Val Burton and Will Jason's "Penthouse Serenade (When We're Alone)" of 1931 and Fats Waller's "Pent Up in a Penthouse" of 1939, which depicted the sequestered apartments as havens of romance and heightened sensation.[14]

By the Depression, penthouses were portrayed contrastingly in the mass media and popular culture as places of deception, criminality, and murder, with frequently featured tabloid stories on the arrests that occurred therein. A typical *New York Times* article of 1933 reported on two former Sing Sing prisoners found by the police, "lounging in their silk pajamas on the terrace of a penthouse," amid closets that "were crammed with new and flashy suits."[15] Several pulp mystery novels that served as the springboards for films echoed these characterizations, highlighting the mysterious deaths of penthouse owners and inhabitants who hobnobbed with members of the underworld and other unsavory types. These included Gwen Bristow and Bruce Manning's 1930 novel, *The Invisible Host* (adapted to film as *The Ninth Guest*), Arthur M. Chase's *The Party at the Penthouse* (1932), Arthur Somers Roche's *Penthouse* (1933, adapted to the film *Penthouse*), and Ellery Queen's *The Penthouse Mystery* (1941, adapted to the film *Ellery Queen's Penthouse Mystery*). Even the cartoon "Penthouse" (David Fleischer, 1933) registers sexual predation as Betty Boop is spied on and then stalked by a monster in her skyward, cottage-like abode, testifying to the ambivalent view of penthouses during the economic downturn.[16]

Design for Living

A new design for living characterized penthouses, replete with heightened aesthetic features, enhanced technological amenities, and human services, which were a hypertrophic version of luxury apartments. Marcia Davenport's "New Apartments" column in the *New Yorker* celebrated all aspects of penthouse architectural space and style, frequently commenting on deluxe characteristics such as private elevators, multiple fireplaces, casement windows, French doors, sweeping stairwells between stories, and outdoor recreational spaces. In addition to sumptuous interior design, these castle-like apartment-hotel hybrids included improved services, such as uniformed doormen, showy lobbies, decorative elevator banks, switchboard operators, and a multitude of servants. Some even offered an array of recreational and commercial facilities on the premises. The London Terrace boasted about its well-equipped gym, its swimming pool, its restaurant with private dining rooms, and the variety of smart shops in its lobby.[17]

Penthouse apartments were most often showcased in shelter magazines devoted to architecture and the home or fashion periodicals, featuring the most stylish interior decor in a variety of foreign and indigenous idioms. Condé Nast's own *Vogue* magazine included a four-page spread on his penthouse in 1928, which was presented as untenanted so that viewers could project their own desires onto the luxurious dwelling.[18] Premier designer Elsie de Wolfe, who had written the influential *The House in Good Taste* (1913) and had previously designed for the Fricks and Vanderbilts, outfitted Nast's penthouse in her characteristic French rococo style with original Louis XV furniture.[19] The ballroom was full of exotic touches and royal splendor, with eighteenth-century Chinese wallpaper from Welbeck Abbey obtained from the home of a marquis.[20]

Yet other essays celebrated the modernist furniture and color schemes of several penthouse dwellings, an approach that was ultimately adopted by a majority of Hollywood set designers, such as MGM's art director Cedric Gibbons, who rendered the penthouse in *Our Dancing Daughters* with the most up-to-date furniture, an acknowledgment that the interior must coincide with the novelty of the architectural typology.[21] In an article appropriately titled "An Apartment in the Twentieth-Century Manner" of 1930, Helen Sprackling argued that the exigencies of the penthouse's architectural design, engineering, and industrial design necessitated a more modern approach to its decor. Well-known furniture and industrial designer Gilbert Rohde created skyscraper bookcases, chrome-accented furniture, and a neutral color scheme for a simple bachelor penthouse in Greenwich Village, which was viewed as the epitome of stylistic efficiency and decorum.[22]

However, modern-style furniture and up-to-date conveniences frequently assumed a more sinister character in Depression-era penthouse films. According to architectural and design historian Donald Albrecht and others, such accoutrements were seen as detrimental to the morality of the nuclear family, signifying waste, excess, and dissembling.[23] The perceived threat to traditional domestic tranquility was exacerbated by a host

FIG. 1.1. Trailer from *Penthouse* (W. S. Van Dyke, 1933).

of technological amenities, which were blamed for freeing women from their supposedly natural feminine duties as housekeepers and for leading men astray, thus disrupting traditional gender expectations.[24] In *The Secret Witness*, *A Shriek in the Night*, and *The Ninth Guest*, stylish skyscraper-shaped cabinets were filled with secret compartments, false fronts, and sinister electrical gadgets, which altered their real functions.

Advertisements, pulp fiction, and film further depicted penthouses as walled-off dwellings that kept their occupants distant from urban noise, grime, and the hustle and bustle of street life, an often-coded effort to high-light their detachment from the lower classes. Penthouses were pitched as presenting a new level of confidentiality and refinement, far removed from the scrutiny and surveillance of prying eyes, where married men and women, bachelors and bachelorettes could indulge in sexual liaisons with impunity, as seen in the trailer for the film *Penthouse*, which proclaimed them "fascinating palaces of pleasure among the clouds" (fig. 1.1) and the "newest abodes of luxury and secrecy."

In Arthur M. Chase's pulp mystery novel *Party at the Penthouse*, the character Mr. Carrington seeks the remote privacy of the Canadian Rockies in the heart of the city. While "the whole huge building . . . in the daytime" was "teeming with clerks and office workers and executives and telephone girls by the . . . thousand," in the evening, it was "empty except for a couple of night watchmen and an elevator runner."[25] Referring to his apartment as the Hermitage and himself as a hermit, Carrington celebrates his isolation and reveals his elitist pretensions. In contrast to an ideology of urbanism later promulgated by Jane Jacobs and others, which was characterized by tenant interaction and public exchange, penthouse promoters valorized individualism and avoidance.

Popular depictions of penthouse living capitalized on this exclusivity, explaining why they were viewed as havens for discreet romance. Typical of the penthouse's amorous reputation is the illustration for the sheet music for Burton and Jason's "Penthouse Serenade (When We're Alone)," featuring a luxuriously dressed couple on their skyward terrace, gazing at the picturesque spectacle of Manhattan by moonlight. The lyrics echo these attitudes:

> Just picture a penthouse way up in the sky
> With hinges on chimneys for stars to go by
> A sweet slice of heaven for just you and I
> When we're alone.
> From all of society we'll stay aloof
> And live in propriety there on the roof.
> Two heavenly hermits we'll be in truth
> When we're alone.[26]

The cinematic penthouse was more frequently an illicit erotic space, a precursor to Hugh Hefner's later *Playboy* pad, which was constructed as a location of promiscuous behavior amid the latest designs and technological appurtenances, where consumption and "aspirational fantasies" prevailed.[27]

Penthouses are also both urban and extraurban, combining the amenities of cosmopolitan living with the illusion of the suburban or even the rural, providing additional removal and refined aesthetic taste. Augmenting the penthouse's commodious interiors are its developed outdoor spaces replete with gardens, terraces, fountains, solaria, and ornate pavilions. Yet as landscape architect Ruth Dean pointed out in 1930, these gardens were as artificial as stage sets, serving as a perfect source for the cinematic set designer. Everything, including soil and plants, had to be imported and carried aloft and arranged to block off unsightly views with decorative vegetation or statuary. Several of these rooftops were so extensive that the *New York Times* reported on penthouse garden tours of Manhattan that commenced in the early 1930s, in addition to those in country locations such as Westchester and the estates of Long Island.[28] A *Vogue* editorial even called for them to imitate the hanging gardens of Babylon. Art critic Mary Fanton Roberts described one such Park Avenue terrace garden, which overlooked the whole city, as replete with tall, latticed fences, half-moon gates, comfortable chairs, concrete flower jars, and birdbaths. In this bachelor's abode, she wrote, "one corner of the garden is a little fountain which plays over colored lights and drips into a pool down over a border of deep ivy which trails to the ground." The effect was so exquisite that Mr. Anderson's friends came there "to rest, dream, or possibly to write a poem," further attesting to fantasies of privacy and self-indulgence.[29]

Lofty outdoor urban living also offered more commanding visual experiences, enhanced by the penthouse's unobstructed panoramic perspectives and sweeping vistas—what Roland Marchand has termed a "magisterial gaze"—which further connoted privilege and upper-class possession.[30] Architectural historian Meyer Wigoder argues further that skyscrapers, especially their roof gardens and observation towers, transformed urban viewers' perceptions, creating new spectators who sought creative expression of their singular identities and visions that were characterized by aesthetic cultivation and detachment.[31] From these high vantage points provided by terraces and French windows, various natural wonders and the urban picturesque were visible. Davenport of the *New Yorker* waxed poetic on such majestic exterior viewpoints, enabled by the "huge windows smiling out over the most expensive views in New York," which appealed to her so strongly that she "stood rooted to the flawless, polished floor, and tussled with the Ten Commandments."[32] Her prescient commentary foreshadows Michel de Certeau's observations on the scenes from atop the World Trade Center that fostered a feeling of omnipotence, "looking down like a god."[33]

While providing outdoor visual marvels of nature and the urban sublime, multiuse penthouses were also admired as havens for the interior and exterior spectacles they afforded, roomy and well appointed for leisure pursuits, especially upscale parties and entertainments. Penthouses are never depicted as mundane spaces in which the vicissitudes of daily life occur; rather they are rendered as spaces of recreation with special focus on commodious dining rooms, ballrooms, outdoor solaria, and gardens for guests. *New York Times* columnist and style editor Virginia Pope stated in 1930 that "a new chapter of social history" was "being written above the roof line." "Balls and dinners" were held during the winter months, while "garden parties," "al fresco teas," and "roof music" mingled with the gushing sounds of fountains in warmer weather.[34]

Penthouse Murder Mysteries and Melodramas

The penthouse plot in cinema emerged during the Great Depression, affected by the popular press reports on economic corruption, resulting in depictions of luxurious spaces of predation and class confusion. The optimistic urban ideology on the advantages of penthouse living proffered by Ferriss, Davenport, and others was dismantled in film and popular fiction, in which the lofty apartments' own structural and stylistic characteristics were seen as opportunities for manipulation. Cinematic penthouses were also depicted as penetrable, places in which heterogeneous classes mingled, where a dissembler or a social climber with a luxurious gown, a dapper suit, or even a feigned accent could claim entrance. Women who populated them were frequently mistresses, chorines, or down-on-their-luck working-class types who were tempted by male benefactors, yet ultimately were demoted to their class roots for their immoral behavior, committed suicide for their shame, or, in a few cases, gained redemption through marriage. Male occupants were often effete, feminized men, including businessmen, corrupt politicians, and playboys, who employed their penthouses as pied-à-terres for illicit affairs or backroom deals. For the criminal element or underworld, penthouses served as refuges of privilege and secrecy, hijacked as havens for profligate entertainments and illegal activities, especially bootlegging, economic subterfuge, and violent crime. For example, the preeminent and appropriately titled Pinnacle Club in *Penthouse* is owned by mob boss Tony Gazotti (Nat Pendleton), who assists lawyer Jackson Durant (Warner Baxter) in apprehending the murderer of chorine Mimi Montagne, who was shot on the penthouse terrace of a rival gangster.

The compromised female aspirant's rise to the penthouse pinnacle is often enacted spatially via cinematography. Gold diggers often begin in a lowly tenement or working-class flat (e.g., Laura Murdock in *The Easiest Way*,

FIG. 1.2. Laura Murdock ascends to the penthouse in *The Easiest Way*
(Jack Conway, 1931).

Whitey Wilson in *Wife versus Secretary*), a factory (Marion in *Possessed*),
or a flophouse (Lily Powers in *Baby Face*) and are tempted to transcend
their class roots by the penthouse's promise of an increase in social and
economic status. The camera explores each successive story of a Manhattan skyscraper's flank in *Baby Face* accompanied by the jazzy score of the
"St. Louis Blues," which adds a risqué flavor to the scene, registering the
heroine's awe and incremental class rise through the metaphor of spatial
ascension. The upward trajectories of both Lily Powers (Barbara Stanwyck) and Laura Murdock (Constance Bennett; fig. 1.2) represent their
exchange of sexual favors with prestigious men who inhabit the skyscrapers' upper stories.

A shift in attitude toward penthouses occurred during the Depression,
when skyscrapers in general, which many viewed as ciphers of American ingenuity and aspiration a decade earlier, came to be regarded as
"tombstones of capitalism" and wanton speculation, frequently linked to
the corruption wrought by the wealthy. Writing in the pages of the *New
Republic*, an anonymous journalist summed up these sentiments: "The

material embodiment of the late bull market remains in our metropolitan structures of towering heights. . . . But the spire on the graph has visibly collapsed. We can still see the buildings; they hover over the plateau of stability, the ironic witnesses of collapsed hopes."[35] Hence the views from the heights of these new mega–apartment buildings and their most luxurious abodes were no longer trained on the sublime; instead their denizens looked down on a city of economic ruin occasioned by speculation, of which they were its most flagrant monuments.

Lewis Mumford was a harsh detractor of skyscrapers as both dwellings and workplaces throughout the 1920s and 1930s. Concerned with the penthouse's impact on the common citizen, he viewed skyscraper apartments as confining, artificial spaces in congested urban spheres. In a direct challenge to Ferriss's futuristic cities that valorized penthouses and the sublime viewpoints they afforded, Mumford was concerned with the common citizen's quality of life. In 1925 he created a fictional dialogue between a critic (himself) and a Ferriss-like architect, in which the former claimed that the terraced buildings' upper apartments, as envisioned by the latter, would serve only the rich "if for no other reason than the cost per room in such a building would be far beyond the pocketbook of the great mass of manual and clerical workers."[36] The critic also claimed that instead of awe and mystical-religious feelings, lofty skyscraper apartments created terror and a sense of obliteration in the average urban dweller.

These attitudes led to a subgenre of film that commenced in 1931—the penthouse murder mystery. A shady male owner is frequently murdered during a party or following a forbidden erotic liaison, connecting the excess of penthouse celebrations directly with decadence and corruption. The idea that penthouses are superior places that provide their wealthy residents with privacy, serenity, and removal from the unsavory metropolis is recast in these murder mysteries and melodramas: penthouses here are portrayed as cloistered and artificial, as a trap set by stealthy criminals who leverage the inaccessible apartment to cause havoc and elude detection. The luxurious, enlarged domestic space of the penthouse that was celebrated by Davenport and others is now seen as confounding, a place where one can get lost, associate with the wrong people, or suffer unintended consequences. For example, in *The Secret Witness* and *A Shriek in the Night*, the murderer appears and disappears in the penthouse's darkened premises and is able to thwart detection, in part, by hiding in its convoluted environs. Lewis Leroy (Ralf Harolde) of *The Secret Witness* is a corrupt politician who kills the philandering penthouse owner, Herbert Folsom (Hooper Atchley), because he seeks to marry Folsom's estranged wife, with whom he is carrying on an affair, and thereby access the family fortune. Leroy conceals himself in various parts of the appropriately titled Crestview Arms, including the penthouse terrace and the building's basement, the former's shadowy underbelly.

The most dramatic depiction of the secluded penthouse as veritable trap occurs in the murder mystery *The Ninth Guest*, in which eight elite members of New York's glitterati are invited to an exclusive party supposedly in their honor given by an anonymous host. The guests include a society matron, a male politician and female lawyer couple, a political party boss, a university president, an actress, a writer, and a former college faculty member, referring to the prestige and heterogeneity of Condé Nast's guest list. Each of them receives an alluring but cryptic Western Union message announcing a party in their honor. The promise of a celebration that is shrouded in secrecy, glorified as a major advantage of penthouse life, lures them to the unfamiliar setting by appealing to their narcissism. Once they arrive, a disembodied voice that emanates from a centrally located, stylish art deco radio informs them that escape is possible only if they outwit their unseen host or the ninth guest, which is death.

Cinematography and set design are employed to underscore the penthouse's isolation from the rest of the city. A tilting shot of the fifty-story Manville Building terminates at its dark, narrow, stepped-back pinnacle, which establishes the detached penthouse's location. Remoteness is further accentuated in another scene, in which college president Dr. Reid (Samuel S. Hinds) builds a fire on the terrace to attract attention in the hope of being rescued but the evacuated building's loftiness ensures that no one at street level will respond to his primitive calls for help.

Once the guests are inside, an enormous electronically controlled iron gate, also viewed from above to suggest an evil, omniscient gaze, snaps shut to underscore that the penthouse is a point of no return, elucidating the negative view of modern conveniences and technology. Guests are later warned that trying to flee through the entranceway or touching the jerry-rigged radio will result in electrocution, a fate that subsequently befalls one of them. Telephone wires have been severed, further guaranteeing the penthouse's separation from the outside world. A reverse-angle, close-up shot displays the face of party boss Jason Osgood (Edwin Maxwell) peering into the radio's prison-like grillwork, as he tries in vain to bribe the disembodied voice to release him.

The interior environs of the cinematic penthouse often mimicked the most commodious and elaborate actual type, a duplex or triplex, characterized by high ceilings (averaging fourteen feet), numerous stories that were often connected by majestic stairwells, and multiple rooms. Traditional domestic house plans with bedrooms on the top story were altered in favor of sleeping quarters on the bottom level and recreation rooms above, which was seen in cosmetic magnate Helena Rubenstein's penthouse at 625 Park Avenue. *New York Times* columnist Virginia Pope reported in "Now the Penthouse Palace Is Evolving" (1930) that penthouse architecture had transformed conventional homes into unorthodox new configurations and arrangements, which might explain its cinematic appropriation as a nonnormative, uncanny space: "Who ever heard of a house with bedrooms on the ground floor, reception halls and sitting rooms on the second, and music rooms in the attic! Topsy-turvy it would have been called," she exclaimed.[37]

New cinematic floor plans underscore this disorientation as guests try to negotiate their way through the roomy, often perplexing penthouse in *The Ninth Guest*, a feeling that is echoed in the entire skyscraper apartment building. The film's penthouse is an intricate web of intrigue as the invitees attempt to discover the source of the commanding, intangible voice that issues its horrific orders from the living room radio. They divide up into groups in order to search its darkened interior for clues, finding hidden stairwells, trap doors, and false entries, one of which contains a dead body. As one of the search parties traverses a hallway, the expressionist-inspired vantage point and a cage-like stairwell seem to impale the silhouetted inhabitants, creating a sense of disembodiment that foreshadows their possible demise. The criminal is further able to capitalize on the penthouse's labyrinthine innards and murky spaces, leaving threatening written instructions throughout the dwelling while remaining undetected. Thus, the cinematic penthouse may be viewed as the Depression era's haunted house, carrying the stain of unresolved class conflicts and jealousies within its very structure, which functions as a return of the repressed.[38]

The mazelike interior space is echoed in the technological amenities and the streamlined furniture that were part of the most up-to-date penthouse interior design. However, technology in the penthouse murder mystery is rendered as a hidden force that can be marshaled for pernicious ends. The killer manipulates electricity to create confusion while he tries to escape (*The Secret Witness*, *The Ninth Guest*, *A Shriek in the Night*). Record players and radios in art moderne–styled cabinets are also harnessed in at least two films to deflect attention from the real criminal. Lewis Leroy in *The Secret Witness* positions the murder weapon in the radio cabinet, which is programmed to discharge and kill penthouse owner Herbert Folsom when the latter turns on the radio.

Despite their elevated economic and political status, each of *The Ninth Guest*'s invitees and the inhabitants of other penthouse films either are dissemblers or shield corrupt pasts. Hence the furniture's veneer serves as an analogue to their artificial identities. The perpetrator's aim is to puncture each elite guest's public persona, thereby exposing a corrupt underbelly. For example, society maven Margaret Chisholm (Nella Walker) is a bigamist who had her husband committed to a mental institution to control his fortune.

Inhabitants of 1930s penthouse murder mysteries and melodramas adopt and perform their acquired identities in order to maintain an appropriate, albeit artificial, upper-class demeanor. Such is the case in *Susan Lenox* and *Possessed*. In the latter, factory worker Marion (Joan Crawford) makes her way to New York City to find a rich husband. Millionaire lawyer Mark Whitney (Clark Gable) takes her to a penthouse restaurant, the St. Maurice Roof, where, upon examining the incomprehensible French menu and its steep prices, she tries to save face by ordering roast beef and mashed potatoes. In the next scene, a close-up of Marion's increasingly bejeweled arm is seen tearing off calendar pages for the years 1928–31, a testament to her new identity and class rise. The now elegant Marion is fully ensconced in Whitney's penthouse, and her name has been changed to Mrs. Moreland to protect her reputation. The once-befuddled neophyte is now the picture of sophistication, supervisor of a bevy of butlers to whom she disseminates orders for a party. Later at the penthouse celebration, the newly fluent Mrs. Moreland even sings a tune in French for her guests.

Jamie Darricott of *Ladies' Man*, who is ultimately pushed off the penthouse terrace by Horace Fendley, begins as a dissembler. Wealthy Mrs. Fendley drops him off at his residence, the Hotel Metropole in midtown Manhattan, where he maintains the illusion that he is well off, ascending in the elevator to the top story. After he steps out, he looks around stealthily to see if anyone is watching and enters a door labeled "exit" that leads to a small, cramped, attic room. Soon after, his benefactor, the lonely

FIG. 1.3. Reenacting a murder from a penthouse terrace in *Penthouse* (W. S. Van Dyke, 1933).

Mrs. Fendley, rewards him with a real penthouse in exchange for companionship and other services.

Covert and desperate behavior is a feature of the cinematic penthouse's outdoor terrace, where much of the hidden intrigue and even death occur. Since they are walled spaces often replete with elaborate vegetation and statuary, terraces serve as perfect environments for concealment or evasion. Sometimes, these ample garden spaces include secret doorways or exits from which villains enter and extricate themselves. In *Ellery Queen's Penthouse Mystery*, criminals who gain access through the terrace entrance murder the occupant, ventriloquist and smuggler Gordon Cobb. Likewise, *Penthouse*'s spiteful mob boss Jim Crelliman arranges to have his two-timing lover murdered by a hit man (who also lives in the building) by luring her onto his terrace during a typical penthouse party and having her shot from the skyscraper setback's projecting apartment above (fig. 1.3). Since Crelliman owns the Oklahoma Building and controls its space, tenants, and invited guests, he is temporarily able to seal it off from the police and manage his alibi.

FIG. 1.4. Corrupt philanthropist pushed from a penthouse balcony in
A Shriek in the Night (Albert Ray, 1933).

The liminal spaces of cinematic penthouse terraces, which are located
between inside and outside, frequently serve as the sites of dramatic falls
by suicide or murder, the spatial obverse of penthouse privilege. Much
like Niagara Falls, their lofty heights and sublime views seem to provide
a dramatic escape to the ineffable. The boundless vantage points afforded
by the terrace, which were linked to godlike possession, are equated with
its reverse, or hell. Depression-era characters are hence punished for enjoying the penthouse and its concomitant material advantages by its very
structural or design properties. For example, the opening scene of *A Shriek
in the Night* begins with a harrowing fall from a penthouse balcony. From
the perpetrator's auditory range and point of view, the audience hears the
victim's blood-curdling scream and witnesses him plunging to his death
and hitting the sidewalk with a loud thud (fig. 1.4). The death of the penthouse's occupant, Mr. Harker, the prominent philanthropist with underworld connections, suggests a just end to his transgressions and initiates a
series of murders in the luxury apartment building.

Several mistresses or fallen women leap to their deaths from penthouse terraces, prompted by their patrons' refusal to marry them and as a consequence of their shame. Miss Jones, the lover of Folsom in *The Secret Witness*, arrives at his penthouse and pleads desperately for marriage, unable to withstand the disgrace of being exposed as a kept woman. While Miss Jones is still present, Folsom's wife arrives at his pied-à-terre and demands a divorce. He replies that the penthouse and their separation affords a "very convenient arrangement for a man of [his] habits." In an act of sadism, he introduces Miss Jones to Mrs. Folsom, sending the young woman into a tailspin. She is shown on the parapet of the penthouse prior to her jump. From her point of view high above, the camera cuts to a street below, foreshadowing her subsequent fall.

A comparable suicide occurs in *Skyscraper Souls* in David Dwight's (Warren William) preeminent office in his eponymous hundred-story building, the tallest in the world, to which his hidden penthouse apartment is attached. Like Folsom, Dwight enjoys a marriage of expediency with Mrs. Ella Dwight (Hedda Hopper), which serves as a perfect cover for his affair with his office wife and right-hand woman, Sarah Dennis (Verree Teasdale). Following Miss Dennis's discovery that Dwight has made advances on her young impresario, Lynn Harding (Maureen O'Sullivan), she threatens to kill him if he continues in his attempted seduction. When he refuses to comply, Dennis shoots and kills him. In the next scene, we view the murderess on the parapet of the preeminent skyscraper. Dressed in funeral black, she extends her arms in a cruciform pose before plummeting to her death, a martyr of the skyscraper and its penthouse privileges.

Conclusion

The Depression-era cinematic penthouse is a place that is most undomestic, haunted with the corrupt circumstances of its acquisition and continued class conflict and gender dysfunction. Although replete with spectacular interior and exterior visual effects and laced with profligate entertainments, a place of desire, it is also the site of secret dealings by unsavory poseurs and criminals who have penetrated its sequestered domain. Spatially, it is depicted as an indecipherable rebus rather than a commodious, multiroomed sphere of domestic relaxation. Characters die or regain their morality, either by quitting the ill-gotten abode in favor of one more humble or by marriage, thereby prescribing traditional class and gender expectations (e.g., *Possessed*, *Baby Face*, *Skyscraper Souls*, and *Penthouse*). A poignant example of such a moral recovery may be found in *The Easiest Way*, in which kept woman Laura Murdock's fate is linked to her architectural surroundings from the film's outset. "Where did you find her?" inquires company president Brockton. "I got her right out of a department store," and her personality is "Park Avenue plus" (showing her suitability for penthouse living) even though "she's right out of the tenements," his executive replies. Brockton then seduces her and moves her into his luxurious abode. Ultimately she is no longer able to live a life of moral turpitude and emotional dishonesty, which prompts her to quit Brockton and his penthouse. On Christmas Eve, the lonely Murdock peers into the window of her married sister's colonial-style house, which has been acquired through hard work and the security of a traditional marriage and which, in contrast to the penthouse, is a cipher of normative domestic felicity and holiday cheer. By abandoning the stained upscale dwelling, she is invited into the wholesome family home from which she had previously been banned. Murdock ends up in architectural limbo or a space between, residing in neither the penthouse nor the middle-class home, but begins the road to her redemption.

NOTES

1. The term "Potemkin architecture" is an adaptation of the Potemkin village, which was an artificial village built by Grigory Potemkin to impress Catherine the Great. The term is still employed to suggest something artificial or meant to deceive others.

2. See Merrill Schleier, *Skyscraper Cinema: Architecture and Gender in American Film* (Minneapolis: University of Minnesota Press, 2009).

3. The "New Apartments" column began on January 29, 1927, and ran intermittently until November 22, 1930. It was initially signed "Duplex." On April 7, 1928, it was signed M. C. On September 22, 1928, the designation "Penthouse" appeared for the first time. Its author was Marcia Davenport (1903–96). In 1928 she was hired on the editorial staff of the *New Yorker*, where she worked until 1931. In 1929 she married Russell Davenport, who became the editor of *Fortune* soon thereafter.

4. Matthew Gordon Lasner, in *High Life: Condo Living in the Suburban Century* (New Haven, CT: Yale University Press, 2012), 5–8, discusses condos as appealing to both individual and collective desires. See also Rebecca Solnit, *Inside Outside* (San Francisco: Artspace, 2006), 11, for a consideration of homes as both sanctuaries and high-stakes real estate.

5. Simon Schama, *The Embarrassment of Riches: An Interpretation of Dutch Culture in the Golden Age* (New York: Vintage, 1997).

6. "Castles in the Air," *New Yorker*, June 4, 1927, 37; Steven Ruttenbaum, *Mansions in the Clouds: The Skyscraper Palazzi of Emery Roth* (New York: Balsam, 1986).

7. Andrew Alpern, *The New York Apartments of Rosario Candela and James Carpenter* (New York: Acanthus, 2002).

8. Hugh Ferriss, *The Metropolis of Tomorrow* (New York: Ives Washburn, 1929), 94.

9. "Gardens and Roof-Gardens in the Heart of New York," *Vogue*, July 15, 1926, 55.

10. Ferriss, *The Metropolis of Tomorrow*, 15, 96. For a discussion of Ferriss's work prior to 1929, see Merrill Schleier, *The Skyscraper in American Art: 1890–1931* (New York: Da Capo, 1990).

11. Caroline Seebohm, *The Man Who Was Vogue: The Life and Times of Condé Nast* (New York: Viking, 1982), 1–3.

12. R. P. White, "What! Penthouses Here? First One Was Built Twenty Years Ago to Perpetuate Real Living," *Los Angeles Times*, April 23, 1933, 18–19.

13. White, "What! Penthouses Here?" See also Holly Meares, "The James Oviatt Building: The Bespoke Brilliance and Pretension behind an Art Deco Masterpiece," KCET, September 6, 2013, https://www.kcet.org/history-society/the-james-oviatt-building-the-bespoke-brilliance-and-pretension-behind-an-art-deco; "Why We Like This Place," Here Comes the Guide, accessed October 19, 2017, http://www.herecomestheguide.com/southern-california/wedding-venues/oviatt-penthouse; Cecilia Rasmussen, "L.A. Then and Now; an Art Deco Jewel with a Glittery History," *Los Angeles Times*, September 10, 2000, http://www.stanthony.ws/archive/oviatt_building_history.pdf.

14. Val Burton and Will Jason, "Penthouse Serenade (When We're Alone)," 1931, available at Lyrics Mania, http://www.lyricsmania.com/penthouse_serenade_when_were_alone_lyrics_arthur_godfrey.html; Fats Waller, "Pent Up in a Penthouse," 1939, recording available at http://sonichits.com/video/Thomas_'Fats'_Waller/Pent_Up_In_A_Penthouse. Even Al Jolson and Cab Calloway, in *The Singing Kid* (William Keighley, 1936), sang "I Love to Sing-a" to each other from atop their respective penthouse terraces, seeming to teeter on the edge in exuberant abandon. See https://www.youtube.com/watch?v=LfiftuUUV8Y, accessed February 9, 2015.

15. "Roundup Nets Two in Penthouse Home," *New York Times*, June 13, 1933, 40. Other articles of this type in the *New York Times* included "Penthouse Raided; Liquor Confiscated," September 14, 1931, 2; "Penthouse Is Raided as Gambling Club," January 21, 1932, 2; "Costly Club Raided as Gambling Place," January 22, 1932, 10; "Penthouse Raided as Gaming Resort," June 2, 1932, 10; "Three Seized in Raid on Park Ave. Penthouse," September 3, 1932, 4; "Trap Policy Gang in Penthouse Raid," February 20, 1934, 44.

16. Gwen Bristow and Bruce Manning, *The Invisible Host* (New York: Mystery League, 1930); Arthur M. Chase, *The Party at the Penthouse* (New York: Dodd, Mead, 1932); Arthur Somers Roche, *Penthouse* (New York: Dodd, Mead, 1935).

Roche's book was first serialized in *Cosmopolitan* from January to June 1933. Ellery Queen, *Penthouse Mystery* (New York: Grosset and Dunlap, 1941).

17. "Penthouse at London Terrace," *New Yorker*, July 19, 1930, 61.

18. "The New York Apartment of Conde Nast, Esq.," *Vogue*, August 1, 1928, 44–47; Marjorie Garber, *Sex and Real Estate: Why We Love Houses* (New York: Pantheon, 2000), 17.

19. Elsie De Wolfe, *The House in Good Taste* (New York: Century, 1913).

20. "The New York Apartment of Conde Nast, Esq." For a discussion of other famous penthouse owners, see Andrew Alpern, *Luxury Apartment Houses of Manhattan: An Illustrated History* (New York, Dover, 1993), 118–34; Elizabeth Hawes, *How the Apartment House Transformed the Life of the City, 1869–1930* (New York: Alfred A. Knopf, 1993), 230; Donald L. Miller, *Supreme City: How Jazz Age Manhattan Gave Birth to Modern America* (New York: Simon and Schuster, 2014), 172; Ruttenbaum, *Mansions in the Clouds*, 100.

21. Hugo Gnam Jr., "Penthouse Acres," *Arts and Decoration* 47 (September 1937): 16–18, 47.

22. Helen Sprackling, "An Apartment in the Twentieth-Century Manner," *House Beautiful*, November 1930, 484–86.

23. Donald Albrecht, *Designing Dreams: Modern Architecture in the Movies* (New York: Harper and Row, 1986), 111; Lea Jacobs, *The Wages of Sin: Censorship and the Fallen Woman Film* (Madison: University of Wisconsin Press, 1991), 56.

24. Gwendolyn Wright, *Building the American Dream: A Social History of Housing in America* (Cambridge, MA: MIT Press, 1981), 141, 145, 151.

25. Chase, *The Party at the Penthouse*, 4.

26. Burton and Jason, "Penthouse Serenade."

27. Bill Osgerby, "The Bachelor Pad as Cultural Icon: Masculinity, Consumption and Interior Design in American Men's Magazines, 1930–65," *Journal of Design History* 18 (2005): 103. See also George Wagner, "The Lair of the Bachelor," in *Architecture and Feminism*, ed. Debra Coleman, Elizabeth Danze, Carol Henderson (New York: Princeton Architectural Press, 1996), 183–220; Bill Osgerby, *Playboys in Paradise: Modernity, Youth and Leisure Style in Modern America* (London: Bloomsbury Academic, 2001); Elizabeth Fraterrigo, *Playboy and the Making of the Good Life in Modern America* (New York: Oxford University Press, 2008).

28. Ruth Dean, quoted in Virginia Pope, "Now the Penthouse Palace Is Evolving," *New York Times*, March 23, 1930, SM5. See also "Penthouse Gardens to Be Open to Public," *New York Times*, May 14, 1933, N5; "Penthouses Bloom for Garden Tour," *New York Times*, May 5, 1939, 24.

29. Mary Fanton Roberts, "A Garden Apartment That Overlooks New York," *Arts and Decoration* 23 (September 1925): 46.

30. Roland Marchand, *Advertising the American Dream* (Berkeley: University of California Press, 1985), 239.

31. Meyer Wigoder, "The 'Solar Eye of Vision': Emergence of the Skyscraper Viewer in the Discourse on Heights in New York City, 1890–1920," *Journal of the Society of Architectural Historians* 61 (June 2002): 152–69.

32. Marcia Davenport, "New Apartments," *New Yorker*, August 11, 1928, 60.

33. Michel de Certeau, "Walking in the City," in *The Practice of Everyday Life*, trans. Steven Rendall (Berkeley: University of California Press, 1984), 92.

34. Pope, "Now the Penthouse Palace Is Evolving," SM5.

35. "Bull Market Architecture," *New Republic*, July 8, 1931, 192.

36. Lewis Mumford, "Towers," *American Mercury*, February 1925, 193–96. For a discussion of Mumford's views toward skyscrapers, see Schleier, *The Skyscraper in American Art*, 93–96.

37. Pope, "Now the Penthouse Palace Is Evolving," SM5.

38. Barry Curtis, *Dark Places: The Haunted House in Film* (London: Reaktion, 2008), especially 58–66. My ideas here were inspired by Curtis, who claims that haunted houses are often replete with unresolved class tensions. Relatives who have been cheated out of their rightful inheritances are unable to rest in peace and often return as ghosts to seek revenge.

2

FROM WALTER NEFF TO C. C. BAXTER

Billy Wilder's Apartment Plots

STEVEN COHAN

Pamela Robertson Wojcik begins her study of the apartment plot by reminding us of the screenplay that Joe Gillis (William Holden) and Betty Schaefer (Nancy Olson) are writing together in Billy Wilder's *Sunset Boulevard* (1950). Their script concerns a man and woman who live in the same apartment, even sleep in the same bed, but never meet because one works during the day and the other at night. Wojcik mentions that this contrived premise offers a parodic twist on Gillis's own situation, as "Joe leaves his apartment, and the independence it represents, to enter the macabre mansion on Sunset Boulevard," where he becomes the live-in gigolo lover of Norma Desmond (Gloria Swanson). Wojcik's purpose in starting with Wilder's film, however, is not to dwell upon "the warped shared-house plot that shapes *Sunset Boulevard*," but rather to link the cockeyed premise of Joe and Betty's fictive script to a new genre emerging at the end of World War II with comedies such as *The More the Merrier* (George Stevens, 1943) and *Apartment for Peggy* (George Seaton, 1948), namely, the apartment plot.[1]

All things considered, Wojcik's rhetorical gambit of starting off with *Sunset Boulevard* to establish the apartment plot as a genre is still surprising. For while she considers film noir, the identifiable genre of this Wilder picture, to be "an especially important parallel to the apartment genre," she takes pains in her introduction to explain how film noir and the apartment plot differ in their epistemology and imaginary landscapes, especially with respect to the urban geographies each envisions.[2] To be sure, in reaction to the migration of middle-class families out of American cities and into their suburbs, both genres present an alternative viewpoint to that emergent suburban sprawl, fashioning their narratives to address the challenges of postwar urban experience. But as Wojcik points out, whereas film noir locates its narrative action in public spaces—"the lonely streets" is the well-worn phrase that instantly describes this genre's familiar urban terrain—the apartment plot remains confined to city residences, the special vantage point from which this genre explores the more private, more literally and symbolically interiorized, domestic spaces of urban life at midcentury. Consequently, whereas "much of noir registers the failure of the protagonist to achieve the ideal of home," often recounting how external forces threaten this ideal, Wojcik stresses how, in example after example, "the apartment plot is uniquely attendant to the experience of *domestic* urbanism."[3]

In Wojcik's nuanced mapping of the apartment genre, single living of the sort indicated by Joe and Betty's script in *Sunset Boulevard*, whether with regard to characters who live alone, with roommates, or in shifts, is a defining characteristic of postwar domestic urban experience and, hence, a prime motivation of apartment plots in movies. But the single life is a narrative component of much film noir, too. Since Billy Wilder worked in both genres, I return to four of his most successful films—along with *Sunset Boulevard*, I look at *Double Indemnity* (1944), *The Seven Year Itch* (1955), and, no surprise here, *The Apartment* (1960)—as a means of tracing the intricate relationship of film noir to the apartment genre through the urban habitat of the single man. When it concerns a bachelor's apartment, I argue, in Wilder's hands one genre builds from but inverts the narrative thematics of the other. His two noir films originate as incomplete apartment plots arising from intrusions upon a single man's domestic space, just as his two fully sustained apartment plots view urban bachelorhood from a cynical viewpoint more characteristic of film noir, despite their stature as sex comedies.

An Apartment of His Own:
Sunset Boulevard and *Double Indemnity*

While *Sunset Boulevard* is obviously a canonical film noir, in its own narrative (as opposed to the script Joe and Betty are writing), Joe's sexual and professional entrapment in Norma Desmond's gothic mansion forecloses upon a possible apartment plot. On the face of it, the crisis that sends him there arises from the urgency with which he has to hide his car from the two repo men. The automobile is his means of movement; having one enables him to make story pitches at Paramount and to track down his agent at a golf course. When, while he is eluding the repo men, the car gets a blowout that inspires him to conceal it in Norma's empty garage, Joe's situation predicts his emasculation as a noir hero—a condition later confirmed when Norma lets his car be towed away. It is therefore telling that, while the film opens at Norma's mansion, the site of his murder and her notoriety in the present time of the diegesis, Joe's flashback takes us back to his furnished single-room digs in the Alto Nido apartment house. From here, the narrative of *Sunset Boulevard* uses Joe's inability to maintain and control his own solitary living space as a marker of his growing dependence on Norma, in effect directing what began as an inchoate apartment plot toward that noirish ending with his corpse floating backside up in the swimming pool.

If the repossessed car symbolizes Joe's imperiled manhood, the furnished bachelor apartment in Hollywood symbolizes his independence. Even when accepting Norma's demand that he sleep in the room above the garage while they work on her screenplay, in Joe's mind, so long as he still possesses his own apartment at the Alto Nido, he remains beyond her control, which is to say he can believe he is the one taking advantage of her sad situation as opposed to it being the other way around. However, rather quickly Norma's manservant, Max Von Mayerling (Erich von Stroheim), pays off the back rent, collects Joe's possessions, and moves him into the garage guest room permanently. Joe loses the solitude and privacy of his apartment—two attractive attributes of his single life that defined his independence, perhaps even more, it turns out, than his automobile. For when rain comes through the garage roof, Max moves him out of that guest room and into the main house. "I didn't much like the idea," Joe reflects in voice-over. "The only time I could have to myself was in that room." Once occupying "the room of the husbands," Joe's fate as Norma's gigolo lover is sealed; worse, because of her past suicide attempts, the door to the husbands' room has no locks. Anyone can enter his room at any time, as Norma later does to stare at him sleeping after he returns from one of his secret nighttime meetings with Betty.

In point of fact, however, neither Joe's one-room apartment at the Alto Nido nor the garage apartment afford him an inviolable sanctuary where he can have uninterrupted time to himself. Before Joe moves into the main house, and consistent with the porousness of residences in an apartment plot, Max has already covertly entered the garage guest room while he slept. More significantly, almost as soon as the flashback begins with Joe in his bathrobe at the typewriter, the two repo men push their way inside, threatening him. The independence connoted by Joe's bachelor life, where he only has to account for himself and can work all day in his bathrobe, is therefore without much foundation. The same is true of the apartment in the script he and Betty are writing, by the way. "How about this for a situation?" he asks with tongue in cheek before they begin in earnest. "She teaches daytimes. He teaches at night. Right? They don't even know each other but they share the same room. It's cheaper that way." The contrived sharing of space, in which roommates occupy even the same bed in shifts, gives each tenant only an illusion of independent single living because someone else is always occupying that space when they are not there. Betty knows Joe is kidding with this preposterous situation, but she still thinks his idea is a good one and even knows how it can fit in with what she has already written on her own.

All of this is to say that Joe's narrative in *Sunset Boulevard* begins as a possible apartment plot that fails to take off because a noir plot subsumes it. Even then, the film's energy as a noir narrative derives from the flashback to his small apartment in the Alto Nido, and his departure from that locale reinforces his inability to own—in the sense of taking control of and financial responsibility for—his social, sexual, and moral independence as a bachelor.

A possible apartment plot functions even more noticeably and, I think, much more complexly in Wilder's earlier *Double Indemnity*. As John Thomas McGuire observes, characters in this film are notable for their "rootlessness." Their mobility across the urban landscape from downtown to Los Feliz to Long Beach characterizes the "urban 'emptiness'" of (probably) prewar Los Angeles.[4] Walter Neff's (Fred MacMurray) job selling insurance relies on his mobility, making an occupation out of his rootlessness. Nevertheless, for the long flashback narrative, the Dietrichson house in Los Feliz establishes a point of origin for Walter's seduction into criminality by Phyllis Dietrichson (Barbara Stanwyck), just as it sets the stage for closure when the murderous couple have their final, fatal confrontation there. During his first visit, Walter observes the house and its interior as an outsider, his voice-over describing it in detail as the camera lingers on the dusty setting and sharply defined shadows of the living room; however foul and corrupt this bourgeois household may be, the insurance salesman is an intruder in a domestic arrangement that excludes him. Likewise, the office building of his employer, Pacific All Risk Insurance Company—the setting that frames the film's noir plot with Walter's voice-over dictation—subjects its workers, including Walter, to panoptic scrutiny and establishes another fixed point of origin for his movement, to which he returns repeatedly. Walter, in this respect, is pulled between these two highly resonant spaces, with one (the insurance company) exerting an institutional, quasi-legal force to contain his criminal desires and the other (Phyllis's house) releasing a libidinal force that unmoors them.

Compared with those settings, the three major scenes taking place in his apartment stand out as a private space where, to echo Joe Gillis, Walter has time to himself. The action happening here reveals how Walter's bachelor status positions him on the margins of a social order personified, on one hand, by Mr. Dietrichson (Tom Powers) due to his patriarchal status and, on the other, by Barton Keyes (Edward G. Robinson), Walter's mentor at the insurance company. Bachelorhood increases Walter's social isolation or anomie, along with his vulnerability to the seductive wiles of the noir femme fatale. The private space of his apartment thus underscores his potential for sexual, moral, and legal transgressions—in deed as well as thought, as it turns out.

Neff's apartment is initially pictured, albeit briefly, as his sanctuary, where he finds relief from work and solitude in which to think. After Phyllis slyly makes her suggestion about murdering her husband, Walter leaves, and his voice-over explains, "She didn't fool me for a minute, not this time. I knew I had hold of a red-hot poker and the time to drop it was before it burned my hand off." He does not return to his office but instead stops at a drive-through for a beer to get rid of the sour taste of the iced tea Phyllis has served him, and then goes to bowl a few lanes to clear his head. Not hungry enough to find a restaurant and not in the mood to see a show, he returns to his apartment. As it gets dark, he leaves the lights off, watches it rain outside, and paces back and forth in his living room.

"I hadn't walked out on anything at all," he reveals in his voice-over, adding, "the hook was too strong" because "this wasn't the end between her and me, it was only the beginning." So when the doorbell rings at eight o'clock, he states that he knows who it is "without having to think, as if it was the most natural thing in the world."

Pause frame for a moment. In contrast with Joe Gillis's furnished single room, Walter Neff's apartment is a more fully realized domestic space, albeit one consistent with his class status as an unmarried working man, connoted by his snappy, sexually charged dialogue and lowbrow taste for beer, bourbon, and bowling—in this setting he gives every indication of finding comfort in a bachelor's solitary life. His living room is clean, well furnished, and neatly arranged; it has curtained windows and even a masculine decor of sorts, since three pictures of boxers hang over the sofa and more pictures with this theme can be seen on other walls. At one point Walter and Phyllis go into the kitchen to get glasses and water for bourbon, and while we do not see a bedroom, we can assume from the layout that there is one. Additionally, the apartment building has its own parking garage and is a short walk to the nearby commercial boulevard.

Walter's apartment, in short, indicates a bachelor's satisfaction with an alternate version of domestic life, which in its privacy and solitude, not to say its licensing of sex outside marriage, greatly contrasts with the unhappy domestic situation of Dietrichson, who bridles under the constraints of marriage, fatherhood, and business debts, and the ongoing agita of Keyes, whose neurotic suspicions of female perfidy have apparently made him an unhappy, dyspeptic, and lifelong bachelor, one mated to his career as an insurance investigator of domestic frauds.

Perhaps more important for the film's narrative, Phyllis envies Walter's single life as she looks around his apartment. "It's nice here, Walter," she comments. "Who takes care of it for you?" He mentions that a cleaning woman comes a couple times a week and adds that he sometimes makes breakfast for himself, squeezing a grapefruit or two, or goes to the corner drugstore. "That's wonderful," Phyllis replies. "Just strangers beside you. You don't know them and you don't hate them. You don't have to sit across the table and smile at him and that daughter of his every morning of your life." Her visit to Neff's apartment makes clear why Phyllis wants her husband dead. She complains that she feels her husband is always watching her, keeping her on a leash so tight she cannot breathe. In a manner of speaking, Phyllis simply wants her own apartment, which as it happens is what Lola (Jean Heather), the detested stepdaughter, gets after she moves out of that house following her father's death: "four walls and nothing to do but look at them," as Walter later describes Lola's "little apartment" in Hollywood, one presumably much like Joe Gillis's in the Alto Nido complex.

Her envy notwithstanding, Phyllis's visit, which climaxes with their having sex offscreen, convinces Walter to go through with the murder. "Yes, I killed him," he confesses to the Dictaphone in the film's memorable opening. "I killed him for money. I killed him for a woman." But he is also motivated by a desire to outwit his employer and "crook the house itself," as he puts it to Phyllis when they are together in his apartment. He has in fact been mulling over a scheme to do just that before meeting her—and presumably he has been doing that thinking in the solitude of his apartment. That is why I infer that Walter's comfortable occupation of his domestic space results in, or perhaps it may be as accurate to say from, his sense of anomie as a bachelor. At least as seen from the moral viewpoint of a good corporate citizen like Keyes, though the man himself is another bachelor, Walter's single life, visualized through his apartment, makes him dangerously marginal to the social order of law and respectability. Keyes's suspicion of Walter's indifference to the rules of a corporate-minded social order, but not yet of his colleague's complicity in the Dietrichson murder, is confirmed when Walter refuses a promotion, preferring his mobility as a salesman to a desk job; it is also voiced through Keyes's mistrust of "Margie," the lady friend Walter invents as a cover for Phyllis. The first scene in his apartment visualizes the social marginality Walter experiences through its framing shots of him looking outside from within his darkened living room. He is there at the window as the scene begins. Phyllis shares the viewpoint with him as she complains about her married life, and he resumes his position at the window to watch her leave after they have agreed to commit the murder (fig. 2.1).

Later, important plot scenes also happen in this apartment. Walter prepares for the murder here: telling Charlie, the garage attendant, that he will be staying in all night; arranging for his alibi by phoning a colleague who lives in Westwood so there can be a record of his making a toll call; dressing in a dark blue suit to be easily mistaken for Dietrichson; placing business cards inside the phone box and doorbell so that, later on, he can tell if someone called or paid an unexpected visit; and finally leaving his apartment by the service exit so that no one will see him depart. In other words, almost everything we see of the preparation for the murder happens in this apart-

FIG. 2.1. Walter at the window of his apartment in *Double Indemnity* (Billy Wilder, 1944).

ment; its privacy offers Walter the shelter as well as the solitude to plan out and then act upon his criminal desires. After the murder, he returns the same stealthy way, checks the phone and doorbell to make sure that no one tried to visit or contact him, and heads down to the building's garage to mention to Charlie that he is going to the drugstore to get something to eat.

Walter's privacy is then intruded upon again after Norton, "the big boss" of the insurance company, unsuccessfully tries to get Phyllis to settle for a decision of suicide rather than accidental death. She calls her lover and coconspirator from the corner drugstore and they arrange for a hasty tryst in his apartment. In preparation for her arrival, Walter closes the curtains on the side window to keep out prying eyes and begins to pick up after himself in the living room. The doorbell rings, but surprisingly, it is Keyes, not Phyllis. He has realized that Dietrichson must have been murdered because the odd circumstances surrounding the accident policy do not make sense, and the obvious suspect, as far as he is concerned, is the widow. Phyllis arrives as Keyes starts to leave, so she hides behind the door while Walter tries to hasten Keyes's departure (fig. 2.2).

FIG. 2.2. Keyes and Phyllis form a triangle with Walter in the hallway outside his apartment in *Double Indemnity* (Billy Wilder, 1944).

Wilder's triangular composition of his three lead actors in the hallway at this point recalls the earlier triangulation of Walter, Phyllis, and Dietrichson when the scheming couple tricks the husband into signing the insurance policy. The paralleled framing of these two scenes is significant: while the murder plot seems to triangulate the husband, his wife, and her lover, the more potent triangle is depicted in the hallway of Walter's apartment, where he is being spatially pulled between, on one hand, Keyes, their friendship, and a sense of legal, social, and moral order; and on the other, Phyllis, their sexual attraction, and his indifference to and then transgression of that order. This triangulation of the three characters drives the entire narrative of *Double Indemnity* and its star casting, too. And this triangulation is most clearly visible for us not in the insurance office building or the Dietrichson house, but outside Walter's apartment. In fact, what may be most striking about the set design of his apartment is that the front door incongruously opens outward into the hall rather than inward into the living room, as would normally be the case. But the strange position of the doorway here visually incorporates Walter's bachelor space into the triangulated action occurring just outside in the hallway. Finally, while all three characters at times openly express their disinterest in normative domesticity, of the three figures Walter is the one with a satisfying if solitary domestic place, as Phyllis appreciates, which accounts for his position as the visual center of the triangular composition. In their different ways, Phyllis and Keyes are each pulling Walter away from the haven of his apartment.

The pattern by which the single man's apartment offers him a place of his own in which to experience the sense of freedom implied by his domestic solitude is not unique to Wilder as an auteur but is present in many noir films. In John Huston's *The Maltese Falcon* (1941), the apartment of Sam Spade (Humphrey Bogart) initially offers the private detective refuge from his partner's murder and his partner's adulterous wife. In short order, though, his apartment is invaded by uninvited guests: two cops intrude to interrogate Spade as a likely suspect; Joel Cairo (Peter Lorre) and Brigid O'Shaughnessy (Mary Astor) meet there and get in a scuffle, and the cops show up again; Cairo, Gutman (Sydney Greenstreet), and Wilmer (Elisha Cook Jr.) surprise Spade and Brigid there, and, eying each other suspiciously, the five wait for the arrival of the black bird; finally, the apartment is the scene of Spade's repudiation of Brigid for killing his partner, and the cops' return to take her away. Likewise, in Howard Hawks's *The Big Sleep* (1946), the apartment of Philip Marlowe (Bogart again) offers the detective sanctuary, where, for instance, he can decrypt Geiger's coded book of blackmail victims only to be interrupted by policeman Bernie Olhs (Regis Toomey); later on, Carmen Sternwood (Martha Vickers) covertly waits for Marlowe in his apartment, presumably for stud service, but, disgusted at having his private space apparently contaminated by her unexpected presence, he violently pushes her outside. The single man's apartment in film noir seems sacrosanct but is nonetheless always subject to intrusion, so, as in an apartment plot, it is never entirely private or solitary, but porous and permeable.

In both Bogart films, too, the hero's position as private detective puts him on the side of restoring lawfulness, even while it highlights his own moral ambivalence in circumventing the law. "Don't be too sure I'm as crooked as I'm supposed to be," Spade explains to Brigid when she asks if he would be turning her in to the police if the Falcon had been real. "That sort of reputation might be good business, bringing high-priced jobs, and making it easier to deal with the enemy." The two Wilder films, by contrast, well illustrate the basis of the noir hero's social, moral, and masculine outlaw identity in a potential bachelor apartment plot that gets subsumed by the dominant film noir narrative although its effects remain on the surface. The bachelor apartments in both *Double Indemnity* and *Sunset Boulevard* highlight how bachelorhood affords the noir hero a domestic space all his own in which to ponder transgressive desires even if he does not act upon them but is acted upon by a dangerous woman. The bachelor's apartment in *Double Indemnity* and *Sunset Boulevard* is therefore not impregnable because the unmarried man cannot escape what, from his outlier viewpoint, is an oppressive moral order that ensnares and potentially dooms him. By the same token, from a generic perspective the stronger if inchoate apartment plots in these two Wilder films reveal the mirroring relation of the two genres, which are not only paralleled but each other's antithesis.

Just Right for a Bachelor?
The Seven Year Itch and *The Apartment*

The presence of an inchoate apartment plot in Wilder's *Double Indemnity* and *Sunset Boulevard* registers how, for film noir, the bachelor's personal space does not simply transgress normative domesticity but offers an alternative formulation of the apartment plot's domestic urbanization. As the long 1950s develop, the single man's apartment carries a different valence on-screen from what it signifies for the bachelors of 1940s noir. On-screen the unmarried male's apartment, a source of envy for Phyllis Dietrichson, turns into the bachelor flat of sex comedies like *The Tender Trap* (Charles Walters, 1957), *Pillow Talk* (Michael Gordon, 1959), and *Come Blow Your Horn* (Bud Yorkin, 1963). In these apartment plots the bachelor's dwelling tends to be well appointed with modern decor, contemporary art, and the newest technologies; the lavish setting highlights the single man's rampant heterosexuality, postwar modernity, upward socioeconomic mobility, and unashamed affiliation with consumer culture. (Even Mike Hammer's high-tech pad in the noir cult film *Kiss Me Deadly* [Robert Aldrich, 1955] shares these elements with the playboy's bachelor apartment.) Setting their plots mainly in this apartment, the sex comedies envision it as a kind of theater where a bachelor entertains women, who come and go with ease for his sexual amusement, and where he performs a newly sanctioned cultural form of virile yet unmarried masculinity, namely, the bachelor playboy.

This male figure was enshrined in Hugh Hefner's wildly successful new magazine, *Playboy*, which began publishing in December 1953.[5] Unlike the articles in *Playboy*, on film the bachelor pad functions as a symptom of the playboy's immaturity, since he fashions a lifestyle out of his refusal to settle down as husband and breadwinner. The comedies therefore view his modern, urban apartment as a sexual playpen, which inevitably has to be replaced by another type of dwelling once the playboy meets but fails to bed and therefore has to wed a nice girl in the form of Debbie Reynolds in *The Tender Trap*, say, or Doris Day in *Pillow Talk*.

Wilder's two bachelor comedies from the period work against the conventions of that popular version of the apartment genre. *The Seven Year Itch* and *The Apartment* both take wannabe but inept playboys for their protagonists, men unable to perform like the bachelors of *The Tender Trap* or *Pillow Talk*. Those other sex comedies initially view the playboy's apartment with admiration for the freedom it represents and the consumables that set it off, yet the bachelor pad's deflation (as when Doris Day redecorates playboy Rock Hudson's apartment in *Pillow Talk*) triggers the plot's resolution. Wilder's two comedies, by contrast, take as their starting point the bachelor's difficulty in just being able to have his apartment all to himself. As Phyllis Dietrichson comments, there is great satisfaction to be had in eating alongside strangers and returning to the comfort and solitude of one's own apartment afterward. Though they live alone, such satisfaction eludes Wilder's two wannabe playboys, Richard Sherman (Tom Ewell) in *The Seven Year Itch* and C. C. "Bud" Baxter (Jack Lemmon) in *The Apartment*. In fact, both films establish their protagonists' discontent, with early scenes of them eating alone without the pleasure envisioned by Phyllis: Richard has an unappetizing meal at a health food restaurant, and Bud, while eating a frozen TV dinner, cannot find anything to watch on the tube except commercials.

To be sure, technically speaking Richard Sherman is not a bachelor. *The Seven Year Itch* plays on the sexual anxiety occasioned by a married man's midlife crisis—a crisis exacerbated by Alfred Kinsey's revelation that a male's sexual potency peaks at a very early age in contrast with a woman's.[6] But Richard is a "summer bachelor," as the narrator puts it in the film's opening: "a typical Manhattan husband whose family is leaving for the summer." He dutifully tries to adhere to his doctors' and wife's orders to follow a healthy lifestyle, renouncing cigarettes, junk food, and alcohol; yet, having "a lot of imagination," as the narrator also states, Richard has one fantasy after another of driving women wild with desire for him and, later on, of seducing the unnamed Girl (Marilyn Monroe) subletting the Kaufmans' apartment upstairs. Her presence in his apartment inspires him to think of his home as a summer bachelor pad where he has license to drink scotch and champagne, smoke cigarettes, and commit adultery— in short, where he can scratch his itch and evade the constraints of postwar domesticated masculinity as personified by his wife and her concern with his health. However, for the screen version of the hit Broadway play, playwright George Axelrod and cowriter Wilder had to reverse its plot, which onstage did allow its hapless hero to bed the Girl before renewing his commitment to his marriage. In the film version, while other summer bachelors—specifically, Richard's boss and Kruhulik (Robert Strauss), the janitor of his apartment building—apparently enjoy their summer bachelorhood without much effort or guilt, Richard fumbles just trying to get to first base with the Girl.

From this significant alteration of its source, there is much reason to conclude that what Wilder's Richard Sherman really wants from his summer bachelorhood is peace and quiet in his own apartment, not a lost weekend of sex, tobacco, and alcohol. After returning home from the train station where his wife, Helen (Evelyn Keyes), and their son, Ricky, have embarked for their summer vacation in Maine, he muses to himself, "I like our house. Why does Helen keep talking about moving into one of those enormous buildings that look like *Riot in Cell Block 11*? So much nicer here. Just three apartments. Ours, the Kaufmans upstairs, and those two guys on the top floor—interior decorators or something." The layout of the Shermans' nicer apartment building, a brownstone cut up into three flats and a janitor's basement, places Richard's domesticated masculinity within "a hierarchy of masculinities supporting [his] position as 'a typical Manhattan husband'" in mid-1950s America.[7] Bruce Babington and Peter William Evans go further to observe that the building's layout "reveals a kind of polymorphous world that Sherman cannot escape": from the crude, sweaty lust personified by the janitor Kruhulik, to the homosexuality implied for those two interior decorators living above, to the "overwhelmingly sensuous Girl" who occupies the space between such masculine extremes.[8] From their perspective, the apartment building places Richard in a landscape of "perverse" desiring, dramatized by his frequent sexual fantasies of being irresistible to women, all the while resisting their aggressive overtures to remain faithful to Helen in these wild daydreams—which may be why the Girl exclaims without surprise when he finally reveals he is not single, "You look married!"

All that said, it is striking that, after verbalizing to himself how much he likes his apartment, this typical summer bachelor goes on to state, "It's peaceful with everyone gone." He then elaborates why: for there is no television blaring *Howdy Doody*, no strong cooking smells, no boring conversation about his uneventful day at the office, no nagging wife. Though a summer bachelor, Richard seems perfectly content to be alone when *The Seven Year Itch* begins. Summer bachelorhood allows him to indulge his overactive fantasy life, without doubt. "Some people have flat feet. Some people have dandruff. I have this appalling imagination," he says to the Girl after recounting a daydream I shall discuss shortly. However, all the intrusions on his privacy interrupt and comically puncture whatever ego-satisfying scenarios his many daydreams stage for him—Helen telephones; the janitor appears twice in an effort to get the wool carpets for summer storage; Tom MacKenzie (Sonny Tufts) shows up to retrieve Ricky's forgotten kayak paddle; and the Girl nearly kills Richard with a falling tomato plant. What is more, she seeks to take partial possession of his space. Pleading that they must think about scandal should anyone see her enter late at night or leave early in the morning, Richard turns a deaf ear to her pleas to sleep in his apartment in order to enjoy his air conditioning and get a good night's rest. Sent away, the Girl reenters in her nightie once she discovers she can access his apartment secretly, avoiding any gossip from neighbors, by removing the wooden board that has closed off the staircase formerly connecting the building's first and second stories. "You know what? We can do this all summer," she announces. Like Goldilocks, the Girl ends up coolly sleeping in Richard's bed while he stays up all night trying to wrap his son's paddle to send to Maine.

In personifying an unselfconscious yet nonetheless aggressive female desirability consistent with Marilyn Monroe's star image, the Girl intrudes upon Richard's solitude. Her presence causes him to be torn between his frustrated desire to stray and his longing for the solitude enabled by his vacation from wife and child. This tension comically inverts the noir hero's seduction by a femme fatale, such as in *Double Indemnity*. This Girl is a naïf, sensuously aware yet innocently unmindful of her impact in triggering Richard's desires; he, in turn, is an inept seducer of a sexy, voluptuous blonde. Her indirect emasculating effect on him mirrors the femme fatale's seduction of a 1940s noir hero. After all, the Girl almost causes serious bodily harm to Richard when she knocks over that tomato plant, and later, what she most wants from him is his air-conditioned apartment.

The Seven Year Itch acknowledges that its apartment plot bears such a suggestive relation to film noir in Richard's final daydream. "Boy, if anyone were to walk in here now, would they get the wrong idea," he boasts to himself as he prepares toast and coffee the morning after the Girl spends the night. Then guilt and paranoia wash over him, as he imagines an unannounced Helen perforating the apartment door with half a dozen bullets. Bursting inside, she declares, "There's a woman in this apartment. I just know there is." Revealing that Kruhulik is really Johnny Dollar, a private eye hired to follow Richard, Helen announces, "I am going to shoot you dead." A whining Richard protests his innocence, but she ignores his entreaty not to shoot. Instead, acting like many a female in film noir, Helen riddles her husband with bullets, "five times in the back and twice in the belly." Following this violent daydream, Tom MacKenzie arrives for Ricky's paddle, and Richard, who now thinks the family friend is a rival appearing with Helen's demand for a divorce, knocks him unconscious.

The violence enacted by both Richard's noir daydream and the subsequent thrashing of his faux rival expresses his barely suppressed rage, which has been building. As Ed Sikov notes, Richard's angry outburst when he slips on Ricky's roller skate, hitting his head on the floor, is "especially strong," and more "extreme" than one might expect from having witnessed his passive interaction with his wife and son at Grand Central Station.[9] Squeezing the skate in his hand, Richard expresses his anger as hostility and paranoia. As he crawls on the floor to look under furniture, he furiously mutters, "Okay, where is it? Where's the other one? I know it's lurking somewhere here to get me." At this moment the door buzzer sounds: it is the Girl, who has forgotten her key to the building. Her first appearance occurs immediately upon Richard's outburst at Ricky for spoiling the peace and quiet of his summer bachelorhood. For all her wide-eyed innocence, she invades Richard's space, threatens his life when she knocks over the tomato plant, reveals his inability to seal the deal with her, exploits his failure to live up to the expectations of summer bachelorhood—and covets his air-conditioned apartment.

Likewise, Richard's final noir fantasy displaces his rage onto Helen, making him his wife's victim. When, as mentioned above, Richard complains about his "appalling imagination" as he recounts this daydream to the Girl, he is explaining why it seemed so real that he believed he was shot and dying. In actuality, he says, his wife is never jealous of other women, a comment that connects his noir daydream back to those earlier ones of women throwing themselves at him; those were fantasies that an imaginary Helen pooh-poohed for being too unbelievable. Informing him that his wife should be "very jealous, very *very* jealous," the Girl delivers a long speech meant to validate the hegemonic value of Richard's "gentle and kind and worried" masculinity, which trumps his lack of sexual aggression and assuages his insecurity in the face of her overwhelming erotic presence. With that ringing endorsement of his domesticated masculinity out of the way, after declaring to Tom that he will bribe judges if necessary to prevent Helen from getting a divorce, Richard repeats the Girl's speech almost verbatim and then socks his supposed rival in the face. So much for being kind and gentle. Turning the irony on its head again, that confrontation and noir daydream convince Richard to join his family in Maine, so he hands over his air-conditioned apartment to the Girl, who gets just what she wanted.

Never the playboy he imagines himself to be, the very married Richard Sherman is an outsider on bachelor life. His multiple daydreams, derived from movie scenes of passionate lovemaking and sophisticated seduction, such as the famous beach scene of *From Here to Eternity* (Fred Zinnemann, 1953), are filmed as if he and sometimes an imaginary Helen are watching and commenting on his fantasy scenarios as they play out like a movie. In *The Apartment*, C. C. "Bud" Baxter is literally an outsider when it comes to his bachelor apartment. He rents "a real nice apartment" just half a block from Central Park, he says in voice-over, "nothing fancy, kind of cozy, just right for a bachelor. The only problem," he immediately adds, "is I can't always get in when I want to."

Bud lends his apartment to his married supervisors for their sexual dalliances, even supplying them with liquor and food, and the expected payback is his movement up the corporate ladder at the insurance company where he works; however, his bosses exploit his good-natured passivity by holding their authority over Bud's head and making veiled threats. For instance, early in the film, Dobisch (Ray Walston) forces a feverish Bud out of bed by reminding him of the upcoming monthly efficiency report, all so that the executive can hook up with a Marilyn Monroe clone he has just met in a bar. Hiding behind the front steps with his overcoat pulled tightly against his chest because of the cold, from the shadows Bud watches as the couple, cocktails in hand, enter his apartment building. He

FIG. 2.3. Unable to remain in his apartment, C. C. "Bud" Baxter has to spend the evening alone on a park bench in *The Apartment* (Billy Wilder, 1960).

leaves once they are inside and spends the remainder of the evening alone on a bench in Central Park (fig. 2.3).

Despite how the four executives regularly evict him from his own apartment so they can use it as a temporary playboy pad, Bud willingly allows the occupants of his building to assume that he is the playboy entertaining women and carrying on night after night. Another executive, Kirkeby (David Lewis), calls Bud just "some schnook that works in the office," but his neighbor, Dr. Dreyfuss (Jack Kruschen), thinks Bud must be "some kind of iron man all around," what with all the booze bottles in the trash and the noise heard from the other side of the wall every night—"and sometimes there's a twi-night double header." Surprised that such "a nebbish like [him]" can keep it up night after night, the doctor even asks Bud if he will leave his corpse to "medical research" since he wants to know what kind of toll the nightly partying has taken on his body. The landlady makes her distaste known more bluntly. Complaining about the noise, she mutters, "What you get from renting to bachelors!" Meanwhile, at the company where Bud works, Jeff Sheldrake (Fred MacMurray), the head of personnel, promotes the underling in order to claim exclusive visiting rights to the apartment for trysts with Fran Kubelik (Shirley MacLaine), who became Sheldrake's mistress when he was one of those summer bachelors of the sort mentioned at the start of *The Seven Year Itch*. Sheldrake assumes as a matter of course that, being single with his own apartment, Bud is another carefree playboy. "You know, Bud," he states, "I envy you. Bachelor. All the dames you want. No headaches, no complications." "Yes, sir," Bud replies with a muted self-reflective irony that Sheldrake misses, "that's the life all right."

Christmas Eve brings this unsatisfying bachelor pose to a point of crisis inside the apartment. Bud discovers that Fran, the woman for whom he has undeclared feelings, is Sheldrake's mistress; he has to find somewhere to go so that Sheldrake can spend time alone with her; he gets plastered at a nearby bar after the company party and for the first time acts like the other philandering men in his office when he picks up a very drunk married woman; back in his apartment, he has to throw that woman out when he discovers Fran in his bed, knocked out by an overdose of his sleeping pills; Dr. Dreyfuss revives Fran, and Bud lets the doctor and Mrs. Dreyfuss believe that he, not the oily Sheldrake, is the reason for her attempted suicide. Ironically, the price Bud pays for pimping his apartment as a means of advancing his rise up the corporate ladder is an undeserved public shaming for callously mistreating Fran, the woman he loves. Furthermore, as Fran and Bud spend the holiday together, he shops, cooks, plays cards with, and waits on his unexpected guest. Far from enjoying his bachelorhood, Bud wants the stability, domesticity, and comfort of being "a typical Manhattan husband."

As an apartment plot, then, *The Apartment* is a series of humbling, even humiliating intrusions upon Bud's residence. Bud schedules time in his apartment for the four executives with the skill of an efficient motel manager, but that ploy for advancement requires him to stay away from his home almost every weeknight until late in the evening—and even then, as we saw, an executive's chance pickup can turn him out in the middle of the night. More distressing for Bud, when Sheldrake claims exclusivity to his apartment, Fran breaks a tentative date with Bud and goes with Sheldrake to the apartment. From this point on, and paralleling Bud's rise to be Sheldrake's underling, Fran becomes the catalyst for the most tumultuous invasions of the apartment. Not too unlike the Girl in *The Seven Year Itch*, Fran rather selfishly lays claim to it when she takes sleeping pills from his medicine cabinet and nearly dies in Bud's bed. As she recovers from her suicide attempt, Bud essentially gives over the apartment to her, functioning there as her "nurse," as both she and Sheldrake call him. On Christmas

Day, Kirkeby tries to push his way inside with a woman but willingly (and leeringly) departs once he sees Fran asleep in Bud's bed. The next day Fran's brother-in-law barges in, interrupts the spaghetti dinner Bud has carefully planned, learns of the suicide attempt, blames Bud, and punches him out. Finally, upon learning that Fran has returned to Sheldrake, Bud refuses to let him bring her to the apartment, a decision that results in Bud's resignation from the company—and his own permanent departure from the apartment.

Consequently, when Fran realizes she does love Bud and rushes to the apartment at the stroke of midnight on New Year's Eve, he has already given notice to his landlady and packed up his things, although he has not decided where he is going or how he will support himself. The couple's reunion therefore only seems like a Hollywood ending, punctuated by Shirley MacLaine's warm delivery of Fran's famous last line ("Shut up and deal"). For as Ben Rogerson points out, "the apartment has never been less homely" in this final scene.[10] Beneath the sentiment, Bud and Fran have no future mapped out, no new apartment to inhabit, and, despite what her remark may coyly encode about her feelings for him, she does not return his open declaration of love.

The Apartment closes with a degree of somber uncertainty that is more characteristic of film noir than of the era's sex comedies, including *The Seven Year Itch*. But then the very premise of *The Apartment* seems shaped by noir attitudes toward postwar urban experience. While residences in the apartment genre typically offer an alternative to the spaces of white- or blue-collar work, the premise here conflates those two distinct spaces: Bud uses his apartment to get ahead at work, and work keeps preventing him from enjoying his apartment. The name of the insurance company, Consolidated Life, suggests the same conflation of public/private, employment/domestic, inside/outside that had become characteristic of corporate America and its consolidation of all aspects of one's life.[11] Likewise, that consolidation registers "the culture of surveillance" that Sheldrake personifies at work and that Dr. Dreyfuss, the steadfast witness to and commentator upon Bud's supposed bachelor misbehavior, does at home.[12] The apartment plot of *The Apartment* thus works quite effectively as a refraction of *Double Indemnity*, complete with Bud's employment in an insurance company, the frequent exchange of *keys* to advance his career, and the casting of Fred MacMurray, Neff himself, as the chief executive and Bud's rival.

Conclusion

While bona fide apartment plots, *The Seven Year Itch* and *The Apartment* each illustrate from their side of the generic mirror how, in Wilder's filmography, noir and the apartment genre function in a dialectic tension with each other. As a director acclaimed for making masterpieces in both genres, Wilder's illumination of this dialectic, I think, is how his auteurship makes itself felt, distinguishing both his noir films and his sex comedies.

Serving as the antithesis of noir, the apartment genre, as Wojcik explains, tends to "marshal utopian fantasies of neighborhood, community, contact, and porousness, even as [these fantasies] present the darker side of urban encounters."[13] Despite their comic surface, Wilder's two apartment plots do more than just hint at the darker side of those utopian fantasies, while his two noir plots find more idyllic value in the bachelor's solitary urban dwelling. In all four films, the apartment promises the male protagonist sanctuary in the form of an impenetrable stillness. For me, the iconic image of that promise is the shot of Walter staring out his window before and after Phyllis arrives in *Double Indemnity*. Similarly, the sight of Bud seated alone on a park bench in *The Apartment* crystallizes a bleaker realization that this promise is not easy to realize, especially in the movies. As narratologists have long shown, stillness retards and even arrests narrativity, which is why, in Wilder's treatment of both genres, the bachelor's apartment cannot remain his private sanctuary for very long, but must be invaded, shown to be porous and susceptible to outside forces. In all four films, it turns out, the most forceful invader of that male space is a female, which raises suspicions about the heterosexual veracity of a bachelor inside his apartment—but that is another type of cultural plot altogether.

NOTES

I thank Roger Hallas and Joe McElaney for their helpful conversations about *Double Indemnity*.

1. Pamela Robertson Wojcik, *The Apartment Plot: Urban Living in American Film and Popular Culture, 1945 to 1975* (Durham, NC: Duke University Press, 2010), 2.

2. Wojcik, *The Apartment Plot*, 6.

3. Wojcik, *The Apartment Plot*, 42 and 39, emphasis in original.

4. John Thomas McGuire, "Exploring the Urban Milieu: Billy Wilder, Four Films, and Two Cities in the United States," *Quarterly Review of Film and Video* 30, no. 5 (2013): 437.

5. For a well-researched history of bachelor culture in the United States, see Howard P. Chudacoff, *The Age of the Bachelor: Creating an American Subculture* (Princeton, NJ: Princeton University Press, 1999). Chudacoff studies the status of the bachelor going back to colonial times, concentrates in depth on the widespread culture of bachelors as an aspect of domestic urbanism in the nineteenth century and the first two decades of the twentieth century, notes the decline of bachelor culture starting in the 1930s, and in his final chapters traces its renewal, when, "from the late 1950s through the 1970s, a newer, more assertive image of bachelorhood came to dominate American styles, and that image emerged from the pages of *Playboy* magazine" (261). Bill Osgerby likewise studies the bachelor through his urban habitat as featured in magazines such as *Playboy*, which celebrates the apartment as a means of highlighting the bachelor playboy's sexual freedom and consumer lifestyle. See Bill Osgerby, "The Bachelor Pad as Cultural Icon: Masculinity, Consumption and Interior Design in American Men's Magazines, 1930–65," *Journal of Design History* 18 (spring 2005): 99–112. See also his book *Playboys in Paradise: Masculinity, Youth and Leisure Style in Modern America* (New York: Berg, 2001), which has a chapter on *Playboy* and another on the swinging bachelor. In *Masked Men: Masculinity and the Movies in the Fifties* (Bloomington: Indiana University Press, 1997), I discuss how, beginning with its first issue, *Playboy* was written for and marketed to a hypothetical bachelor reader, and I also look closely at its two-part article from 1956 detailing the perfect bachelor penthouse apartment, which makes the theater aspect of the playboy's dwelling very apparent (267–75).

6. For a more detailed treatment of *The Seven Year Itch* in relation to 1950s discourses about masculinity crisis, see Cohan, *Masked Men*, 56–68.

7. Cohan, *Masked Men*, 65.

8. Bruce Babington and Peter William Evans, *Affairs to Remember: The Hollywood Comedy of the Sexes* (Manchester: Manchester University Press, 1989), 224.

9. Ed Sikov, *Laughing Hysterically: American Screen Comedy of the 1950s* (New York: Columbia University Press, 1994), 127.

10. Ben Rogerson, "Wilder's Mensch: United Artists and the Critique of Fordism," *Arizona Quarterly* 70, no. 1 (spring 2014): 70.

11. Rogerson, "Wilder's Mensch," 70.

12. Ian Brookes, "The Eye of Power: Postwar Fordism and the Panoptic Corporation in *The Apartment*," *Journal of Popular Film and Television* 37, no. 4 (November 2009): 158.

13. Wojcik, *The Apartment Plot*, 40.

3

ALAIN RESNAIS, TSAI MING-LIANG, AND THE APARTMENT PLOT MUSICAL

JOE MCELHANEY

I

In the late 1990s, two major examples of the musical film's modernist strain were released, *On connaît la chanson* (Alain Resnais, 1997) and *The Hole* (Tsai Ming-liang, 1998). While made by two filmmakers with markedly different approaches to cinematic form, the films share several points of contact: for the musical numbers, the actors lip-synch to well-known, preexisting recordings; both are set in urban environments (respectively Paris and Taipei) that assume a central function in relation to the films' larger concerns; and, of special relevance to this essay, apartments become central expressive terrains, particularly in terms of the function of song and dance. Using these two films as a framework, I wish to explore the implications of what Pamela Robertson Wojcik has termed the apartment plot when such a plot is situated in relation to the musical.

For Wojcik, this figurative plotting is capable of cutting across genres. Wojcik is careful not to make a case for the apartment plot as one that can supplant more widely accepted genre categories. Rather, she argues for a "dense and porous model of genre" in which films may engage in a "productive conversation" with one another."[1] Wojcik's attention is on American cinema within a defined historical period—1945 to 1975—and the majority of her examples are films set in New York. My essay operates within the general framework established by Wojcik. But in its emphasis on the musical, it returns to more traditional generic issues even as it addresses broader contexts. However, what follows here is not simply an analysis of two highly self-conscious, late manifestations of the musical. I also want the films to engage in a "productive conversation" with each other and with musicals that long precede them.

I have already referred to the films (in an almost automatic way) as modernist, which would presuppose that there is a classical musical with which they may be contrasted. The classical musical (in most readings of the genre) valorizes community and the romantic couple. This valorization reaches its ultimate expressivity through song and dance, even as these musicals seek to hide the materiality of their discourse in the name of entertainment as a transparent spectacle.[2] Such manifestations may be contrasted with the modernist musical, which, as Jane Feuer has put it, "*systematically* deconstructs the classic syntax of the genre" and expresses far greater skepticism about the value of community and the romantic couple.[3] For Feuer, *Pennies from Heaven* (Herbert Ross, 1981), with its intertextuality, deconstructionist gestures, and sound-image disjunctions, is the "furthest development" of this possibility.[4] *On connaît la chanson* is dedicated to the memory of Dennis Potter, the author of the screenplay for *Pennies from Heaven*, itself an adaptation by Potter of his six-episode television series, originally broadcast by the BBC in 1978. Both the Resnais and Tsai films make use of the most remarked-upon strategy of the television and film version of *Pennies from Heaven*: performers lip-synching to voices that are not their own.

The forms of the Resnais and Tsai films clearly indicate their modernist status. Such a status, however, is itself subject to variables: The modernism of Resnais is tied to immediate postwar French culture, marked by knowledge of the concentration camps, the atomic bomb, and the war in Algeria (all of these subjects of Resnais's films of the 1950s and 1960s) and by concomitant developments in the arts that often took it upon themselves to testify to this history in forms that reflected a search for new meanings. Tsai, not emerging until five decades after Resnais's first films, has an equally strong tie to Taiwanese culture of the late twentieth century, a period of increased democratization and accelerated, late capitalist expansion. Nevertheless, both directors, a year apart from one another, coincidentally made musicals in which classical and modernist distinctions that have been applied to the genre are at once confirmed, expanded, and challenged. That these films are also apartment plot musicals will be central to what follows here.

II

Let us begin with the classical period and an ingenious but neglected Hollywood musical, *I Love Melvin* (Don Weis, 1953). The film reunites Debbie Reynolds and Donald O'Connor, stars of the iconic *Singin' in the Rain* (Gene Kelly and Stanley Donen, 1952). *I Love Melvin* is a comparatively low-budget affair, its small scale also part of the film's charm. The setting is New York, the social environment decidedly middle class and family oriented. Judy (Reynolds) lives with her parents in an apartment on the Upper West Side, plays a human football in the production number of a Broadway show, and is being wooed by Melvin (O'Connor), a photographer's assistant for *Look* magazine. In one sequence, Melvin photographs Judy in the living room of her apartment, culminating in a duet, "Where Did You Learn to Dance?" The transformative impulses of the classical musical often manifest themselves in the treatment of a film's interior environment, this environment becoming raw material elevated to another dimension through singing and dancing. Such elevation occurs in this number but in a way that has specific implications for the apartment plot. Most obviously, there is the question of scale.

In *Singin' in the Rain*, Reynolds (as Kathy Selden) and O'Connor (as Cosmo Brown) join forces with Gene Kelly (as Don Lockwood) for "Good Morning," a number set on the ground floor of Lockwood's Hollywood mansion. Their performance takes in a fair amount of territory, as they sing and dance from the kitchen out to the dining room, living room, up and down a flight of stairs, over to a bar, and back to the living room again, making use of costumes and the decor in a manner consistent with the transformational gestures of the genre. The spaciousness of Lockwood's home allows for this territorial excitement to occur. But such an impulse may literally find itself frustrated by the cramped quarters of an apartment, and, consequently, more ingenious measures must be taken. In "Where

Did You Learn to Dance?" mastery of a domestic environment is again attempted as it faces the additional challenge of moving two performers through a song-and-dance routine with very little space and decor at its disposal. But this tiny space also contains within it a coffee table and a wood floor, most of the latter covered by a rug. Across the number's three and a half minutes, eight camera setups are employed and the mobile framing, closely tied to the performers, creates an impression of fluidity. There are several points of interest here in terms of the concerns of this essay.

First, the coffee table is used as a tiny dance floor. Dancing on tables may be found in many musicals, serving as a kind of lyrical domestic anarchy. All that is of interest for this essay in relation to *I Love Melvin* is the smallness, even structural vulnerability, of the table within a confined living room set. Judy and Melvin are no sooner on this table than they move off it and return to the floor. However, the floor is itself problematic for dancing in that it is extensively covered with a rug, limiting the ability to tap. Consequently, Judy and Melvin often move to the edge of the living room, just beyond where the rug ends, so that their taps can solidly hit a wood floor. They eventually move to an archway that connects the living room with the dining room and where there is no rug. The couple here enjoy a particular freedom, arms happily extended out and over their heads, and Melvin grabs a stool for Judy to sit on as they playfully re-create the gesture of Melvin photographing her. But they do not move into the dining room, and instead return to the living room, revisiting and revising many of their earlier steps. In contrast to the expansive movements of "Good Morning," in *I Love Melvin* it is as though Judy and Melvin prefer to confine themselves to one small section of an apartment in order to explore the implications of the tiny space as fully as possible. But in a manner typical of many classical musicals in which domestic space may assume a key function, this is the only apartment number in *I Love Melvin*. The film otherwise moves about a variety of locations, all of this framed by a conception of New York as a space of boundless opportunity.

On connaît la chanson and *The Hole*, on the other hand, extend and intensify the possibilities of musical apartment dwellings. Apartments are central to the narrative situation of the Resnais film, for example, rather than simply one setting among many: Odile (Sabine Azéma) is looking for a bigger apartment and employs the services of real estate agent Marc Duveyrier (Lambert Wilson), who, in the midst of the apartment search, begins romancing Odile's sister, Camille (Agnès Jaoui); Camille is being simultaneously wooed by Duveyrier's assistant, Simon (André Dussollier), even as the married Odile begins to reignite an attraction to one-time close friend Nicolas (Jean-Pierre Bacri), also married. While the film is not solely preoccupied with the search for a new apartment, it nevertheless frequently returns to this search, necessitating sequences set in various apartments and within which several musical numbers occur; and the extended final sequence, its de facto finale, is set in Odile's new, large Paris flat. In *The Hole*, it is one working-class apartment building that dominates, and the film only leaves that building in order to go to an underground shopping area where the film's unnamed male protagonist (Lee Kang-sheng) works in a food store. The film otherwise confines itself to his small apartment and to one of an also-unnamed female protagonist (Yang Kuei-mei), who lives in the space underneath him. Over the course of the film, a strange courtship develops between them through this proximity. As in *I Love Melvin*, apartment living and the formation of romantic couples are essential to *On connaît la chanson* and *The Hole*. But the implications of urban space undergo a shift in these later films, and the notion of the urban world as a hypothetical playground for romance and social success likewise undergoes a shift.

III

In contrast to the urban ecstatic sensibility of *I Love Melvin*, the Taipei in Tsai's film is suffering from an epidemic of uncertain origin, resulting in the city being evacuated and an order to cut off all water in quarantine zones in seven days, on January 1, 2000. In the midst of this, the rain never stops falling. *The Hole* is a film of perpetual rainfall and of water in various manifestations (sewage, drinking water, bathing). Such a preoccupation with water is central to Tsai's cinema. Apartments also recur in his films prior to *The Hole*, most notably in *Vive l'amour* (1994), a film that addresses the disastrous overdevelopment in Taipei and the many vacant apartment buildings that stood in the wake of this. With *The Hole*, though, we are almost entirely in the realm of allegory, a realm that Tsai continues to draw upon, to varying degrees, up through his most recent work. The recasting of such concerns in the form of a musical, though, allows both Tsai's cinema and the musical genre to engage with one another in a very particular manner. The musical has historically been a genre of modernity, a celebration of the urban and the technological. In its classical incarnations it may allow harsh social and economic realities to be addressed. But these films must finally show the overcoming of social realities through the force of creative energies. In *The Hole*, however, we find a modernity on the brink of extinction as it faces the impending millennium. Whereas the New York of *I Love Melvin* is constantly renewing itself as it makes way for the Judy LeRoys of this world, the Taipei of *The Hole* is being literally and symbolically washed away.

Within the context of the classical musical, rain is a temporary inconvenience and can ultimately allow for a further strengthening of a couple, now brought together for shelter through a sudden downpour. In *Top Hat* (Mark Sandrich, 1935), for example, the first duet between Jerry Travers (Fred Astaire) and Dale Tremont (Ginger Rogers) occurs because the couple seeks protection from a cloudburst. In a park bandstand, as the rain comes down, their romance takes its first major move toward solidification as they sing and dance to "Isn't This a Lovely Day (to Be Caught in the Rain)?" But in *The Hole*, the rain not only never stops but finds its way into the apartments. This torrential rain, combined with the mysterious virus that is contaminating what is left of Taipei, turning some of its inhabitants into cockroaches, would appear to be a refusal of the temporary setbacks of the classical musical, setbacks to be overcome through the will of the imagination or a shift in philosophical perspective. In *The Hole*, the combined problems of omnipresent water and an insidious virus are so insurmountable that a simple song and dance or change in attitude is, on one level, ludicrously inadequate. And yet such a bleak reading does not quite capture the experience of the film.

In the film's opening sequence, the male protagonist, wearing only white briefs and white T-shirt, is lying asleep on a black leather couch in his apartment. A coffee table is in front of the couch, but unlike the table in *I Love Melvin*, at no point in the film is it used for singing and dancing. The man is awakened by a plumber who has (miraculously in the midst of the apocalypse) arrived to fix a water leak that is spreading into the apartment below. (We later discover that the plumber is having an affair with the woman in that apartment.) The plumber locates a source for the leak in the floor's center and, in the process of ostensibly repairing it, leaves behind an enormous hole. Within the syntax of the classical musical, as we have already seen with *I Love Melvin*, a floor is a privileged surface in that it also becomes a surface for dancing. But a floor may also serve as a prelude to romantic seduction and is occasionally lyricized through song. In *Top Hat*, Jerry and Dale first meet when he boisterously dances to "No Strings" in the hotel room that is above hers, waking her and causing her to come upstairs to his room in order to complain. He apologizes, and after she returns to her room he puts her back to sleep by doing a soft shoe on the same floor, now sprinkled with sand. Nevertheless, the white-on-white luxury of *Top Hat*'s hotel, while offering the possibility for performance, is not domestic. And it is precisely the transient nature of a hotel that differentiates it from the apartment even as the apartment, placed within the shared living space of the apartment building, is less permanent in its implications than a house.

In contrast to *I Love Melvin*, the working-class apartments in *The Hole* are closer to the apartment plot tradition of the urban dwelling for young unmarrieds.[5] But in *The Hole* these are not bachelor or bachelorette digs, glamorizing the urban single. Instead, the decor in *The Hole* is threadbare, the apartments virtually identical with one another, save for the red-painted entrance door for the apartment of the man. These apartments, as Amy Herzog argues, "bear the marks of the historical conditions that brought them into being—the by-products of a technological, aspiring capitalist state that has overextended itself."[6] How, then, can a musical number arise amid such apparent negation? The impulse to perform in this film is not situated in the manner of *I Love Melvin*, in which the songs naturally arise from the story. Taipei is not a city for the protagonists' taking (not that they would want it anyway). In the absence of any sense of community, the numbers emerge (as in *Pennies from Heaven*) through a type of psychological projection in which a protagonist envisions herself in a musical number that is outside of the time and space continuum of the narrative world. Such placement is not, in the most general sense, terribly new but is traceable to the fashion for dream ballets and fantasy numbers that recur in musicals from the classical period: Judy's "Lady Loves," with which *I Love Melvin* opens, is one example of many.

What the *Pennies from Heaven* approach involves is an intensification of this, in which virtually every number is situated in a subjective manner, and a sense of community is gone. We are in a world in which the gap between the dreams and desires offered to us through the popular culture of music and cinema cannot be reconciled with a given material reality. *The Hole* is less emphatic in its intent than *Pennies from Heaven* but also more restrictive in the ways that it positions its numbers. Whatever its modernist inclinations, *Pennies from Heaven* clearly locates the precise moment to which a musical number is responding and is equally clear in its indications that we are now back to reality once the number ends. In *The Hole*, the woman likewise leaves her apartment through the force of her imagination, although the precise cues indicating a passage from reality into song and then back again are less clear-cut than in *Pennies from Heaven*.

Moreover, all of the songs that she lip-synchs to are from the same performance source, the film and pop music star of the 1950s and early '60s, Grace Chang. The music in *Pennies from Heaven* is consistent with the period in which the film is set, the Great Depression. In *The Hole*, Chang (who retired from performing in 1964) becomes less a nostalgic emblem than an unseen force for the utopic possibilities of song and dance, given a specific female emphasis here that gradually incorporates the possibility of a male-female couple. Chang is a mythic star within postwar Chinese popular culture, and this status is occasionally passed into the body of *The Hole*'s female protagonist. In one of Chang's earliest and most popular films, *Mambo Girl* (Wen Yi, 1957), Li Kailing (Chang), like Judy in *I Love Melvin*, lives with her family in a middle-class apartment building. Most of the numbers in the film are ensemble in nature, set in public spaces, with Li always taking the lead. But when Li discovers that she is adopted, she sings a ballad on the rooftop of her building, in which an imagined version of her biological mother as a peasant descends from the sky and sings to her. But the film offers no songs within the apartment itself. It is as though the apartment is inadequate for both Li's exuberance in the early scenes and for her melancholia once she acquires knowledge of her adopted status.

The first four musical sequences in *The Hole* occur either within various transitional spaces of the building (elevators, stairs, hallways) or in the passages of the shopping area. In its need to get away from the confines of the apartment, then, *The Hole* does not entirely abandon the basic syntax of the classical apartment plot musical. At the same time, the film goes no farther than the building itself, as though, in the midst of the devastation, it is unable to conceive of a concrete alternative beyond these apartments. All of the numbers present certain challenges in terms of the restricted space. Of the first four, the most interesting of these for the concerns of this essay is the first, "Oh Calypso," originally performed by Chang in *Air Hostess* (Wen Yi, 1959), where it is staged in a very different manner

FIG. 3.1. The woman performs "Oh Calypso" in an elevator in *The Hole* (Tsai Ming-liang, 1998).

Oh Calypso, Oh Calypso

from what we find in *The Hole*. *Air Hostess* uses a variety of camera setups and movements as Chang performs in a large social space, being viewed by dozens of people, as she moves about the room in a seductive, tight-fitting red lamé gown. The space in which the woman in *The Hole* performs the song is far more restricted: an elevator (fig. 3.1). For the song, though, it is transformed into a magical box of performance, the walls covered with blinking lights and the woman outfitted in a showgirl costume with feathers. In contrast to the way that the number is shot in the Chang vehicle, Tsai films this in one extended take, the camera starting at some distance from the elevator and then slowly tracking forward. When the camera, in its forward tracking, eventually comes close to the woman, she makes a move as though about to step out of the safety zone of the elevator. As with Melvin and Judy resisting the temptation to dance beyond the living room, her (potentially fatal?) step does not occur, and instead the camera begins to reverse its forward movement, as though it wishes to echo a lyric in the song that refers to taking one step forward and then one step back. While this number is not technically staged within an apartment, its lyricizing of confined space is in itself indicative of the apartment plot musical's potential for resisting the expansiveness otherwise typical of the genre, at least in its classical manifestations.

The three subsequent numbers, while reasonably restricted in spatial terms, do not go to the extremes of "Oh Calypso." "Tiger Lady" shows the woman moving down a hallway and through various emergency stairs, accompanied by an all-female trio; in "I Want Your Love" she is on the exterior walkway of the building, singing to and chasing the man who keeps eluding her grasp; and the most elaborate one of all, "Ahchoo Cha Cha," is staged on the stairs that lead down to the shopping arcade, the woman surrounded by male and female dancers. While acknowledging that these musical interludes represent the female protagonist's "inner world," Tsai also sees them as "weapons . . . to confront the environment at the end of the millennium." For Tsai, the musical offers a "passionate desire, naïve simplicity" now suppressed within an advanced technological present and envisioned nightmare future.[7] Unlike *Pennies from Heaven*, which repeatedly underlines the impossibility of the fantasies engendered by singing and dancing, *The Hole* refuses a didactic fantasy/reality split. The end of "Oh Calypso" does not return us to a point of origin for the woman, forcing her to confront the futility of her illusions. Instead, there is a cut to presumably the same elevator, returned to its earlier state, the woman now gone and the man passed out on the floor as the elevator door opens and then closes. While on a first viewing the moment might indicate a return to reality, the film's overall structure resists such an interpretation.

Whereas "Oh Calypso" is not directly cued by a moment in the film's narrative, the succeeding numbers gradually become more aligned with the heroine's inner world, even if they do not arise from the diegesis in the fluid manner of a classical musical. For example, when she spots the man peering at her through the hole, she takes an aerosol can and sprays him in the face. This moment cues "Tiger Lady," with its lyrics repeatedly telling an unseen male figure that he is a nuisance who must go away. Beyond this, a trajectory is detectable in which a romance between the man and the woman, only fitfully articulated in the nonmusical sections, develops as the woman increasingly pursues the man across the numbers. At the close of "Oh Calypso," the shot of the passed-out man is followed by another shot of him staggering down an external hallway as he grabs a fire extinguisher from the wall. Another cut takes us into his apartment, as he continues to hold the extinguisher and then vomits through the hole in the floor and into the woman's apartment. What such a seemingly revolting moment foreshadows, however, is not a return to reality signaled through bodily functions. On the contrary, the film moves toward, on the one hand, further abstraction: this hole becomes both a metaphor for urban devastation and an extension of the human body, an orifice. On the other hand, this orifice will ultimately be tied to bringing the man and woman together, culminating in the film's finale.

IV

Tsai's cinema is obsessively associational, and virtually all phenomena (including apartments) become simultaneously concrete and metaphoric. As Herzog notes of *The Hole*, "The woman's relationship with the apartment is so tightly woven that the differences between them are indistinguishable."[8] But if the woman is linked with the apartment, she is also linked with the man, the film engaging in its own ironic variation on the formation of the couple. Some of the film's effects in this regard are relatively simple: cross-cutting between apartments as they both eat noodles; later, her extended crying sequence is followed by his. But the linkages also assume other, more corporeal articulations. At one moment in "I Want Your Love," for example, the man grabs a fire extinguisher off the wall and throws it at the woman. Unfazed, she holds the extinguisher and continues to perform after his departure, lovingly cradling the extinguisher in her arms and then using it as a dancing partner. Such a use of the object is, as can be seen in the "Good Morning" number, a trope of the classical musical. But within the context of Tsai's film, the extinguisher is also a stand-in for the body of the male object of desire, as Chang's voice calls out for him to "come a bit closer."

In *Top Hat*, Jerry dancing on the floor above Dale is an act of aggression before it eventually becomes an act of seduction. In Tsai's film, the floor's potential for seduction is no less potent and even more blatantly erotic. But *Top Hat* uses its floor as a traditional inciting incident for its narrative. Near the end of *The Hole*, in a strange, initially failed courtship ritual, the man inserts his leg into the shared hole between the two apartments. The insertion begins as an agonized push before the leg finally makes its complete insertion and then dangles through the floor, a kind of leggy feminine seduction but here enacted by a man. (It is almost an echo of the opening shot of "I Want Your Love," where the woman's leg emerges from around a corner.) Sadly, she does not notice this body part in front of her, preoccupied as she is with going to the bathroom and flushing the toilet. In *The Hole*, one must wait for romantic formations. One must wait, in fact, until the end of the film. Here the man reaches down through the hole, offering the woman a glass of water and, in a transcendent moment, lifts her up into his apartment, their drab clothes miraculously changed in the process, as she is now wearing a red chiffon gown and he is in a white tuxedo. The wind lightly blowing, the couple performs a slow dance to Chang's "I Don't Care Who You Are," with its lyrics promising "days of carefree springs." In contrast to the other numbers in the film, performed in a presentational style, the man and woman here never acknowledge the camera but look only at one another. Within the context of the apartment plot musical, however, this moment is of some significance. In contrast to most classical apartment plot musicals, apartments in *The Hole* are not points of origin one must master before moving beyond these spaces in order to conquer the world. Instead, performing in an apartment is the culmination of the journey, its poetic end point. By the end of *The Hole*, Taipei is effectively gone, as the Last Man and Last Woman dance together in his apartment, facing either the end of civilization and their own imminent deaths (there are indications that the woman herself has begun to show symptoms of the virus) or the beginning of a new millennium, a new world (the film's visual language is so figurative that it resists attempts to explain its intent in literal terms; that is, this is a despairing conclusion because the woman is dying).[9]

The apartments in *The Hole* do not so much motivate a plot (the film has none to speak of) as clarify the film's intent. The film's allegorizing tendencies override the more localized victories of the classical musical. The man and woman here do not explore the space of the apartment in the happily confined manner of Judy and Melvin in *I Love Melvin*. The man and woman's slow dance occurs within one tiny area of the apartment's living room. At the same time, the energies of an *I Love Melvin* are far from negated, even if their rhythm in *The Hole* is of a very different nature. In its emotional and musical intensity in the midst of chaos and death, this final sequence from *The Hole* is a magisterial representation of the musical's utopic impulses. The man and woman do not seem to go anywhere as they dance, the lyricizing of a small space typical of the apartment plot musical taken to its absolute limit. One must now, in a sense, simply slow down, move tentatively, and push a bit harder.

V

In contrast to the decay of *The Hole*, *On connaît la chanson* is situated within a vibrant and somewhat touristic contemporary Paris that is, as Emma Wilson writes, "mapped as a location of encounters and interconnections."[10] The film opens with a prologue in which, on a comically theatrical set, Dietrich von Choltitz (Götz Burger) is in his Paris office during the Nazi occupation, refusing to follow Hitler's orders to bomb the city. The sequence culminates with Choltitz lip-synching to Josephine Baker's "J'ai deux amours" (1930), a song that expresses, in Baker's American-accented French, her love for Paris as her second home. Choltitz's performance is interrupted after only a few bars as we abruptly transition to the present day. We there find Camille acting as a tour guide outside of the building that served as Choltitz's headquarters. (Her voice can already be heard during the credits, immediately before the prologue, speaking to what will turn out to be this tour group.) "Paris was not destroyed," she says in relation to Choltitz's decision, "but it was a close thing."

With *On connaît la chanson* we are not at the end of history but in the midst of it, with Camille as both literal tour guide and a scholar of the most obscure French historical data: she has just completed her thesis on the yeomen at Paladru Lake in the year 1000. Moreover, the film offers an abundance of plot: complications, criss-crossing action, coincidences and misunderstandings, the film's rhythm one of great speed and energy. Here characters not only have names but they are written and performed in a style that gives the characters specificity, backstories, blood ties. Far from being washed away, *On connaît la chanson* shows us a world still capable of being researched and catalogued. (Among Camille's tour group is Simon, who writes radio plays with French historical topics.) But if *On connaît la chanson* does not represent a world facing immediate extinction, it nevertheless does, through its prologue, show us that such an extinction was (and remains) a "close thing."

In spite of Resnais's repeatedly expressed admiration for the Hollywood musical, neither this film nor his subsequent musical, *Pas sur la bouche* (2003), owe a debt to American models. Moreover, French cinema has little in the way of a classical musical film tradition for Resnais to draw upon. Rather, it has scattered titles of interest, such as the René Clair films of the early 1930s (their use of song, dialogue, sound effects, and musical underscoring as part of a playful soundtrack fabric loosely anticipates Resnais's film) or something like the Josephine Baker vehicle *Princess Tam Tam* (Edmond T. Gréville, 1935). French cinema engages in its most significant intervention much later, through its modernist reworkings of the musical, beginning in the 1960s with *A Woman Is a Woman* (Jean-Luc Godard, 1962) and Jacques Demy's films. *On connaît la chanson* is part of this later history and, moreover, a history in which the apartment is a frequent domestic space for a reconceived notion of the genre.[11]

As it is for Tsai, the apartment for Resnais is, from *Muriel ou le Temps d'un retour* (1963) to *Cœurs* (2006), a privileged location. For Wilson, the "spatial paradigm" of *On connaît la chanson* is the new apartment into which Odile and her husband Claude (Pierre Arditi) move.[12] The apartment itself is clearly a studio set, the view consisting of an artificial backdrop of the city, this backdrop, in its hallucinatory artifice, looking like something out of *An American in Paris* (Vincente Minnelli, 1951). The apartment move, though, does not occur until the film's final thirty minutes, when this space is the setting for a party that Odile gives in order to celebrate her purchase. Prior to this, we have seen the apartment, minus any furniture, when Marc shows it to Camille. Other empty apartments are also part of the unfolding action, when Simon shows them to Nicolas, the latter newly arrived in Paris. The bourgeois characters of *On connaît la chanson* face neither the social nor the economic stagnation of the Tsai film. Nevertheless, all of the apartments, aside from the final one, are thought by the protagonists to be too small or too large or too gloomy. Simon shows at least thirty apartments to a perpetually dissatisfied Nicolas, and even Odile's final one, for all its square-foot advantages, will soon feel closed in, a real estate disaster, due to a high-rise building that Odile discovers (to her horror, in the midst of her party) is being constructed opposite it.

Wilson notes that the protagonists of the film are rarely at home and that the apartments themselves are "unsettling or cluttered."[13] If in *The Hole* apartments are a precarious refuge from the destruction and disease that lie beyond them, *On connaît la chanson* presents us with apartments in which it is difficult to remain still, a nervous agitation that dominates much of Resnais's cinema. The characters of *On connaît la chanson* suffer from palpitations, fainting spells, and manic-depressive behavior, the possibility of death almost as certain as in *The Hole*: Adjacent to Odile's office building is a cemetery (a startling, surreal image), and she hurriedly passes through it on her way to look at her new apartment. Immediately after this cemetery walk she observes an old man on the street, just narrowly missing being killed by a speeding car—another "close thing." The classical apartment plot musical's impulse to briefly lyricize an apartment but only as a springboard for movements that are finally beyond domestic space is given another variation in Resnais's film. Even though the film moves about various Paris locations and shows us several different apartments, the futile search for the perfect apartment—a utopic space—dominates. The apartment plot's concern with spontaneity, play, and simultaneity is more aggressively present here than in *The Hole*, even as the tone of the film is, for all of its apparent lightness, itself unsettled. If in *The Hole* a collapsing of the spatial and temporal occurs through the film's concern with a slow, sometimes agonized experience of duration, *On connaît la chanson* creates an atmosphere of frantic simultaneity.

Unlike Tsai, Resnais is a montage filmmaker. Even in Resnais films in which the montage is relatively muted, the cut having a particular rhetorical, temporal, or spatial force remains. And this has implications in terms of the treatment of apartment space. Some of Resnais's effects in *On connaît la chanson* are playful. For example, there is the sequence in which Simon shows Nicolas the umpteenth apartment, this one decreed to be too large due to Nicholas's sudden revelation, at the end of the three-minute mobile take with which the sequence begins, that he would now prefer a studio flat: his wife no longer wishes to join him in Paris. A reaction shot of a disappointed Simon follows, with Simon finally sinking into the bottom of the frame. There is then an impossible match on action, as both Nicolas and Simon sink down not to the floor of the dining room where they had been standing but on the edge of a tub in the bathroom. Here they sit and perform a duet over their anguished love for two different women, the voice emerging belonging to a single female performer, Jane Birkin, singing "Quoi" (1985) (fig. 3.2).[14] However, this notion of a song being so powerful that its continuity is challenged by ellipses in the spatial organization of the number through montage is not uncommon in the classical musical. Resnais's boldest strategies in the film lie elsewhere.

In *On connaît la chanson*, the strong sense of a cut is present not only within the images but also on the soundtrack. However different the implications of the songs are in *The Hole* from the Potter approach, that film (like *Pennies from Heaven*) stages each song from beginning to end. This sense of completion never occurs in the Resnais film. There are no production numbers; there is no dancing. Even though props are sometimes used during songs, these props are never (as they continue to be in *The Hole*) transformed in the manner of a classical musical. Instead, the decor remains immutable. And unlike the sustained use of a single performer source for *The Hole*, *On connaît la chanson* draws upon more than fifty years of French popular music. However, the recordings are only heard in snippets, as they quickly arise from and then disappear back into the dialogue, all in a matter of seconds. Working out of a statement by Resnais and Bacri (the film's coscreenwriter, along with Joui), Wilson argues that the songs "work as indicators of, or interference from, the characters' mental lives . . . representing the imaginary and emotional life of both individuals

FIG. 3.2. An impossible match on action places Nicolas and Simon on the edge of a tub as they begin their duet in *On connaît la chanson* (Alain Resnais, 1997).

and collective groups."[15] Such a description is still close to what may be found in Potter. But the music itself is also another type of montage, moving beyond the fixation on a single mythic diva in Tsai's film to a multiplicity of voices across French history. This audio landscape creates its own layer of simultaneity, at once individual, collective, and historical, so that in virtually any given sequence we might hear voices from across a fifty-year span.[16] In the same sequence in which Nicolas and Simon sing "Quoi," they also perform to Léo Ferré's "Avec le temps" (1970) and Henri Garat's "Avoir un bon copain" (1930). *On connaît la chanson*'s emphasis on a collective French cultural imaginary in the music extends to the film's larger treatment of space and time, in which the apartments likewise become implicated.

VI

Five minutes into *On connaît la chanson*, we see the film's first apartment, the one out of which Odile wishes to move and where she and Claude are now entertaining Nicolas. In this early sequence, Resnais would seem to be observing the rules of analytical editing, the action occurring within a rigorously observed 180-degree line, the three protagonists carefully and theatrically positioned at the dining room table so that none of them have their backs to the camera. In fact, throughout the rest of the film we are never given a reverse angle of this apartment, an apartment that would appear to be, given the presence of a bed in the living room, a studio. But its actual size is not clear, as the only cuts or movements that open up the space occur in relation to a character's limited actions. Not until later in the sequence, when Nicolas begins to feel feverish, do we fully see the immediately adjacent living room, as Odile walks over to it and, in a panning and tracking movement, opens a window through which we can see, in the window of the apartment of the building next door, a man visible. (He is slightly visible but out of focus behind Claude, sitting at the table, in an earlier single.) This sight reinforces the sense of enclosure as well as foreshadowing the blocked view that Odile will eventually face in her more luxurious new surroundings.

At the same time, Claude's alienation from the moment, as Odile and Nicolas exchange intimate memories, is articulated not so much through dialogue as through the relationship between the camera and the space of the apartment. The establishing shot of the sequence, for example, is less classically spatial than rhetorical and psychological. As the sequence begins, Odile walks toward the table from a kitchen in the rear of the shot, the camera following her in a slight reverse tracking movement. The camera stops as she reaches the table but not in order to frame the principals in a three-shot. Instead, the camera frames Nicolas at the far left, Odile in the center, and only the barely visible folded hands of Claude at the far right bottom of the frame. (The film has not yet introduced Claude as a character.) When Nicolas complements Odile on her beauty, he looks off camera, as does Odile when she serves food to Claude. But there are no eyeline match cuts or a camera movement that would bring Claude into this moment. Instead, Odile and Nicolas begin lip-synching to Dalida and Alain Delon's "Paroles, paroles" (1973).[17] As the song excerpt abruptly ends, the camera tracks backward as Claude simultaneously leans forward, and he at last becomes fully visible, the camera settling into a wide three-shot. Here and throughout the film, apartments are constructed as much through the montage as through production design. For the spectator, this can create a sense of anxiety, a feeling that the film withholds spatial acclimatization. The magical, expansive properties of a song or dance in a classical musical are present here in only the most fleeting of ways. Otherwise, a song can close down a space as much as open it up.

The modernist design of Odile's new apartment stands in contrast to most of the other apartments of the film: Odile literally and symbolically ascends to her high-rise flat, a Paris of the past, present, and future now hers to conquer after the claustrophobia of her studio. Throughout most of the party sequence, the framing is tight, the bodies of the party-goers filling the frame, making it difficult to experience the much-touted spatial grandeur of this new apartment. But even before she receives the announcement of the high-rise opposite that will soon block her view, there is a strange image of jellyfish swimming across the screen that occurs at every dissolve during the party sequence. Resnais has explained this aesthetic decision as his way of saying "something of the common unconscious, of the ripples which move between individuals in a circle or community."[18] Prior to the appearance of the jellyfish, the aquatic element has been introduced in small ways: the clam sculpture outside the building itself, for example, or the aquarium in one of the many doctors' offices visited by Nicolas. This rippled community, though, is markedly different from the conception of community we find in the classical musical. What creates the "common unconscious" of this nervous community, its romantic couples tentatively forming and breaking apart even during its conclusion, is ultimately invisible, resistant to direct representation. Unlike the water imagery of *The Hole*, the jellyfish images are irrational and cannot be explained through either literal or symbolic meanings. Nevertheless, their periodic placement over shots of the party suggests that this community does not have the capacity to master nature so much as to be engulfed by or return to it, Odile's apartment, looking out upon a soon-to-be-blocked fantasy image of Paris, likewise subject to the same contingency.

VII

The widest view of Odile's apartment is a high-angle shot in the film's coda. The party is over and the father of Odile and Camille (Jean-Paul Roussillon) is alone, surveying the wreckage. He sits down, picks up a CD, and there is a cut to the film's final shot, a close-up of him looking into the camera and asking, "Does anyone know that song?" An old man holds a technology (the compact disc) that came into existence many years after his birth, as he moves about a one-time fantasy space, all of its major protagonists now gone. The happy ending of *I Love Melvin* is, within the logic of the classical musical, fully achieved: a romantic couple is definitively formed, the urban world beyond now rightfully theirs for the taking. But by the time it has reached its conclusion, *I Love Melvin* no longer needs its apartment. That space is now too small, too confining. As modernist apartment plot musicals, by contrast, *The Hole* and *On connaît la chanson* cannot let go of or move beyond the apartments that are central to both films, as the search for the ideal song or dance continues. All that is left by the end are, on the one hand, a slow-dancing couple and, on the other, a very old man, all of them moving within worlds that may be, in different ways, close to death. But the need to lyricize space through song or dance persists, now situated amid ruined apartments that once served as vital containers of the dream of something better.

NOTES

My thanks to Steve Barnes for his help on this essay.

1. Pamela Robertson Wojcik, *The Apartment Plot: Urban Living in American Film and Popular Culture, 1945–1975* (Durham, NC: Duke University Press, 2010), 10.

2. See Rick Altman, *The American Film Musical* (Bloomington: Indiana University Press, 1987), 129–327.

3. Jane Feuer, *The Hollywood Musical*, 2nd ed. (Bloomington: Indiana University Press, 1993), 129.

4. Feuer, *The Hollywood Musical*, 126.

5. Wojcik, *The Apartment Plot*, devotes two separate chapters to such urban, postwar American apartments, one on those inhabited by single men, "'We Like Our Apartment': The Playboy Indoors," 88–138, and the other on those inhabited by single women, "The Great Reprieve: Modernity, Femininity, and the Apartment," 139–79.

6. Amy Herzog, *Dreams of Difference, Songs of the Same: The Musical Moment in Film* (Minneapolis: University of Minnesota Press, 2010), 196.

7. David Walsh, "An Interview with Tsai Ming-liang, Director of *The Hole*," World Socialist Web Site, October 7, 1998, https://www.wsws.org/en/articles/1998/10/tsai-007 .html.

8. Herzog, *Dreams of Difference*, 196.

9. Robin Wood offers an agonized reading of the film in this regard. Robin Wood, "*The Hole*," *Cineaction* 48 (1998): 54–57.

10. Emma Wilson, *Alain Resnais* (Manchester: Manchester University Press, 2006), 188.

11. Apartment settings dominate the Godard film as well as Demy's *Les Parapluies de Cherbourg* (1964) and *Une chambre en ville* (1982).

12. Wilson, *Alain Resnais*, 189.

13. Wilson, *Alain Resnais*, 189.

14. In one scene later in the film, it is Jane Birkin who will play Nicolas's wife as she lip-synchs to her own recording of "Quoi."

15. Wilson, *Alain Resnais*, 184.

16. That many of these voices are either those of actors who sing or singers who also became actors (Arletty, Josephine Baker, Simone Simon, Jacques Dutronc, Charles Aznavour) cannot be incidental, given Resnais's love for the specific texture and rhythm of an actor's speaking voice.

17. Delon does not sing in this duet but merely responds to Dalida by reciting.

18. Wilson, *Alain Resnais*, 187. One may also be reminded here of Henri Laborit's statement in Resnais's *Mon oncle d'amerique* (1980): "We are nothing but others."

4

MOVEMENT AND STASIS
IN FASSBINDER'S APARTMENT PLOT

MICHAEL DEANGELIS

Across a career of thirteen years and more than forty feature films and television series, Rainer Werner Fassbinder wrote and directed a great number
of domestic melodramas with plots centering upon the urban apartment.
In these films, Fassbinder demonstrates that fluidity and permeability—
central features of urban space and urban domestic living activated by
the apartment plot—are invariably inflected by class and social relations
that determine one's ability to move freely through the public and private
cityscape. In his cinema, the urban apartment becomes a crucial anchor
point in an elaborate system of movement and stasis that both enables and
compromises human agency and intervention. Within, toward, and away
from their central apartment dwellings, and always orchestrated by elaborate mise-en-scène and a cinematography that foregrounds both clearances and obstacles to motion, simple attempts at character movement
in Fassbinder's urban apartment plot function synecdochically to signal
larger-scale problems of urban interpersonal relations, inexorably illumi-

nating the power differentials perpetuating systems of social oppression that the close and populous city spaces exacerbate. If critical work on Fassbinder has historically highlighted his critique of human relations under capitalism, the model of the apartment plot provides keen insight into an elegant, kinetic system that he devises to demonstrate, through a focus upon movement, a contention that fluidity and permeability in urban domestic spatial relations can never be politically neutral or universally accessible concepts, but rather mechanisms that are always already bound up in a self-perpetuating system of social relations harboring privilege and disadvantage. His handling of urban domestic space thus expands our understanding of a crucial sociopolitical dimension of the apartment plot.

Henri Lefebvre's conceptions of space help to illuminate Fassbinder's stylistically vibrant and formally challenging reimagining of the apartment plot—foremost, his suggestion that space is never space in itself, and that it can only be said to exist to the extent that it becomes socially activated. As Lefebvre describes it, "Space is social morphology: it is to lived experience what form is to the living organism, and just as intimately bound up with function and structure."[1] The mode of spatial activation that Fassbinder articulates is one that focuses upon principles of motion and movement. If, for Lefebvre, "to say 'urban space' is to say centre and centrality," Fassbinder designates the urban apartment as centralized space that both enables and impedes actual and potential movement not only within it, but also toward and away from it.[2] If space requires navigation and movement in order to be activated, Fassbinder's manipulation and disruption of movement in the apartment plot constitutes his singular political critique of urban space—a critique, as I will demonstrate, that is frequently steeped in the dynamic between seeing and being seen that recurs so consistently in his filmmaking practice. This study focuses upon five domestic dramas that most clearly demonstrate this problematic of movement through the urban space in and around the apartment dwelling: *Warum läuft Herr R. amok?* (*Why Does Herr R. Run Amok?*, 1970, cowritten and codirected by Michael Fengler); *Die Händler der vier Jahreszeiten* (*The Merchant of Four Seasons*, 1971); *Angst essen Seele auf* (*Ali: Fear Eats the Soul*, 1974); *Mutter Küsters Fährt zum Himmel* (*Mother Küsters Goes to Heaven*, 1975); and the made-for-television film *Angst vor der Angst* (*Fear of Fear*, 1975).

Committed to a politically engaged cinema, Fassbinder often confronted timely historical and national issues, including the terrorism prevalent in the national landscape during the late 1970s (*Deutschland im Herbst / Germany in Autumn*, 1978; *Die Dritte Generation / The Third Generation*, 1979), the concerns over the perpetuation of National Socialist Party ideologies in the German postwar era (*Die Ehe der Maria Braun / The Marriage of Maria Braun*, 1979), and the exploitation and plight of Turkish and Moroccan *Gastarbeiter* in the wake of a mid-1970s economic downturn, and especially after the tragic events at the 1972 Munich Olympics (*Ali: Fear Eats the Soul*). Even in the more topical, overtly issue-oriented narratives, however, the political nature of Fassbinder's cinema is rarely a mere function of subject matter choice; more consistently, the films are politicized through their dialectical approach to illuminating the dynamics of personal, interpersonal, and social relations under capitalism. As Thomas Elsaesser argues, Fassbinder "deployed conventions, stereotypes and genre formulas in order to capture a truth whose validity may have been emotional but also could be read as political. . . . Especially *The Merchant of Four Seasons* was often cited as an example of political cinema, accessible to the mass public, while subtle and formally complex in the way it secured this accessibility."[3] The intimacy of this interaction between the relational and the political is perhaps nowhere more pronounced than in his melodramas, which, as Peter Ruppert suggests, evoke a "dialectical structuring" of identification and distance that requires viewers to actively negotiate their emotional and political investment, and to discover an inherent yet never-represented "utopian potential" by imagining social and political structures that might transcend the constraints of economic exploitation and subjugation that his protagonists so consistently endure.[4] According to Ruppert, the objectifying glances so prevalent in Fassbinder's cinema "function to recall us to our own positions as viewers, similarly engaged in the act of looking."[5]

And it is in Fassbinder's melodramas and domestic dramas where one finds the clearest sense that, as Wojcik explains, "the apartment not only hosts but motivates action."[6] Action here takes the form of directional movement that implies a traversing and activation of space in ways that reference Michel de Certeau's explication of this process in *The Practice of Everyday Life*. There, de Certeau contrasts the abstraction of representational mapping of urban space with the more cogent realities attained by individual movement and carving of routes by moving through the urban grid.[7] If it is only the process of traversing space that produces the difference or distinction between one's location now and moments earlier, Fassbinder conveys movement cinematically through a highlighting of spatial distance—the space separating one point from the next, or the space that would require traversing in order to arrive at one's destination. As will be demonstrated, Fassbinder conveys this sense of distance in a variety of ways: by the representation of the actual movement of characters, by camera movement that traces its own path through space, or by the representation of discrete spaces separated (and linked) by cuts. Just as integrally, his films often register distance by foregrounding the act of looking, whether the look emanates from a character within the diegesis or from the outside perspective of the viewer. "Fassbinder often makes us—more or less uncomfortably—aware of our invisible presence, and by extension, of the fact that the 'frame' is not a window on the world outside," argues Elsaesser, adding, "Two structures—the viewer/film relation and the relation of the characters to the fiction itself—mirror each other infinitely and indefinitely."[8] Critical work on Fassbinder has also demonstrated how he foregrounds crucial functions of the Lacanian gaze—the reciprocated look that emanates from the perspective of the object viewed—emphasizing how the subject's looking out at an object of vision itself marks a locative distinction between two specific points in space. Curiously, as Kaja Silverman demonstrates, in Fassbinder's films this gaze is often represented as detached or dislocated from the originating look.[9]

In Fassbinder's domestic dramas, the locative distinctions established through the process of traversing (and thus creating and activating) urban space correlate dialectically with one of the functions of the urban apartment—as destination, as a place where (at least for some characters) the impetus for movement might be permitted to lessen or even momentarily cease. Character movement toward or away from one's apartment consists of directed, motivated movement, but the completion of the path toward home brings with it the sense that one has arrived somewhere—that one has ultimately been properly situated, and this serves as a call or justification for a change from motion to stasis. This principle is perhaps nowhere more clearly illustrated than in the opening sequences of *Fear of Fear*: while the pregnant, physically uncomfortable housewife Margot (Margit Carstensen) darts ambiently and directionlessly among the rooms of her upper-middle-class apartment in Bonn, her husband Kurt (Ulrich Faulhaber) stations himself in a comfortable leather easy chair, reluctant to move from his situated station even when Margot exhibits signs of early labor. Indeed, Fassbinder confines the action to the apartment in this film so intently that he entirely elides the representation of the labor scene itself, and practically the only scenes that occur elsewhere involve Margot's occasional journeys to the pharmacy across the street.

This example also demonstrates another important function of the apartment in Fassbinder's urban spatial design—as anchor point, or, in terms of movement, as endpoint of a vector that traces paths to or from locations outside the parameters of the domestic setting. Such vectors are sometimes linked to actual movement (leaving one's apartment and walking, as Margot does, to the pharmacy), or potential-yet-unactivated movement (from Margot's apartment window, she sees the pharmacy across the street, realizing the proximity and distance between it and her without actually activating this spatial route by walking there). As lines connecting two points—lines that activate or imply movement from one point to the other—directional vectors are also created by the act of being looked at. One cogent example of this phenomenon occurs on the morning following the first time that the Moroccan guest worker Ali (El Hedi ben Salem) spends the night at the apartment of the much older, widowed cleaning woman Emmi (Brigitte Mira) in *Ali: Fear Eats the Soul*. With the camera positioned facing the couple from the opposite side of the street, they are shown leaving the apartment building together, and on the sidewalk in front they depart in opposite directions. Immediately afterward, the camera pans up and to the right to reveal Frau Kargus (Elma Karlowa), the concierge of the apartment building where Emmi lives, who has been looking down at the couple from her own apartment window, the trajectory of her look tracing (in reverse) the exact trajectory initiated by the path and direction of the pan. The couple has not witnessed Kargus's look, but her act of looking back, in conjunction with the camera's initiating movement, creates another vector that links the couple to Kargus's judgmental scrutiny, and to the dominant position from which she looks out.

In Fassbinder's conception of urban space, the notion of proximity becomes crucial to the apartment's function as an anchor point in relation to actual or anticipated movement. Although these domestic dramas are all set in major German cities (Munich, Frankfurt, or Bonn), none of the films orients the viewer to the urban landscape via panoramic overview; instead, Fassbinder emphasizes the contiguity or relative accessibility of spaces by motivated or implied movement within the urban setting at the level of what Jane Jacobs calls "the street neighborhood network," a microscale urban environment that provides a sense of intimacy, ready access, and the impression that all of the places one might need or elect to visit beyond one's home are close by, often even visible from one's apartment window, as they are for Margot in *Fear of Fear*, or for Hans (Hans Hirschmüller) in *The Merchant of Four Seasons*, who positions his fruit vending cart strategically in the courtyard of neighboring apartment complexes as well as his own, proximity and access accentuated by the melodic tone of his bellowing voice calling his customers down to the street level below them to make their purchases.[10] Proximity is also a function of the immanently traversible nature of urban space: even when characters cannot see their destination from their apartment residence, they can walk there or readily navigate a route that gets them there expeditiously. In fact, of these five domestic dramas, it is only in *Ali: Fear Eats the Soul* that ready traversibility of urban space is ever compromised. From the start it is made clear that Ali and Emmi do not live close to one another in the city of Munich, and the fact that we are never granted visual access to his tenement housing or the neighborhood where it is located emphasizes Ali's social marginalization. Indeed, aside from the scenes in the Asphalt Bar, where the couple first meets, and in its owner Barbara's (Barbara Valentin) adjacent apartment, our experience of the city is confined to Emmi's neighborhood and apartment, and their arrangements to meet there must be negotiated as a function of spatial distance and the routes and timetables of the urban transit system. In fact, Emmi's suggestion that Ali stay at her apartment after their first evening together is framed as a matter of practicality and convenience, since by the time that they are ready to say their goodbyes, the last tram to Ali's neighborhood is about to leave, and their economic status does not allow for privately arranged transportation. Aside from this exception, however, although the urban landscape itself may be vast, most often in Fassbinder films, for better or worse, cities make citizens and their destinations accessible to one another.

At the same time, however, Fassbinder strategically undermines the notion of accessible, fluid, and potentially traversible space even as he highlights the conditions that appear to facilitate movement along these vectors. It is by such means that his films postulate a critique of urban space through an interrogation of the politics and sociology of the urban apartment and its residents. This strategy, which involves many of the hallmarks of Fassbinder's stylistic practice, is best illustrated through an analysis of two key scenes from *Why Does Herr R. Run Amok?*, a film that methodically brings spatial movement and momentum to a point of crisis, linking its gradual impeding of physical movement to the diminution of its protagonist's agency in the face of normative bourgeois life conditions, the progressively more oppressive nature of which he never gains the opportunity to articulate. Herr R. (Kurt Raab) diligently conforms to materialist notions of success: he has a beautiful wife (a character never given a name, played by Lilith Ungerer) and a son, Amadeus; the luxury of his own car (which Frau R. has once again dented as the plot begins); a stylish apartment with contemporary furnishings; and a steady job at a graphic design agency with prospects of promotion and greater monetary rewards clearly in view. Yet Fassbinder consistently subverts these conditions of economic advancement through the stifling nature of the film's mise-en-scène and cinematography. On the basis of the number of guests who visit in the course of the plot—on separate occasions, a childhood friend of Herr R., his parents, and a group of Frau R.'s friends—it is clear that movement in and out of the couple's apartment does transpire, yet we are presented almost exclusively with only the results of movement, entering each scene as character positions have already been fixed within the living room, to which our perspective is largely confined. Visible space is further constricted by high-angle framing, close camera distance, and a mise-en-scène whose cramped, cluttered feel is accentuated by the placement of characters immobilized on connecting sofas around two sides of the frame's perimeter, distinctive coffee tables and wall-hung artwork added to fill in any remaining empty space. On the rare occasion that a character mobilizes (as Frau R. does to bring drinks back to the table), the camera remains fixed on the remaining inhabitants and guests, none of whom ever acknowledges the departure or arrival.

Motion in *Why Does Herr R. Run Amok?* is limited almost exclusively to two scenes occurring outside the apartment. The film begins as Herr R. and his four work colleagues leave their office via an alley: the group tightly assembles as a single, leisurely moving unit. Each person (except for Herr R.) tells a joke that elicits laughter from the others (again, except for Herr R.), and the closely framed reverse tracking shot substantially neutralizes any sense of figure movement. As the group turns into another alley, the camera briefly tracks them from behind before gradually coming to a stop, the sluggish progression of the group now accentuated by the protracted time elapsing before they reach the street, the gait and pace of their movement unaltered even by the sudden presence of an automobile approaching and then abruptly backing out away from them in the alley. The other, much longer scene uses similar stylistic strategies of spatial containment, compromising momentum through the reverse tracking shot that follows Herr R., Frau R., his parents, and Amadeus on a leisurely walk down a snowy path after their visit to the R.s at their apartment. The close framing of Frau R. and her faultfinding mother-in-law—both of whom share the foreground of the frame with Amadeus—accentuates an already rising tension that is suddenly exacerbated when they realize that Amadeus has disappeared from the group. The mother-in-law, who has already been berating Frau R. for her extravagant spending habits, now launches into more heated invective regarding Frau R.'s parental irresponsibility even after the boy is located (he had simply wandered away from the group to climb a tree), the camera ultimately ceasing to follow their movement as they recede into the depths of the frame.

Although mothers (and mothers-in-law) in Fassbinder's domestic dramas tend to be nagging and overprotective, the concerns that Herr R.'s mother expresses are less fundamentally misgivings about her daughter-in-law's actions than uneasiness about how these actions might be perceived by others. In *The Merchant of Four Seasons*, when Hans expresses his desire to learn a mechanic's trade, his mother (Gusti Kreissl) raises similar concerns, expressing that she does not want her son to be seen doing a job requiring that he get his hands dirty. Thomas Elsaesser argues that "all human relations . . . manifest themselves along the axis of seeing and being seen," and the manifestation of these problems of human perception within this dynamic find their most intensely cinematic elaboration in *Ali: Fear Eats the Soul*, where they are framed as problems of constrained movement, whether actual or potential.[11] That the narrative initially establishes this dynamic in a public setting is crucial to the subsequent domestic manifestations of movement that we encounter. In the film's noted opening scene, sensitivity and hyperawareness of the perception of others is accentuated from the moment that Emmi stops and decides to enter the door of the Asphalt Bar on her way home from work one night, her body relegated to the far background of the deep space composition, the length of the establishment highlighted by the row of empty tables with deep red tablecloths extending from Emmi's position into the extreme foreground of the frame. The shot / reverse shot editing further isolates Emmi from the space of the bar owner Barbara and the other six customers, grouped singly and in pairs at the far end of the bar, all of them spatially fixed and staring back at the intruding customer, the intensity of their cumulative look substantiated as the camera cuts back to a medium shot of Emmi taking a seat at the nearest table. The vast empty space here is bridged only after the volley of cuts concludes, when a tracking shot traces Emmi and Ali's route as they walk together through the vast expanse to the dance floor.

This opening scene's intricate dynamic of movement and stasis is prescient in relation to the film's overall spatial design. While in one sense the scene configures space metaphorically to underscore the culture clash between Germans and Moroccan outsiders in Germany, it simultaneously establishes as a precondition of this cultural disparity the terms of its own reconciliation. Emmi's appearance in a place where other Germans are unlikely to visit is not entirely accidental: as a justification of her presence there, she explains to Barbara that yes, it was raining outside that night, but also that she has been walking past the bar every night and is curious about the "foreign music" she hears. Her position upon entering the bar situates her as a spatial anchor once she decides to remain inside to continue probing the space (and this other culture) rather than immediately running out the door upon sensing that her presence is unwelcome. Her expressed justification confirms that she is attracted to the space because of these differences rather than in spite of them. Rather than just an attempt to assert control over a protected spatial domain, then, the customers' gaze back at Emmi is also an acknowledgment of their own sense of also being looked at, a reminder of their own outsider status regarding which they have no reason to consider Emmi's unanticipated intrusion as anything less than a challenge. If, as Avery Slater suggests, the film "provides a useful analytic for thinking through how noncitizen migrant workers and refugees come to be structurally positioned as stateless individuals," it is equally important to note that this opening scene also establishes the "thereness" of all of these characters present at the bar, including Emmi.[12] The reciprocal nature of the looks and gazes exchanged confirms Kaja Silverman's observation that in this film, no one gets to "possess" the gaze, and yet the dynamic of seeing/being seen also marks the characters' sense of positionality—they may not get to possess the gaze, but they remain spatially located, fixed, and anchored by it, and the seemingly incidental movement of the tracking shot following Emmi and Ali's short walk to the dance floor marks a contestation of the seeming polarity that the reciprocated looks establish, a contestation that actualizes space kinetically rather than perceptually.[13]

As the remainder of the narrative demonstrates, however, this potential for kinetic disruption of a seemingly closed system of looks and gazes is enabled only in instances where the fixed positions of those who look and those who look back are mutually avowed by both parties, and the potential for movement depends upon the acknowledgment of both spatial anchors organizing the dynamic between seeing and being seen. That the Asphalt Bar is unique, at least early in the film, as a setting that enables such contestation becomes apparent in many of the scenes in which Emmi's apartment serves as a more central spatial anchor point in conjunction with destinations outside of the domestic sphere. The most striking example entails a scene in which motion vectors become snagged in a slow zone established by Ali and Emmi's successive tracings of the short path between her apartment building and the grocery store across the street and owned by Herr Angermayer (Walter Sedlmayr). Emmi first sends Ali there with a grocery list that includes Libelle, a new brand of margarine; repeatedly feigning his inability to understand Ali's request, Angermayer blames Ali's less than fluent German for the communication problem even after his wife (Doris Mattes) reconfirms to her husband that Libelle is indeed what Ali has been referencing as "gleiche für Butter" (like butter). After Ali is shown having returned to the apartment exasperated and empty-handed, Emmi's outrage propels her to retrace the path back across the street to the grocery store, her movement toward the destination marked only by a simple cut. After a heated exchange in which Emmi accuses him of racism, Angermayer ejects her from the store and vows to no longer serve her as a customer.

Emmi's very short journey back to the apartment is, however, hindered by a series of gazes that impede the progress toward her destination. First, as she leaves Angermayer's grocery, the camera cuts to a position immediately within the apartment building's entranceway and looking out, the door propped open just wide enough to witness Emmi approaching the building at a brisk pace through the narrow center fifth of the frame, the wider left and right portions of the image consisting entirely of the door and frame themselves. The surreptitious nature of the shot suggests that her movements are being monitored from the inside, but the subsequent match-on-action cut reveals Emmi racing up the stairway from the vestibule with two

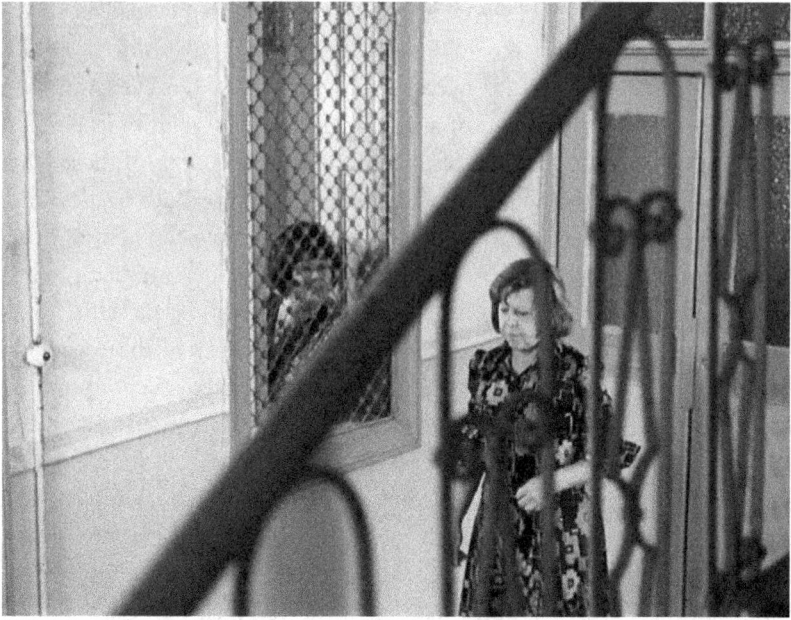

FIG. 4.1. Trapped in the slow zone of entrapment: Frau Kargus interrogates Emmi in *Ali: Fear Eats the Soul* (Rainer Werner Fassbinder, 1974). Filmverlag der Autoren.

of her meddling neighbors positioned halfway up, staring intently at her and barely making way as she passes by them and reaches Frau Kargus, who calls to Emmi from behind the grating of the concierge's office. Emmi is now barely visible between this grating and the lattice of the wrought-iron stairway railing that leads back to her apartment (fig. 4.1). As the three women explain that they and the other tenants have reached an agreement that Emmi must clean the staircase twice a month because of the recent infiltration of dirt in their building since Ali moved in, a volley of cuts reveals Emmi now trapped between women's judgmental gazes before and behind her. As Emmi scowls and accuses Frau Kargus of jealousy, the scene ends with Emmi moving offscreen, the sound of her footsteps completing the trace of the path back up the stairs and to her destination.

Occurring roughly midway through the film, this scene rhymes with the opening sequence in the Asphalt Bar while also evidencing a crucial shift in the seeing / being seen dynamic: unlike in the earlier sequence, Emmi resists avowing each of the gazes cast back at her—not only of the three women, but also the seemingly unanchored gaze at her through the narrow opening in the doorframe. Despite her resistance, however, she is consistently hailed or lured by each of these gazes, all of which originate from looks (both human and cinematic) that are not objectified via outsider status, and who, unlike the Moroccan patrons of the Asphalt Bar, do not assume the fixed identity of an other. In terms of movement, these gazes construct a series of checkpoints that must be recognized before signal clearance can be obtained for Emmi to move ahead to the next point along her trajectory, the short distance between points of origin and destination only intensifying the slowed progression of motion along these vectors.

This scene from *Ali: Fear Eats the Soul* clearly demonstrates Lefebvre's contention in *The Production of Space* that "the form of social space is encounter, assembly, simultaneity."[14] Applying these principles of spatial convergence to the sociology of urban domestic space, Wojcik asserts, "Rather than be dominated by nostalgia for other forms, the apartment plot substitutes a revitalized sense of neighborhood and community. This sense of community is . . . inherent to the apartment, for good or bad. It relates to the porousness and permeability of apartment living, to the knowledge and awareness residents have of each other, through sight, sound, gossip, and other encounters. Rather than solely emphasize the alienating effects of urban life, the apartment plot tends also to emphasize the erotic possibilities for accidental and surprising encounters in the city, for simultaneity and play."[15]

Fassbinder foregrounds these principles of the urban apartment's porousness in *Ali: Fear Eats the Soul*, but rather than focus on erotic potential, he concentrates on surveillance operations obtaining from power relations of race and class. Emmi's urban apartment certainly qualifies as a haven that accommodates romantic entanglement, and her status as a working-class woman who labors at night to clean up the dirt that middle-class office workers leave behind during their day jobs actually becomes the requisite condition that enables the entirely unplanned encounter that initiates her relationship with Ali. The couple can never meet at his residence—a small room that he shares with six other Moroccan Gastarbeiter—so that her apartment might be said to serve as a hideaway of sorts were it not for the fact that this urban domestic space allows almost nothing to remain hidden for very long. If Frau Kargus and disapproving neighbors exchange gossip and assemble in common vestibules, corridors, and stairways awaiting the next opportunity to berate Emmi, the conditions of surveillance are revealed to be just as oppressive inside, behind closed and locked doors. In the first half of the film, Emmi and Ali learn quickly that their privacy within the apartment can be permeated without notice; they are constantly rendered susceptible to the next unwelcome visit—from her coworker Paula (Gusti Kriessl), who leaves the apartment abruptly in disgust once she spots Ali; from the landlord Herr Gruber (Marquard Bohm), who accuses Emmi of violating her rental agreement by taking in undocumented boarders; and from the Munich police, who are summoned after neighbors complain about the noise that a group of Ali's invited Moroccan friends are making one night.

While this sense of constant scrutiny dominates their relationship outside and within the walls of the apartment in the first half of the film, the second half activates an aspect of the apartment's porousness that at first seems more welcoming and less anxious. Rather than receiving visits from others who voice complaints and restrict the couple's movement, after their return from vacation the domestic space accommodates more fluid movement to, from, and within the apartment. Upon the now married couple's return from vacation, Emmi immediately receives a warm, undisruptive greeting on the stairway from a resident who had earlier complained about the presence of more dirt there; her welcoming acknowledgment of Emmi serves, however, only as the pretext for a request to use some of Emmi's extra storage space. A similarly motivated congenial visit follows from her son Bruno (Peter Gauhe), who apologizes for having destroyed her television set upon learning about her marriage to Ali and now asks for his mother's help with babysitting. In conjunction with the change of heart that the family and neighbors now evidence, however, Ali appears reduced entirely to a utilitarian function, as Emmi's accessory more than her partner, as she commands him to help the neighbor with the preparation of the storage unit, or to have his biceps squeezed by her coworkers who meet in the apartment to discuss wage negotiations. The apartment has certainly become the site of convergence—there are no noise complaints, no sarcastic comments, and no more slow zones. Couched as it is in the rhetorical context of friendship exploitation, however, the convergence and more fluid movement within this new urban social configuration do little to dispel any feelings of alienation and loneliness, especially for Ali, whose more frequent solo journeys from the apartment building now become progressively longer, and the conditions of his return less predictable.

Repeated instances of this convergence enabled by the urban apart-ment emerge in the other Fassbinder narratives as well. With its unrelenting focus upon individual and interpersonal alienation, *Why Does Herr R. Run Amok?* offers a searing commentary on dysfunctional communication practices in contemporary urban social gatherings. Groups are always assembling in the R.s' apartment, yet the clustering and accumulation of human bodies only further conveys the profound sense of interpersonal fragmentation, disjointedness, and distance. The group of five family rela-tives remains assembled together on the living room couch throughout most of the scene of the parents' visit, yet the cinematography emphasizes separation and distance, despite the tight quarters evoked by framing: with R., his father, and Amadeus on-screen in an extended static camera shot, the soundtrack includes only the extended, mostly offscreen con-versation about opera and culture that is being conducted by his mother and his wife. When R.'s father and Amadeus subsequently discuss a book that the boy is reading, the on-screen presence of the silent and unmov-ing Herr R. seated beside his conversing family members serves to isolate him further. The camera occasionally traces a slow pan across the group, and even at one point a cut from one end of the couch to the other, yet throughout the scene the cinematography conveys stasis, as if the camera's blank, frozen stare were mimicking the sense of alienation and remove that Herr R. is experiencing.

If the porousness of the urban apartment is held in check by static cin-ematography in *Why Does Herr R. Run Amok?*, other Fassbinder domestic dramas configure movement within urban space in terms that can best be described as functionally mechanical and that relate directly to Lefeb-vre's concept of space as an animate, permeable machine. In *The Produc-tion of Space*, Lefebvre disrupts the notion of a given domestic dwelling as "discrete, solid, immovable space," suggesting that once the semblances of solidity have been peeled away, such a dwelling "would emerge as perme-ated from every direction by streams of energy which run in and out of it by every imaginable route: water, gas, electricity, telephone lines, radio and television signals, and so on. Its image of immobility would then be replaced by an image of a complex of mobilities, a nexus of in and out conduits."[16]

Fassbinder's perhaps most elaborate and celebrated illustration of this notion of circuits and flow occurs in the final sequence of *Die Ehe der*

Maria Braun (*The Marriage of Maria Braun*, 1979), which orchestrates the dissolution of a marriage (after its eponymous heroine has moved up from an apartment dwelling to an expansive single-family residence) to the discordant yet synthesized tempos of water flowing from faucets, radio waves broadcasting the final soccer match of the World Cup, and the gas flowing through open lines that ultimately causes a deadly explosion upon the distracted lighting of a cigarette. In the apartment plot of *Mother Küsters Goes to Heaven*, the circuits of energy flowing through permeable, urban domestic space take on a different set of forms. The narrative begins as Emma Küsters (Brigitte Mira) struggles with how to inform her son Ernst (Armin Meier), her daughter-in-law Helene (Irm Hermann), and later, her daughter Corinna (Ingrid Caven) that their father Hermann has just killed his foreman and committed suicide after an announcement of mass layoffs at the chemical plant where he was working. From its opening images, Mother Küsters's apartment is identified as an immanently permeable and dynamic setting—the film begins with close-ups of hands assembling a series of small components into electrical sockets; as the camera cuts to a series of medium shots, the hands are identified as belonging to Emma and Ernst, who execute this in-house factory assembly on the Küsters's kitchen table, quickly reconverting the assembly line to a dining table with Helene's assistance once Emma is finished cooking dinner (fig. 4.2).

The sense of the apartment as a private domain rendered public is reinforced once news of Hermann's crime is disseminated, after which circuits of information begin to flow more freely throughout these rooms and corridors. Unlike in *Why Does Herr R. Run Amok?*, where convergences and assemblies of guests transpire by invitation, or *Ali: Fear Eats the Soul*, where the unwelcome intrusions of others are at least signaled in advance by loud knocks on the door, *Mother Küsters Goes to Heaven* obfuscates the boundaries or borders between the infiltrators of social networks and the apartments that they invade—infiltrators who appear there but who are rarely shown arriving. For example, on the day of the tragic incident at the chemical plant, Emma returns home only to find photographers and reporters who are interviewing Helene and Ernst in the living room. The matter of privacy subsequently becomes the domain of journalistic scrutiny: on the day after the incident, the reporter Niemeyer (Gottfried John) returns to Emma's apartment to continue his investigative enterprise, equipped with his camera and ready to capture the inside story of the

FIG. 4.2. The kitchen as factory: Ernst assembles electrical sockets on the dining room table while wife Helene (*right*) and mother Emma Küsters (*left*) cook dinner at the start of *Mother Küsters Goes to Heaven* (Rainer Werner Fassbinder, 1975). Filmverlag der Autoren.

place that housed a renowned murderer/suicide. Seeking to reveal its mysteries, Niemeyer fuses the operations of surveillance and journalistic inquiry, probing the rooms of the apartment one by one, and keeping Emma in character by prompting her to reflect upon life with her recently deceased husband as his camera distills her identity through a series of action photos. Emma is asked to pose as Niemeyer directs her to assemble an electrical outlet, and then again to make her bed. His careful orchestration leaves room for spontaneous, unplanned developments: "If you could just turn towards me," he asks, when Emma finds herself reduced to tears as she holds a framed picture of her husband.

While these spatial intrusions at first appear to be motivated only by morbid public curiosity, it becomes clear that much more is at stake once Emma connects with Herr and Frau Thälmann (Karlheinz Böhm and Margit Carstensen), the upper-middle-class Communist Party couple who also make a conspicuous appearance at the apartment on the day of the murder, but who strategically bide their time before revealing their intentions to Emma. By vindicating Hermann's action as a valiant response to unfair labor practices at the chemical plant, they guide Emma to construct an image of her husband not as a criminal but as an inspiring revolutionary hero. Before long, they have elevated Emma to the position of spokesperson at a Communist Party gathering, but when the Thälmanns subsequently put Emma's case on hold in pursuit of more urgent causes, Emma is approached by the anarchist Knab (Matthias Fuchs), who advises her that the Thälmanns are only using her for their own political purposes, and that the true path to her husband's vindication is to "take action," just as Hermann did. What becomes clear through this progression of encounters—with journalist, communists, and anarchist—is that Emma is being used by all of them. The case is perhaps most apparent with Niemeyer, whose extended real-life photo sessions literally reduce Emma to an object of vision for public scrutiny and consumption, to the status of a being-seen that delimits her role as a domestic, nurturing, yet ultimately obtuse figure with a blind, unquestioning devotion to an unknown psychopath. Curiously, however, Fassbinder refuses to distinguish this form of abuse from the strategy of the Thälmanns, whose disingenuous empathy and patronizing expressions of concern for Emma mask their intellectual, class-based assumptions of superiority as they carry out their grander design of molding her into a suitable instrument of propaganda.

In terms of movement and motion vectors, circuits of information and energy flow openly in *Mother Küsters Goes to Heaven*, but they consistently flow in the same direction: inward, coalescing and accumulating within the urban apartment, whose dual role as the site of labor paid (the assembly of cogs) and unpaid (the mother's maintenance of the domestic space) attracts these diverse political factions so intent upon transforming the space for their own ends while offering nothing to Emma in return. The machine of the apartment plot here is revealed as a mechanism of pure consumption; indeed, even Emma's own family participates in this machinelike process of feeding off the energy of this domestic space, especially her daughter-in-law Helene, who resides there with her husband out of convenience, who insists that she and Ernst proceed with their scheduled vacation plans despite the inconvenience of Hermann's tragedy, and who ultimately forces Ernst to comply with her decision to move out once extended family living no longer suits her. Indeed, the machine of consumption in *Mother Küsters Goes to Heaven* situates the urban apartment as a processing plant, with Emma serving as the fuel that keeps the domestic-political engine in motion as long as it can. No longer deemed important or essential to the needs of family, the Thälmanns, or Knab, by the end of the film she is discarded as waste, her act of protest to attempt to force Niemeyer to retract his damaging and sensationalist article having failed, and her family having abandoned her entirely.

If *Mother Küsters Goes to Heaven* evidences a form of capitalist internal combustion engine (in which even communists feel at home participating), motion vectors elsewhere in the world of Fassbinder's domestic dramas direct the flow of energy sources differently in the permeable domestic setting, via principles of substitution. *Why Does Herr R. Run Amok?* aligns this energy flow with the static compositions that ultimately drive the plot toward inertia, as is especially apparent in a scene that assembles Frau R.'s neighbor friends in the cinematographically cramped confines of the living room couch. As Frau R. prepares drinks in the kitchen offscreen, the neighbors speculate upon the R.s' ability to afford this "very nicely furnished" apartment. ("She doesn't work, does she?" one of the women asks.) Upon Frau R.'s reentry, a ritual of comparison and contrast ensues among participants whose residence in virtually identical apartment spaces in the same building exacerbates their inability to afford the R.s' lifestyle, and who—in a most neighborly way—reveal their scorn over the privileges that have transformed her space into something unique. When Frau R. boasts that she and her husband will not be residing in the building much longer because Herr R. "hopes to better himself," the spirit of envy dominates more overtly, with the neighbors' ensuing expressions of concern about Herr R.'s health, his weight, and their son's school issues, and with questions such as "Will you be able to use this furniture in the new apartment?" driving the conversation. The scene elegantly illustrates the narrative logic of spatial substitution and interchangeability at work here, as the primacy and constancy of domestic spatial settings under capitalism are set against the inherently transitory nature of any given set of inhabitants' stay of residence. As the R.s move up and out, others will move in to replace them, with either more or less impressive sofas and wall hangings, until they too find their way (or not) to the next, more desirable apartment space.

Principles of substitution permeate the apartment plot of *The Merchant of Four Seasons* as well, revealing once again the facility with which the engine of capitalist enterprise drives Fassbinder's narrative momentum.

Here, too, the logic of spatial substitution is driven by class differentiation and the prospects of moving up. Fired from his job as a police officer after being caught having casual sex with a criminal suspect, and subsequently reduced to providing for his family by hawking fruit and vegetables throughout the city, Hans is despised by most of his family until the heart attack that renders him incapable of continuing to perform this strenuous work becomes the requisite condition for a change in class status. Ordered to stop working, he simply advances himself to the position of overseeing the work of others, hiring out the working-class labor and substantially increasing the flow of his revenue stream in the process of exerting very little physical effort. His wife Irmgard (Irm Hermann) and family become more pleased, even as Hans himself progressively disengages, his new role as overseer draining him of any sense of motivation for movement. After being invited to move into Hans's apartment, his close friend Harry (Klaus Löwitsch) gradually begins to serve as Hans's surrogate, both at work as he handles the heavy pushing and lifting with the fruit cart, and at home as he helps Hans's daughter Renate (Andrea Schober) with her homework. Before long, Harry is assuming Hans's place at the dinner table as Hans himself stares unresponsively out the kitchen window (fig. 4.3). Hans ultimately carries out his decision to drink himself to death, and the film concludes with his funeral, immediately after which Harry blankly complies with Irmgard's invitation to stay on with her and Renate—an invitation neither extended nor accepted out of any predetermined romantic scheme, but instead emerging entirely out of logic and convenience, as the seemingly natural next step in the process of perpetuating the engine of production at work and at home. The easy substitution of Harry for Hans in the roles of father, husband, and provider is the constant in the world of *The Merchant of Four Seasons*—serving an interest of maintaining and improving one's class status at all costs that transpires at the expense of reducing this film's central protagonist from a state of motion to sheer inertia.

Virtually everywhere in Fassbinder's apartment plots, then, the potentially liberating and invigorating aspects of urban living are held in check by the realities of human exploitation that govern class, social, and interpersonal relations under capitalism—relations that the dynamics of movement and motion through urban space illuminate. From the German nationalists who police domestic slow zones as they deem themselves superior to foreign guest workers; to the journalists, communists, and

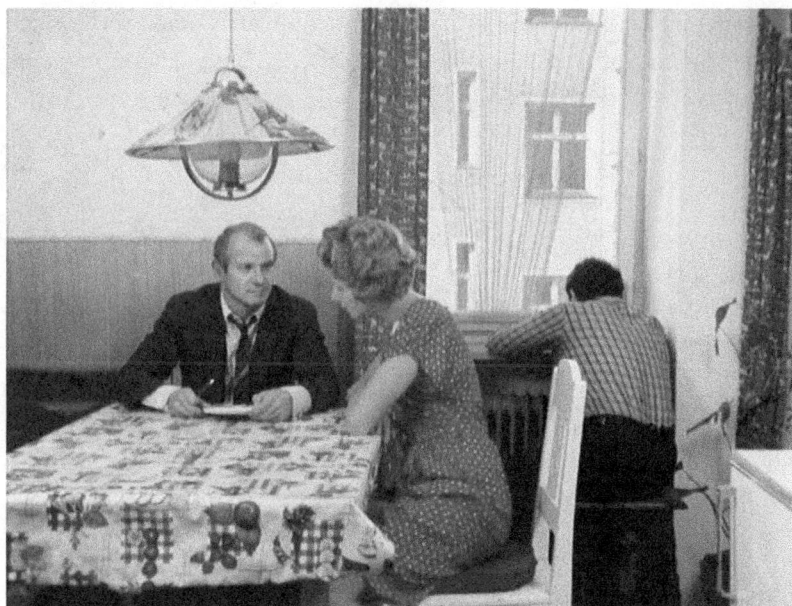

FIG. 4.3. Substitution and alienation: Harry (*left*) and Irmgard discuss finances while her husband Hans (*right*) stares out the kitchen window in *The Merchant of Four Seasons* (Rainer Werner Fassbinder, 1971). Tango Film.

anarchists who designate the apartment space as the site of a machine that feeds off the labor of a traumatized German working-class widow; to the stasis and inertia that ensue from a street produce vendor's unforeseen opportunity for class advancement, Fassbinder always foregrounds the obstacles to movement through urban domestic space that obtain in networks of power relations. Aside from the progression of two unlikely lovers walking together toward a dance floor, it is both ironic and tragic that one of the only instances of unconstrained, liberated movement occurs in the climactic scene of *Why Does Herr R. Run Amok?*, when the eponymous protagonist wanders aimlessly among the rooms of his stylish apartment dwelling, killing off everyone in his path before hanging himself in the office bathroom the next morning. The system of movement and stasis that Fassbinder devises in his version of the apartment plot is so elegantly structured that, from the perspective of his central protagonists, it becomes largely impermeable. Yet while Fassbinder's narratives rarely provide his protagonists with a way out of the network of capitalist social relations in which they seem fated to operate, his foregrounding of this network's intricate, self-generative structure ultimately empowers his audiences to imagine alternative, more equitable, and less polarizing systems of movement through urban space.

NOTES

1. Henri Lefebvre, *The Production of Space*, trans. Donald Nicholson-Smith (Oxford: Blackwell, 1991), 94.

2. Lefebvre, *The Production of Space*, 101.

3. Thomas Elsaesser, *Fassbinder's Germany: History, Identity, Subject* (Amsterdam: Amsterdam University Press, 1996), 51.

4. Peter Ruppert, "Fassbinder, Spectatorship, and Utopian Desire," *Cinema Journal* 28, no. 2 (winter 1989): 28–47.

5. Ruppert, "Fassbinder, Spectatorship, and Utopian Desire," 37.

6. Pamela Robertson Wojcik, *The Apartment Plot: Urban Living in American Film and Popular Culture, 1945–1975* (Durham, NC: Duke University Press, 2010), 7.

7. Michel de Certeau, *The Practice of Everyday Life*, trans. Steven F. Rendall (Berkeley: University of California Press, 2011), 91–110.

8. Elsaesser, *Fassbinder's Germany*, 37.

9. Kaja Silverman, "Fassbinder and Lacan: A Reconsideration of Gaze, Look and Image," *Camera Obscura* 7, no. 1 (1989): 57–59. See also Silverman's discussion of Lacan and Fassbinder in *Male Subjectivity at the Margins* (New York: Routledge, 1992), 125–56.

10. Jane Jacobs, *The Death and Life of Great American Cities* (New York: Random House, 1961), 119–21.

11. Elsaesser, *Fassbinder's Germany*, 60.

12. Avery Slater, "*Jus Sanguinis, Jus Soli*: West German Citizenship Law and the Melodrama of the Guest Worker in Fassbinder's *Angst Essen Seele Auf*," *Cultural Critique* 86 (winter 2014): 93.

13. Silverman, "Fassbinder and Lacan," 59.

14. Lefebvre, *The Production of Space*, 101.

15. Wojcik, *The Apartment Plot*, 40.

16. Lefebvre, *The Production of Space*, 93.

5

HOUSEWORK, SEX WORK

Feminist Ambivalence at
23 Quai du Commerce, 1080 Bruxelles

ANNAMARIE JAGOSE

In memory of Chantal Akerman, 1950–2015

I wrote this essay in 2015 while a visiting fellow at the Institute for Cultural Inquiry (ICI), Berlin.[1] Three weeks to the day before I was scheduled to present it as part of the ICI-Berlin's Errans lecture series, Chantal Akerman killed herself. No expert on Akerman, I had nevertheless spent several months that year with her *Jeanne Dielman, 23 Quai du Commerce, 1080 Bruxelles,* and that, together with the timing of my public presentation of her work, drew me unexpectedly close to the event of her death. In preparing to speak to an audience that included not just scholars but also friends of Akerman's, I was visited by a different form of feminist ambivalence from the one I had, with diagnostic cockiness, laid hold of for my subtitle. It was not so easy to critique the way in which the feminist reception of Akerman's film was ambivalently structured through an imagined mother-daughter relation once her suicide was frequently linked in the international public commentary to her low spirits following the death of her own mother, Natalia Akerman, a constant artistic principle for Akerman, the previous year. As I have had cause to write once previously, and "as is often sorrowfully noted, the work of mourning must feel its way inside newly unstable structures of address as the usual conventions of tone, tense, and even nomination buckle under the relational effects of death's transformations of the person."[2] On that occasion, I proposed a collective silence of three minutes twenty-one seconds, fashioned after the length of the film itself, to mark Akerman's death in the durational experience of our shared time. Here, and more conventionally, Akerman is remembered in my epigraph.

INCLUDED AS PART of the Official Selection in the Directors' Fortnight at the Cannes Film Festival in 1975, *Jeanne Dielman, 23 Quai du Commerce, 1080 Bruxelles* brought the then twenty-four-year-old Chantal Akerman to international attention. Critically acclaimed and modestly successful in foreign box office terms, the film established Akerman "as one of Belgium's bankable auteurs."[3] Despite Akerman's being claimed for a national cinema, however, the aspects of *Jeanne Dielman* that have warranted the most attention—the film's small number of repeated and fixed camera positions and the consistently medium framing and lengthy duration of its shots, for example, or its sustained attentiveness to the grindingly real time of quotidian female domestic routine—have tended to be annexed as markers of an international style and claimed for either experimental or feminist filmmaking. Yet in turning away from this global positioning of the film to resituate these strikingly characteristic aspects of *Jeanne Dielman* within the specific geocultural and material coordinates of its production, an interestingly different iteration of the apartment plot film becomes visible.

Prominent in the urban architecture of Brussels since at least the mid-nineteenth century, the apartment was key to a number of Belgian social revolutions before Akerman recruited it in the mid-1970s for the purposes of second-wave feminism. A brief historical overview of the role of the apartment in Brussels affords a better understanding of how the spatial coordinates of the apartment in *Jeanne Dielman* are temporalized for a feminist project. An important strategy in forging a national identity following the 1830 secession of Belgium from the Netherlands, the architectural and infrastructural redesign of Brussels as a major European capital in the last decades of the nineteenth century was "largely inspired by the Haussmann-planning in Paris" and—like Haussmann's renovation of Paris—took the apartment house as the default for modern domestic life in the city.[4] A century later, post–World War II attempts to reimagine Brussels and the role it might play on the world stage led to large-scale demolition of earlier urban architectures, including the Haussmann-inspired apartment blocks that had once signaled the city's modernity. In preparation for Expo '58, the first significant international exhibition since the war, the government supported major infrastructural and transportation projects that radically accelerated the modernization of the city. There was also a scramble to meet the urgent and increasing real estate requirements of new European institutions that made their headquarters in Brussels.[5] Urban planning was so poorly regulated in Brussels at this time that the phenomenon of haphazard urban redevelopment enabled by municipal entrepreneurship, unenforced zoning regulations, land speculation, and nontransparent alliances between politicians and developers became known as Brusselization.

Coined as a term by those who resisted the postwar destruction of historically coherent architecture—much of it residential—in established urban quarters to make way for governmental and commercial interests, "the concept of 'Brusselization' came to the fore in 1968, when public protests arose against two specific projects: the Manhattan plan in the Northern Quarter and the European Headquarters in the Leopold Quarter."[6] The vision of the Manhattan plan was to cleanse the city center of run-down housing stock along with the low-socioeconomic-demographic populations they housed, including the elderly and noncitizens, in order to clear space for high-density construction at the heart of the city.[7] "A symbol of urban planning only based on land speculation and realized in a guilty mix of public and private interests," the Manhattan plan centered on a substantial site in the Northern Quarter between Willebroek Canal and the Gare de Bruxelles-Nord, just north of the R20 ring road. The center of prominent and successful populist antiplanning protest through the early 1970s, this site lies less than a kilometer north of the address nominated as Jeanne's apartment at 23 Quai du Commerce just to the south of the city center.[8]

Filmed on location in an actual apartment, Jeanne's home is neither one of the subdivided, formerly grand, nineteenth-century apartment houses or terraced townhouses being razed in the city center nor one of the glass-and-chrome apartment blocks being flung up among the office towers and hotels that came to characterize the clogged central business district. It is instead part of an interwar apartment block in a mixed residential and commercial precinct. Neither obsolete nor contemporary, Jeanne's apartment signifies as something that persists in a temporal moment that is nevertheless not indicatively its own. Only recently returned from several years in New York, Akerman might not have been aware of the symbolic valence of the apartment in the high-profile grassroots protests that successfully challenged urban planning in Brussels in the early to mid-1970s. Nevertheless, the chronotope of the interwar apartment in a chaotically modernizing Brussels affords a new perspective on an issue that also but differently animates the feminist film reception of *Jeanne Dielman*—namely, how to engage the dense particularities of spatiotemporal experience across historical difference.[9] For if the apartment space at 23 Quai du Commerce most obviously enables Akerman's durational experiment in marking the passage of quotidian time, it does so with recourse to historical time, capturing habits and styles of everyday female life practices at the tremulous and sometimes fraught moment of their passing from relevance.

DESPITE THE SLIGHTNESS of most of the action of *Jeanne Dielman*, it seems few accounts of the film—popular or scholarly—can resist the impulse to plot summary. Whether abstractly or minutely realized, such descriptions focus largely on the eponymous protagonist's enclosure in her apartment and the iterative cycles of housework that characterize the passage of time there. Given that Akerman's film is more read about than watched, it may come as something of a surprise to the critically informed spectator how engaging, eventful, and beautiful the film is to watch. Having been primed to expect a durational experiment in low-incident, low-affect domesticity, spectators encounter instead in "Akerman's minimal hyperrealism" a richly rendered seam of everyday life, at once incidental and monumental.[10] This might partly be an effect of the differences between watching the film and accessing it via the often labored narrative summaries that characterize responses to it with their marked tendency to remediate the film's plot. Acknowledging this desire in her own critical practice, Janet Bergstrom comments, "The temptation is to retell the plot step by step, as if the clarity of the succession of gestures and elisions carried with it an understanding of the film's strength and its importance for feminist filmmaking."[11] Succumbing to such temptation, however, is a short lesson in medium specificity. No matter how lengthy or descriptively effective, such plot summaries fall short of the thing they attempt to capture, the durational immersion in everyday domestic practice.

Set across three days with each reprising the last, the film's action consists almost entirely of the domestic routines of Jeanne Dielman, played with a radiant affectlessness by Delphine Seyrig in housewife drag. Across more than three hours, Seyrig—"an international symbol of haute bourgeois chic" with "a screen presence comparable, perhaps, only to Garbo"— peels potatoes, shines her son's shoes, makes her bed, turns lights on and off as she enters and leaves a room, washes dishes, minds a neighbor's bassinet-bound baby, has sex with her clients, shops for a button, prepares veal escalopes, and bathes herself.[12] Although the film famously ends with Jeanne murdering her third client, her everyday life practices are for the most part the manifest action of the film, which plays out largely in the tight confines of her one-bedroom apartment. Setting the representational coordinates for the rest of the film, in the opening scene Jeanne stands at the stove in the far left corner of a medium-long shot of a compact and tidy kitchen. Immediately laid open to the glance, the kitchen remains available to more leisurely viewings as the camera and its equally immobile lens stay fixed in the same position for the duration of the scene.

Inside the motionless frame of this shot, Jeanne salts a pot of water on the stove and lights the gas ring beneath it. In a more plot-driven narrative feature film, such a slight event might be either overlooked as inconsequential stage business, the background to some alternate action or dialogue, or, conversely, by dint of being included in the field of vision, recognized as laden with a significance yet to be narratively explicated. In *Jeanne Dielman*, however, it initiates a gestural vernacular that is operational across the film in which Jeanne's unremarkable routines are the film's main action, stitching together from scene to scene a recognizable although seldom apprehended domestic everyday. So loyal is the camera to its perspective through the kitchen doorway that as Jeanne moves about—returning a wooden salt box to its spot on the rear windowsill, unbuttoning her pale blue housecoat in response to the door bell, washing and drying her hands on a towel—she sometimes is only partially in shot or even altogether out of frame, the built space of the empty apartment kitchen and the offscreen sounds of her footsteps or a running tap having

FIG. 5.1. The camera is more loyal to the apartment space of *Jeanne Dielman* (Chantal Akerman, 1975) than to its protagonist.

to hold everything together as a scene in the more conventional sense (fig. 5.1).

Considering its close attention to the quotidian gestures of housework, a common critical observation across the contemporary feminist reception of Akerman's film is to note how *Jeanne Dielman* registers in its field of vision aspects of women's everyday that are conventionally deemed so unimportant as to not warrant representation.[13] In Marsha Kinder's succinct phrasing, "Akerman cultivates the unseen."[14] It is less *Jeanne Dielman*'s inclusion of the domestically trivial nonevents of its protagonist's life, however, than its unblinking, full-frontal, fixed-frame attention to the durational qualities of that housework that drew feminist praise. Analyzing from a psychoanalytic perspective feminist films that venture to create a new filmic language, Mary Ann Doane elaborates this point, arguing that Akerman's work "constructs its syntax by linking together scenes which, in the classical text, would be concealed, in effect negated, by temporal ellipses. The specificity of the film lies in the painful duration of that time 'in-between' events, that time which is exactly proper to the woman (in particular, the housewife) within a patriarchal society."[15] Similarly, Teresa de Lauretis describes the film as "engaged in the project of transforming vision by inventing the forms and processes of representation of a social subject, women, that until now has been all but unrepresentable."[16] The degree to which *Jeanne Dielman* was recognized as a welcome exemplification of a newly theorized feminist cinematic sensibility depended not simply on its focus on Jeanne's housework but on its bringing that domestic labor to visibility via formal experimentation with strategies of cinematic representation.

Angela McRobbie has noted the tight fit between Akerman's work and a particular type of 1970s feminism: "Akerman's films have been linked with feminism ever since the early 70s, when *Je, tu, il, elle* (1974), followed by

Jeanne Dielman, 23 Quai du Commerce, 1080 Bruxelles (1975), were taken up by theorists and film critics as reflective of the new feminist politics. Her work was also seen as pioneering in that it seemed to herald the development of a distinctively feminist aesthetic."[17] Certainly, feminist critics made much of the way the film's minimalist narrative was imprinted with the iterative and durational temporalities of Jeanne's everyday actions via Akerman's formal preoccupations with a fixed camera, lengthy medium shots, a frontal theatricality, real-time sequences, and single-take scenes that eschew the conventionally suturing nip-and-tuck of the shot reverse shot or the close-up. Widely acclaimed for its thematic and formal originality, the novelty that Akerman's film offered was nevertheless immediately recognizable to this new generation of feminist film scholars, who were, in that same mid-1970s moment, taking up psychoanalytic models to theorize relations between femininity and its cinematic representation.

In the same year *Jeanne Dielman* premiered at the Cannes Film Festival, Laura Mulvey published her influential—if subsequently contested—essay "Visual Pleasure and Narrative Cinema." While Mulvey did not reference Akerman's film, *Jeanne Dielman* has been subsequently claimed as "an almost literal realisation of the critic's vision."[18] In her essay, Mulvey famously argues that "the unconscious of patriarchal society has structured film form" to the extent that the visual pleasures associated with mainstream cinema temporarily enable a non-traumatizing resolution of the necessary psychic tensions between sexual instincts and processes of identity formation for the presumptively male spectator.[19] Her call for nothing less than "a new language of desire" prompted an energetic proliferation of feminist film scholarship bent on exploring what she identified as the potential of avant-garde or experimental film techniques to revision spectatorial relations with regard to spectacularized images of women. Understanding Akerman's formal strategies to resonate strongly with Mulvey's closing claim that "the first blow against the monolithic accumulation of traditional film conventions (already undertaken by radical film-makers) is to free the look of the camera into its materiality in time and space and the look of the audience into dialectics, passionate detachment," much of this work took *Jeanne Dielman* as a key text, reading its apartment plot as a more general critique of the social marginalization of Western women.[20]

For some critics, the film's full and "drily pugnacious title"—*Jeanne Dielman, 23 Quai du Commerce, 1080 Bruxelles*—with its uninflected specification of occupant's name and apartment address is sufficient clue to the domestic containment of its protagonist.[21] In Kinder's analysis, "the full title of the film immediately tells us that Jeanne Dielman is defined and circumscribed by the space she occupies—'23 Quai du Commerce—1080 Bruxelles.' The patterns of her life have been determined by the social-economic structures of her society. . . . The consciousness and body of the female protagonist are identified with her rooms and house: all are empty spaces waiting to be entered and activated by the male visitor."[22] Mary Jo Lakeland similarly emphasizes the way that the title captures Jeanne's emplacement both literally within a specific domestic setting and figuratively in relation to economies of sexual exchange: "Beginning with the film's title, we see the chief character not simply named (as in *Marnie*), nor named and claimed (as in Alfred Hitchcock's *Marnie*), but named and put in a place. The frequent practice of referring to this film by the shortened title of *Jeanne Dielman* overlooks the heavy burden of signification implicit in the address— Quai du Commerce. The complete title not only locates Jeanne Dielman in an explicit geographical sense, but also defines her mode of existence."[23] Such representations of Jeanne as symbiotically bound to the apartment in which she lives are not idiosyncratic; other feminist critics similarly note various ways in which "Jeanne's relationship with her apartment marks her as a social victim."[24]

Despite—or, perhaps, because of—Akerman's insistence on Seyrig's evenly unemotional performance of everyday tasks such as the brushing of hair or the making of coffee, feminist film scholars have tended to understand Jeanne as trapped in domestic servitude in an apartment the repressiveness of which is self-evident. For Jayne Loader, the apartment itself has an almost characterological force in the domestic plot, anthropomorphically animated by the energies of Jeanne's housework: "The apartment seems to have a life of its own, to have needs and demands which manipulate Jeanne and structure her day much more substantially than do the needs of either her living son or once-living husband. . . . It is the apartment that makes clear and tangible demands: it must be cleaned, its dishes washed, its furniture polished, its rooms aired of unpleasant odors, its voracious appetite for human attention, love, and labor appeased."[25] On account of *Jeanne Dielman*'s sustained attentiveness to the microgestures of quotidian female domestic routine, the apartment has largely been read as a space of containment, the perfect mise-en-scène for the claustrophobia and psychological repression that feminist film critics routinely presumed was the apartment's psychic corollary.[26]

Similarly, feminist critics tended to understand the film's iterative three-day cycle as key to its representation of a brutalizing everydayness, noting the way that the subtitled shifts to the second and then the third day both make clear the cyclical nature of Jeanne's labor and induct the spectator into her deadening regimes of habituation. Bergstrom sees the repetitive and routinized housework activities as key to *Jeanne Dielman*: "The film's sense depends very much on the strict, chronological progression of its events. One task and its habitual movements is followed by the next in a routine which is already familiar by the second day."[27] With the relatively lengthy film focused on the everyday techniques of Jeanne's housewifely activities and the camerawork designed to tether the spectator to their durational specificities, feminist critics frequently remark on their own experience of being gradually drawn into the predictably patterned world of Jeanne's apartment, often against the force of their resistance to such scenes of domestic quietude. As Loader notes, "We are initially bored with [the film's] slow pace, which admits no music, no camera movement, and no opticals as distraction, but we are ultimately carried into the rhythm of Jeanne's life: empathy is virtually unavoidable."[28] Similarly, having commended *Jeanne Dielman* for being "the first film to scrutinize housework in a language appropriate to the activity itself, showing a woman's activities in the home in real time to communicate the alienation of women in the nuclear family under European postwar economic conditions," B. Ruby Rich goes on to observe that "we internalize these rituals, learn to count to her rhythm of gestures, come to feel instinctively the precise calibrations of her daily routines."[29]

Unsurprisingly, being drawn into the phenomenological experience of everyday female alienation marks a moment of ambivalence for much of the film's feminist criticism. Although not owned as such in the criticism, this ambivalence attaches properly to the subject of everyday life itself, which is famously "characterized by ambiguities, instabilities and equivocation."[30] As can be traced in its historic deployment, the notion of the everyday has operated across a dialectic, either celebrated for its inventive engagements with massified power or lamented as an alienated space of repetition and meaninglessness. If feminist film scholars have tended to read *Jeanne Dielman* in relation to the more pessimistic framing of everyday life, that is in large part overdetermined by the ways in which femininity itself has been associated in a number of critical traditions with the negative declensions of the everyday.[31] In an influential essay that critiques the masculinist biases evident in some definitions of the everyday, Rita Felski ventures "an alternative definition." "The temporality of the everyday," she writes, "is that of repetition, the spatial ordering of the everyday is anchored in a sense of home, and the characteristic mode of experiencing the everyday is that of habit."[32] This definition resonates strongly with the everyday of *Jeanne Dielman*, which across its three consecutive days takes the tight confines of the apartment on Quai du Commerce as its seat, each of its internal spaces—kitchen, foyer, corridor, bedroom, dining room— becoming habituated across the film's unhurried 201-minute span through the encounter with repeatedly performed household activities.

Repetitive, domesticated, and habituated: these characteristics cumulatively describe something that feminist criticism of *Jeanne Dielman* is drawn to as an aesthetic style but disidentifies with as a subject position. Although she suggests an empathetic spectatorial relation with Jeanne is almost inevitable, Loader also notes more anxiously that "the static camera traps us as completely as Jeanne's static life traps her, and studying that world, we become a part of it."[33] If study brings the feminist spectator uncomfortably close to her abjected other, however, it is also the feminist spectator's studiousness—or, at least, her analytical capacity—that differentiates her from the alienated housewife. In an unpersuasively upbeat and almost proselytizing conclusion, Kinder makes this point rather awkwardly in the closing sentences of her article when, with the turning up of the house lights, she releases the spectator into a new and improved feminist consciousness by way of a temporary overidentification with the unsalvageable figure of Jeanne herself: "Of course, when the film is over, unlike Jeanne, we are released from the trap; yet our own susceptibility to the routines and resistance to the new have been demonstrated. We have experienced the trap from the inside and, as a result, our own perception and consciousness have been expanded. The film makes us see our own daily routines in a new way; it leads us to re-examine the relationship between our identity and our actions. Most important, it makes us more receptive to what is new and liberating in our experience."[34] In its fairly bald subscription to the idea of the politically transformational encounter with art, Kinder's comment coarsely captures the principle that elsewhere implicitly underwrites the feminist reception of Akerman's film: that *Jeanne*

Dielman is a work of ideology critique, making visible the stultifying trap that everyday domestic life is for women.

In bringing to representation the minutiae of female domestic labor—sometimes even in the real time of those labors—Akerman is praised for denaturalizing the everyday by basting it with a close attention that is the very opposite of the casual lack of regard and distracted disengagement that more commonly characterize the embodied experience of everydayness. A feminist object lesson, Jeanne Dielman is nevertheless beyond the reach of feminism herself. In her account of the film's organizing logics, Bergstrom makes clear that Jeanne is structurally the opposite of a feminist, an alternative declension of femininity: "There is a split here between character and director, two discourses, two modes of the feminine: the feminine *manquée*, acculturated under patriarchy, and the feminist who is actively looking at the objective conditions of her oppression—her place in the family."[35] Routinely called out as "robotic and automaton-like, incapable of creatively investing herself in the world or of taking a step back, frozen in habit and repetition," Jeanne is mired in the routinized conditions of her everyday life, enslaved to repetition, and therefore unable to grasp her situation analytically.[36]

Of course, it is a common human capacity to recognize more easily the pointedness of critique when it is pointed at someone else. Nevertheless, it is worth noting the strong whiff of disavowal or, at least, self-protectiveness in the ease with which a second-wave feminism stakes its radicalism and the newness of its project on a sharp differentiation with the previous generation of women. As Bergstrom writes, "*Jeanne Dielman* is the image of the old viewed actively, with fascination."[37] Once again, Kinder expresses this in the plainest terms, her praise of the film dependent on a generational divide that is traversed by the triumphal narrative of succession. Referring to Akerman's recent return to Europe from New York, Kinder writes, "She takes her expanded consciousness home to Brussels and concentrates it on the narrowest of subjects—a woman from her mother's generation who is trapped in the very conventions that Akerman has escaped."[38] Kinder's characterization of the relation between Akerman and Jeanne Dielman as generational subscribes to a broadly held feminist view that *Jeanne Dielman* is "a film made from the daughter's point of view" and throws into prominence the temporal logics that enable a feminist disidentification with the older women who are nevertheless required to stand as feminism's prehistory.[39] The young, globally mobile director, buoyed along on the bubble of her burgeoning consciousness, is associated with the opportunities of feminism, while left behind in her wake is the previous generation of women—domestically bound, drained of agency, and trapped in meaningless cycles of repetition—for which condition the perfect domicile is presumed to be the small apartment on Quai du Commerce.

IN ORDER TO THINK a little further about the temporal logics of the feminist reception of *Jeanne Dielman*, I want to read two scenes against each other—the first, the much-analyzed, overdetermined, but, given Akerman's distinctive cinematic style, radically uncharacteristic representation of Jeanne's orgasm and subsequent murder of her third client in the film's penultimate scene; the second, the seldom-discussed instance in which Jeanne prepares crumbed veal escalopes, the typicality of this scene's real-time rendition of yet another household task seeming to attract no particular attention.

While the camera stays discreetly outside the closed bedroom door for the temporally elided afternoon visits of Jeanne's first two clients, on the third day, when her routines have already been disrupted by a series of minor mishaps such as the burning of potatoes and the misbuttoning of clothing, it moves inside the bedroom, recording Jeanne's partial undressing, the sex she has with her client, her getting dressed again, and her stabbing of her client in the neck with a pair of scissors as he lies on her bed. Although interpretations vary as to its effect, many commentators have noted that both the orgasm and the murder occur in an explicitly fictional order of representation, in contrast to the rest of the film and the realist claim it exaggeratedly lays to the everyday events it records. For reasons that derive from the built specificities of the actual apartment in which the film was shot, the shooting and editing of this scene also differ from the aesthetic style previously established across the first three hours of the film. As becomes clear with the 2009 release of the "director-approved" restored digital transfer DVD from Criterion, which includes Sami Frey's documentary "Autour de *Jeanne Dielman*," shot during the filming of Akerman's film and edited nearly thirty years later by Agnès Ravez and Akerman, as well as new interviews with Akerman and her cinematographer, Babette Mangolte, the scale of the apartment was such that it was barely able to accommodate the technologies of reproduction that meticulously recorded it (fig. 5.2).

FIG. 5.2. The cramped apartment space barely accommodates the camera and film crew on the set of *Jeanne Dielman* (Chantal Akerman, 1975).

Unable to put much distance between the camera and her subject anywhere in the tight confines of the small apartment and further constrained by the fact that it had such low ceilings that there was only clearance of two and a half feet for the tungsten lighting and all the electrical cabling that she ran on the ceiling to keep it out of shot, Mangolte relied heavily on a wide-angle lens. The inflexibilities of the built space were even more challenging in the bedroom, where the furniture took up most of the small footprint such that the sex-and-murder scene was recorded without the sound boom since there was no room for it outside the image frame.[40] Given the bedroom's ungenerous internal spaces, the bracketing shots of Jeanne undressing and redressing are accomplished via angled reflections in the dressing-table mirror (fig. 5.3). For the intervening sex scene, Akerman's lower-than-standard camera height—indexed by the director to her own stature and physical perspective and hence widely celebrated as an indicator of feminist filmmaking practice—is abandoned as the camera tilts from a height over the footboard to show Jeanne gently convulsing on the bed beneath her client, an even less kinetic man in a white singlet.[41]

It is widely presumed in feminist film scholarship—no doubt because it has been asserted many times by Akerman herself in interviews—that the event that initiates Jeanne's slow process of coming undone is an off-screen orgasm she has with her second client.[42] This sexual experience is represented in the scene with the third client where, demonstrating none of her usual competent proficiencies for tasks frequently enacted, Jeanne alternates between ineffectually pushing at the dead weight of the man on top of her and gently squirming beneath him, rumpling the bedspread in her clenched fist. Female orgasm and murder are limit events in the sense

FIG. 5.3. Due to the bedroom's small footprint, Akerman abandoned her usual shooting style for angled reflections of the action via the dressing-table mirror (*Jeanne Dielman*, 1975).

that they cannot be brought to representation in the hyperrealist style so comprehensively established across the previous three hours of Akerman's film. As such, they raise questions of motivation, both characterological and directorial, that demand a different kind of attention than that extracted so strenuously from spectators by the film up to this point. Why does Akerman have Jeanne orgasm? Why does she have her kill her client?

Even allowing for the unreliable resource that cinema has been for representations of the everyday techniques and temporalities of female sexual pleasure, the diegetic motivation for Jeanne's orgasm is implausibly scant, with her client lying in an apparently postcoital languor on top of her, any effective movement undetectable. And if, extradiegetically, its function is to motivate the murder, then such a neat economy of closure still seems at odds with the already established narrational rhythms of Akerman's scenes, the beginnings and endings of which are disconcertingly unsynchronized to human action. Nevertheless, the break that murder effects in *Jeanne Dielman*'s hyperrealist representational order has tended in feminist readings to be taken, satisfactorily or not, as an indication of the coordinates of the film's narrative closure.[43] In the generational terms that characterize the feminist reception of the film, Jeanne's orgasm and her killing of the client is fantasized as the mother's break with an oppressive social order, "a repressed sexuality erupting as jouissance" that "must be annulled in the act of murder, in the abolition of the phallus."[44]

The tidiness of this analysis is thrown into suspicion by Ivone Margulies's claim that "much of the writing on Akerman (with notable exceptions) tends to shift from detailed textual analysis to conclusions about her work's politics that seem to come from somewhere other than the films themselves. In the more articulate criticism, this 'elsewhere' is usually feminist psychoanalytic theory."[45] Here, the question of motivation gets a different answer as, under cover of that story and its well-known points of oedipal reference, feminism stages a different, unspectacular but no less violent, break: the daughter's break with the mother. For if the film is ostensibly taken to represent Jeanne's violent rupturing of an individualizing erotic repression that stands in synecdochal relation to a more broadly worked societal oppression, that break is proprietarily taken up by and for a feminist interpretative frame that derives its force from the distance it takes from its analytic object. Not the true or even logical figure of the film's negative affect, the murdered client is more a fall guy, an externalization of an implicit violence bent on renouncing continuities between mothers and daughters, between women of an older generation and feminists of the second wave.

The disidentification with the figure of Jeanne evident in the feminist reception of Akerman's film has, as Frey's documentary also reveals, an interesting corollary in the fact that many of the female everyday life practices used to characterize Jeanne were already only patchily recollected by Akerman to an extent that threatened to compromise her capacity to capture them representationally. Given the conventions already well established in *Jeanne Dielman* for the representation of household labor, the veal escalope scene is formally unsurprising. Squared frontally to a fixed camera and across the time it takes to accomplish the unelided sequence of actions, Jeanne scatters flour on the kitchen table, pours bread crumbs from a canister into a plate, unwraps two pale pink escalopes, breaks an egg into a flat bowl before beating it with a fork, and then coats each piece of veal with flour, egg, and bread crumbs. As with all her household activities, Jeanne performs her task in a matter-of-fact and routinized way that suggests she has undertaken these exact actions so many times previously that they are habituated in her person at the level of muscle memory. As becomes clear in Frey's documentary, however, neither Akerman nor Seyrig had much of an idea as to how to bread veal escalopes.

Although Akerman has frequently claimed that her familiarity with domestic business in her own childhood home as well as those of her various aunts allowed her to specify in her script every aspect of the film's action down to the smallest detail—"chaque geste, chaque geste, chaque geste"—in the rehearsal of this scene there is so much uncertainty about how to prepare a breaded escalope that Seyrig is moved to say it's a shame Akerman's mother didn't teach her how to do it.[46] They debate whether or when to season the escalope, in what order the flour, bread crumbs, and beaten egg should be applied, how to grasp the veal during the breading process, and whether it is wrapped in aluminum foil for refrigerator storage, with Akerman applying to the authority of her aunt and Seyrig to Éliane (presumably Éliane Marcus, the makeup artist) in support of their countervailing opinions.[47]

Although Jeanne's production of the cutlets is flawless, each gesture run through with a seeming proficiency that implies frequent recurrence, it is useful to understand Seyrig's performance as a historical reenactment in which the meticulous re-creation of skills no longer securely held speaks to the dynamic of generational difference that animates both the film's feminism and its feminist reception. Of course, all performance is to some extent reenactment, in the sense captured by Richard Schechner's concept of restored behavior. "Performance means: never for the first time," writes Schechner. "Performance is 'twice-behaved behavior.'"[48] Necessarily coming late to the scenes it would reanimate, reenactment emphasizes the way in which Seyrig's performance references an archive of historical gestures that have already passed from everyday practice. Reenactment is gesturally haunted by the events to which it lays representational claim. "Pre-occupied with the minutiae of daily life—dress, diet, bodily maintenance, domestic space, material objects, the management of human relationships, and the organization of time," reenactment's "mode is agglomerative—discrete pieces of information are gleaned and corroborated through firsthand experience."[49] Foregrounding the affectivity of investments in the past alongside the historical discontinuities such investments must negotiate, the concept of reenactment brings to critical attention the processes of temporal disidentification intrinsic to *Jeanne Dielman* and the feminist interpretative frameworks that have been its most significant reception contexts.[50]

ON ITS RELEASE, Akerman's apartment film was celebrated for its cinematic articulation of "a consciously feminist sensibility."[51] Yet the initial feminist reception of Akerman's film hinged ambivalently on *Jeanne Dielman*'s apartment plot and its representation of the temporalities of a female everyday. Not often explicitly interested in issues of temporality, the feminist film critics who wrote about *Jeanne Dielman* often emphasized the interventionist force of Akerman's lengthily held shots of culturally insignificant housework activities, as if subscribing to a folk-Bazinian faith in the aesthetic value of the deep-focus long take. Yet the feminist championing of Akerman's film style enabled a covert subscription to a different order of temporality, endorsing a sense of lived time animated by the generational divide between second-wave feminism and the women it succeeded. Coined as a term for the unsystematized yet emphatic wiping out of accrued patterns of living in the quest for modernization, *Brusselization* might also work figuratively to recall at one remove the kind of unacknowledged violence with which the feminist criticism of *Jeanne Dielman* breaks with a previous generation of women in its urgent desire to clear some space for new and improved ways of life. Acknowledging the complicated temporal disidentification feminist film criticism expressed for the figure of Jeanne Dielman allows in turn a broader recognition of the ways in which *Jeanne Dielman*'s apartment plot functions. For all its obvious pleasures in being shaped by tight architectural confines, the apartment plot of Akerman's film is not simply or even primarily spatial; it is, as importantly, temporal, and not just in its celebrated attention to the durational span of everyday domestic gesture. As can be seen in its almost anthropological capture of everyday practices as they pass from lived experience, *Jeanne Dielman* seizes the apartment plot to thematize the passing of historical time in order to indenture the present moment to feminism.

NOTES

1. Warm thanks to Christoph Holzhey and Claudia Peppel for inviting me to the ICI-Berlin, and to them and the resident fellows for providing me with an intellectually engaged and socially welcoming environment for six months.

2. Annamarie Jagose, "Thinkiest," *PMLA* 125, no. 2 (2010): 378.

3. Catherine Fowler, "*Jeanne Dielman 23 Quai du Commerce 1080 Bruxelles / Jeanne Dielman*," in *The Cinema of the Low Countries*, ed. Ernest Mathijs (London: Wallflower, 2004), 131.

4. Evert Lagrou, "Brussels: Five Capitals in Search of a Place—the Citizens, the Planners and the Functions," *GeoJournal* 51, no. 1/2 (2000): 99.

5. Carola Hein, *The Capital of Europe: Architecture and Urban Planning for the European Union* (Westport, CT: Praeger, 2004), 135–59. The two key institutions were the European Economic Community and the European Atomic Energy Communities. Less than a decade later, these two organizations merged with the older European Coal and Steel Community to form the European Communities, whose commission was "the most powerful entity in the European community," 135.

6. Katarzyna M. Romanczyk, "Transforming Brussels into an International City: Reflections on 'Brusselization,'" *Cities* 29, no. 2 (2012): 127.

7. Aylin Orbasli, *Tourists in Historic Towns: Urban Conservation and Heritage Management* (London: Taylor and Francis, 2002), 11.

8. Lagrou, "Brussels," 106.

9. While the chronotope is Bahktinian, it has more recently been revitalized for a theorization of the cinematic rendering of apartment space. See Lee Wallace, *Lesbianism, Cinema, Space: The Sexual Life of Apartments* (New York: Routledge, 2009), 1–12.

10. Ivone Margulies, *Nothing Happens: Chantal Akerman's Hyperrealist Everyday* (Durham, NC: Duke University Press, 1996), 65.

11. Janet Bergstrom, "*Jeanne Dielman, 23 Quai du Commerce, 1080 Bruxelles* by Chantal Akerman," *Camera Obscura* 1, no. 2 (1977): 116.

12. Judith Weinraub, "She Looked Good Being Passive, But . . . ," *New York Times*, July 31, 1976, 31; Vincent Canby, "*Jeanne Dielman*," *New York Times*, March 23, 1983, C25.

13. This essay concentrates on the initial feminist reception of *Jeanne Dielman*. Given that distribution across different national territories was uneven, however, initial reception is an elongated period that includes criticism published between 1975, the date of the film's premiere at Cannes, and 1983, the year it opened commercially in the United States. For brief accounts of the film's distribution history, see Annette Kuhn, *Women's Pictures: Feminism and Cinema* (London: Routledge and Kegan Paul, 1982), 188–89; Hamid Naficy, *An Accented Cinema: Exilic and Diasporic Filmmaking* (Princeton, NJ: Princeton University Press, 2001), 51.

14. Marsha Kinder, "Reflections on *Jeanne Dielman*," *Film Quarterly* 30, no. 4 (summer 1977): 5. In a 1978 roundtable discussion of feminist film style, however, Anna Marie Taylor cautions against any too simple equation of feminism and such bringings to visibility. Immediately following a discussion of *Jeanne Dielman* and reflecting on the discussion so far, Taylor says, "It sounds as if we are all saying that a feminist aesthetic or a feminist kind of filmmaking is the process of making the invisible visible. I don't think we want to take making the invisible visible too literally." For Taylor, visuality is better understood as a convenient metaphor for addressing the operations of ideology: "We have to talk about ideology because that's what we're really talking about when we say women filmmakers should make the invisible visible or the unthinkable thinkable." Michelle Citron, Julia Lesage, Judith Mayne, B. Ruby Rich, and Anna Marie Taylor, "Women and Film: A Discussion of Feminist Aesthetics," *New German Critique* 13 (winter 1978): 103.

15. Mary Ann Doane, "Women's Stake: Filming the Female Body," *October* 17 (summer 1981): 34. For similar accounts, see B. Ruby Rich's claim that "the activities of shopping, cooking, and cleaning the house are presented without ellipses, making visible the extent of time previously omitted from cinematic depictions"; Ruth Perlmutter's assertion that "in its extreme attention to Jeanne's domestic activities, the film not only articulates the reality of most women's experience, but also challenges the way in which their mundane reality has been elided in the conventional narrative"; and Annette Kuhn's insistence that "the very fact that the film shows a woman doing housework sets *Jeanne Dielman* apart from virtually all other fiction films.

Domestic labor has probably never been documented in such painstaking detail in a fiction film." B. Ruby Rich, *Chick Flicks: Theories and Memories of the Feminist Film Movement* (Durham, NC: Duke University Press, 1998), 68; Ruth Perlmutter, "Feminine Absence: A Political Aesthetic in Chantal Akerman's *Jeanne Dielman, 23 Quai de Commerce, 1080 Bruxelles,*" *Quarterly Review of Film Studies* 4, no. 2 (1979): 129; Kuhn, *Women's Pictures*, 174.

16. Teresa de Lauretis, *Technologies of Gender: Essays on Theory, Film, and Fiction* (Bloomington: Indiana University Press, 1987), 145.

17. Angela McRobbie, "Passionate Uncertainty," *Sight and Sound* 2, no. 5 (1992): 28.

18. Marion Schmid, *Chantal Akerman* (Manchester: Manchester University Press, 2010), 48.

19. Laura Mulvey, "Visual Pleasure and Narrative Cinema," in *Movies and Methods*, vol. 2, ed. Bill Nichols (Berkeley: University of California Press, 1985), 305.

20. Mulvey, "Visual Pleasure and Narrative Cinema," 315. Other films that are frequently discussed in this context are *Lives of Performers* (Yvonne Rainer, 1972), *Riddles of the Sphinx* (Laura Mulvey and Peter Wollen, 1977), *Thriller* (Sally Potter, 1979), and *Daughter Rite* (Michelle Citron, 1980).

21. Patricia Patterson and Manny Farber, "Kitchen without Kitsch," *Film Comment* 13, no. 6 (1977): 48.

22. Kinder, "Reflections on *Jeanne Dielman,*" 5. Similarly, Claire Johnston writes, "The film charts with an ethnographic precision three days in the life of a Belgian housewife/prostitute: the fixed identity encapsulated in the name and address of the title." Claire Johnston, "Towards a Feminist Film Practice: Some Theses," in *Movies and Methods*, vol. 2, ed. Bill Nichols (Berkeley: University of California Press, 1985), 325.

23. Mary Jo Lakeland, "The Color of *Jeanne Dielman,*" *Camera Obscura* 3–4 (1979): 216.

24. Jayne Loader, "*Jeanne Dielman*: Death in Installments," in *Movies and Methods*, vol. 2, ed. Bill Nichols (Berkeley: University of California Press, 1985), 333.

25. Loader, "*Jeanne Dielman,*" 331.

26. This is not a universal reading of the film. Without the interpretative frame of feminism, critics sometimes found it difficult to make Jeanne's actions meaningful. Jonathan Rosenbaum, for instance, struggles to identify the axis of oppression taken as self-evident in the feminist reception of the film: "An easy conclusion would treat [Jeanne] as a simple social victim à la Fassbinder, her act of violence as spontaneous rebellion. But rebellion against whom or what? What we *see* in the film appears self-imposed, a way of life that seems partially designed to rule out the possibility of extended thinking." Jonathan Rosenbaum, "Edinburgh Encounters: A Consumers/ Producers Guide-in-Progress to Four Recent Avant-Garde Films," *Sight and Sound* 45, no. 1 (1976): 23.

27. Bergstrom, "*Jeanne Dielman,*" 115.

28. Loader, "*Jeanne Dielman,*" 330.

29. Rich, *Chick Flicks*, 67, 171.

30. Ben Highmore, *Everyday Life and Cultural Theory: An Introduction* (London: Routledge, 2002), 17.

31. An important exception to this tendency is Judith Mayne's emphasis on the ambiguity of *Jeanne Dielman* and its "competing levels of agency, identification, and pleasure." "Certainly," she writes, "the film traces the restrictive conditions of housework, the dehumanizing effects of continuous labor and servitude, while it portrays Jeanne as an unmistakable compulsive. Yet it also produces an equally unmistakable sense of pleasure in the rituals of everyday life." Judith Mayne, *The Woman at the Keyhole: Feminism and Women's Cinema* (Bloomington: Indiana University Press, 1990), 203, 207.

32. Rita Felski, "The Invention of Everyday Life," *New Formations* 39 (1999–2000): 18.

33. Loader, "*Jeanne Dielman*," 330.

34. Kinder, "Reflections on *Jeanne Dielman*," 8.

35. Bergstrom, "*Jeanne Dielman*," 117.

36. Loader, "*Jeanne Dielman*," 330.

37. Bergstrom, "*Jeanne Dielman*," 118.

38. Kinder, "Reflections on *Jeanne Dielman*," 3.

39. Mayne, *The Woman at the Keyhole*, 211.

40. Babette Mangolte, interview, supplementary material, *Jeanne Dielman, 23 Quai du Commerce, 1080 Bruxelles* (Criterion, 2009), DVD.

41. Insofar as its representations of the apartment are themselves often visibly shaped by the apartment's spatial dimensions, *Jeanne Dielman* is an intriguingly material instantiation of Wojcik's observation that "the apartment plot entails more than setting: the apartment not only hosts but motivates action." Pamela Wojcik, *The Apartment Plot: Urban Living in American Film and Popular Culture, 1945 to 1975* (Durham, NC: Duke University Press, 2010), 7.

42. The widespread subscription in the feminist criticism to Jeanne's orgasm with her second client, an event that does not have any even connotative representation in the film, is also explicable in terms of the degree to which orgasm is more broadly held in the modern period as interpretatively key to many orders of epistemological truth. For a discussion of the cultural work of orgasm in the long twentieth century, see Annamarie Jagose, *Orgasmology* (Durham, NC: Duke University Press, 2013).

43. See, for instance, Claire Johnston, who understands the orgasm and murder in terms of a repression-countering jouissance, and Jayne Loader, who reads them as a capitulation to mainstream cinematic protocols and masculinist values of violence. Johnston, "Towards a Feminist Film Practice," 315–27; Loader, "*Jeanne Dielman*," 327–39.

44. Johnston, "Towards a Feminist Film Practice," 326.

45. Margulies, *Nothing Happens*, 6.

46. Chantal Akerman, interview, supplementary material, *Jeanne Dielman, 23 Quai du Commerce, 1080 Bruxelles* (Criterion, 2009), DVD.

47. Sami Frey, "Autour de *Jeanne Dielman*," supplementary material, *Jeanne Dielman, 23 Quai du Commerce, 1080 Bruxelles* (Criterion, 2009), DVD.

48. Richard Schechner, *Between Theater and Anthropology* (Philadelphia: University of Pennsylvania Press, 1985), 36.

49. Vanessa Agnew, "Introduction: What Is Reenactment?," *Criticism* 46, no. 3 (2004): 330.

50. Arguing that *Jeanne Dielman* has no articulable context in any aesthetic movement, including alternative national cinemas, Judith Mayne contends, "one of the most important contexts for *Jeanne Dielman* is contemporary feminism," where that feminism is understood as preeminently psychoanalytic. "Akerman's film responds more directly to a feminist context, one in which the notion of the 'primitive' has surfaced in fairly controversial ways. From the resurrection of the pre-oedipal and the attendant mother-child bond in feminist psychoanalytic writing, to the insistence on the body in discourse in *l'écriture féminine*, to the conceptualization of a female aesthetic defined in so-called pre-aesthetic terms, contemporary feminism has been obsessed with the excavation of a space, an area, somehow prior to and therefore potentially resistant to the realm of the patriarchal symbolic." Mayne, *The Woman at the Keyhole*, 202.

51. Rich, *Chick Flicks*, 67.

Never court a wee lassie with a dark and roving eye.
—"Courting Is a Pleasure," folk song

6

HOME'S INVASION

Repulsion and the Horror of Apartments

VERONICA FITZPATRICK

The opening credits of Roman Polanski's 1965 film *Repulsion* pass at canted angles over the surface of an open eye, until the closing directorial credit, "directed by Roman Polanski," cuts clear across the center, resembling, as Lucy Fischer has remarked, the infamous eye slice of Luis Buñuel's *Un Chien andalou* (1929).[1] In the first minute of Buñuel's surrealist film, a straight razor is used to cut a woman's eye; the film abruptly cuts to a dark cloud slicing the moon, and the cuts of eye and film and moon constellate a spectatorial lesson: not that the image of a cloud replaces the image of a razor, evoking in euphemism the violence previously shown, but that the cloud *is* the razor—such that, in the film that follows, familiar distinctions between filmed objects and film images will not obtain. *Repulsion*, too, typifies a mode of film that's expressly concerned with the futility of boundaries or, more significantly, of boundary logic: that which reduces the distributive impulse of taxonomy to an either/or arrangement.

Cinematic horror lends itself to compartmentalization and taxonomy at several levels: globally, in terms of inclusion criteria, for example, *this* counts as horror while this does not; and locally, in terms of a film's temporal organization, that is, this is a scare, as if a scare is a finite, stable episode, more like a shot than a scene. One of the most durable examples of this logic in genre criticism is the theorization of monstrosity, most notably by Noël Carroll, who argues in *The Philosophy of Horror* that to qualify as horror proper (rather than as a neighboring but distinct genre), films require a scientifically inexplicable monster and must provoke sensations of both fear and disgust in their spectator.[2] Carroll's work on horror constitutes a major contribution to the development of concrete defining criteria for a genre whose variations engender instability and ambiguity, but the disadvantages of this framework are also well documented.[3] In the case of a film such as *Repulsion*, a critical approach that privileges horrific monstrosity assigns authority to causality, asking what, specifically, is to blame for protagonist Carol's (Catherine Deneuve) gradual mental disintegration. Is the threat primarily internal (her psychosis) or external (in her apartment), or a symbiosis of both, in which her troubled mental state manifests a materialized threat? This essay suggests that such an inquiry, concerned as it is with the measurement and maintenance of boundary, is scarcely equipped to account for instances of horror that complicate or otherwise fail to conform to generic criteria, even as they exhibit a thematic and formal coherence that warrants theorizing.

Critical work on Polanski's apartment trilogy films, of which *Repulsion* is the first, followed by *Rosemary's Baby* (1968) and *The Tenant* (1976), has focused largely on the coexistence of these films' apartment settings with art-cinematic modes of form and narrative, on one hand, and their depictions of complex psychological unraveling, on the other. In other words, despite the apartment trilogy classification, and the centrality of a haunted house trope that owes to a Gothic tradition as well as to horror, the generic significance of these films' urban domestic spaces is relatively neglected. In his "Polanski and the Horror from Within," for example, Tony McKibbin grounds his analysis of the apartment trilogy in character psychology, arguing that the films distinguish Polanski as an "interior horror" filmmaker, generating fright not through physiologically primitive startles, but through psychologically complex characters. For McKibbin, psychic complexity elicits a correspondingly complex spectatorial interaction, as opposed to the simple embodied response (e.g., a shudder) to a filmic startle.[4] McKibbin comes closer to what I find crucial in *Repulsion* in his interpretation of a not-strictly-apartment film: Polanski's *Death and the Maiden* (1994), which he reads as inverting the woman-in-peril trope (of *Repulsion* and *Rosemary's Baby*) such that a female character (rape survivor Paulina Escobar, played by Sigourney Weaver) faces peril not as a threat in the present, but as a recollection of the past kept alive only in her mind. The atemporality of past traumatic experience and present remembrance acts on both character and spectator such that "any startle here is essentially the shiver of recollection."[5] Though working to productively foreground trauma in his analysis of fear, McKibbin adheres to divisions between past and present, and event and memory, to the point of over-dichotomizing these categories. To collapse here/now with recollection/then elides the ways in which what's recalled is never truly, safely, not-now and not-here.

Writing on *Repulsion*, Tarja Laine also lingers with character (i.e., what happens to Carol) in order to land with the spectator. For her, the titular emotion/sensation is not a stop en route to catharsis, but is as much a container as the apartment itself, such that "the film imprisons its protagonist in madness and disgust."[6] Laine distinguishes her approach from McKibbin's by attempting to focus out on the world of the film, rather than in on character psychology: "By contrast [to psychological readings of the film], I suggest that *Repulsion* is about being ultra-sensitive to the world and the resulting state of insane fear of intimacy, into which spectators are directly induced by the film itself."[7] Yet Laine's very reading remains relatively insensitive to the material specificity of that world, particularly as that world bears a fear of intimacy on its sensible surface.

Missing from these strands of conversation is a sufficiently close reading of the details of Polanski's *Repulsion* specific to its expression of urban domesticity—including Carol's interactivity not only with her shared apartment but with her place of work (the salon) and the surrounding city of London, all of which become increasingly mutually permeable. As her salon's hallways resemble domestic corridors, and the sidewalks' cracks mirror splits in the apartment walls, *Repulsion*'s mise-en-scène disperses. The apartment is not simply a setting or even a narrative motor, but a generic machine: dissolving distinctions between setting, plot, and character, and thus urging us to recalibrate our understanding of what is explicit and implicit, objective and subjective, and apparent and submerged.

Repulsion participates in and typifies not only what Pamela Robertson Wojcik defines as the apartment plot, nor simply so-called modern cinematic horror, but a subgeneric form I'll call *domestic horror*: texts in which horror within the home works to formally surface an as-yet-submerged encounter with past sexual trauma.[8] In these films, the gradual mutation of an ostensibly safe space into something not only potentially gruesome but ontologically unstable expresses the particular horror of violence experienced and violation undergone in the supposedly safest, most familiar milieu: that of the family. As a formative domestic horror text, *Repulsion* signifies said mutation in primarily textural terms, probing, with a hairline wall crack as with its hallway of grasping hands, how cinematic mise-en-scène signifies at what depth specific fears are felt.

More Than Setting

In Wojcik's analysis, in the apartment plot "the apartment is *more than setting*: it motivates or shapes the narrative in some key way." In other words, thinking the apartment plot requires further dismantling the familiar boundary between formal feature—in this case, setting as an aspect of mise-en-scène—and filmic narrative. The apartment thus understood is not simply a container for plot events and figural relations, but an active, if potentially ambient, participant in itself. Key to that participation are the ways in which the apartment's mode of domesticity is distinct from that in keeping with the house; Wojcik accords the apartment values of visibility, density, community, contact, impermanence, and porousness, in contrast to the containment, stability, and privacy of a permanent home. The apartment's fundamental cellular structure results in not only proximity to, but various kinds of ongoing contact with, hallways, neighbors, the surrounding city, and whatever else just exceeds the visible walls.

A domestic space as more than setting is familiar ground for film criticism, and horror has proved particularly susceptible to allegorical interpretations of filmic space.[9] Often, we scrutinize space specifically for its capacity to materialize a mental state: for instance, the Victorian home as a shell, that which, in Walter Benjamin's words, "bears the impression of its occupant."[10] Space thus understood is primarily reflective; it is altered or shaped, discernibly, by its inhabitant. *Impression* goes further still to imply a tactile relation, whereby the home does not simply mirror but is pressed upon, and thus superficially or even structurally changed. A phenomenological approach to film setting imagines an impression that is not only sensible but mutual, as in Laine's description of the *Repulsion* flat as an organism unto itself, a "lived body in the Merleau-Pontyean sense . . . both a physical (architectural) and a mental (conscious) structure with an agency and intentionality of its own, aiming to drive Carol insane."[11] Both Benjaminian and phenomenological readings of on-screen space take up the expressionist notion of figure, wherein surroundings extend toward and into one another, resisting definite boundaries and mutual self-containment.

Domestic interiors are particularly supple sites of query with regard to cinematic horror. We can look back on the long, literary tradition of the Gothic domicile: vast, cold castles and manors, foreign to their new or temporary (or soon to be temporary) occupants, presenting and producing an atmosphere both literally and figuratively tomb-like.[12] We can also recall modern horror's Terrible Place, the exemplar for which is the dilapidated homestead of Tobe Hooper's *The Texas Chain Saw Massacre* (1974): a farmhouse, seemingly abandoned and yet magnetic, as even the camera is moved to stalk and corral the film's teenagers into the fatal family home.[13] In the Terrible Place, "outside" (i.e., not exclusively the home's exterior but also the material, sensible indoor space) reflects what's inside (the space itself is repulsive, carpeted and even furnished with bodily remains); in *The Texas Chain Saw Massacre*, the house's spatial practice is such that the family's cannibalistic legacy obtains in each polluted surface.[14]

Where Clover's spatial theory most crucially innovates is in its suggestion that the Terrible Place is legible: it not only disgusts and frightens; it conveys and informs. So for an unlucky visitor to apprehend the inhabitants' nature through the space inhabited, she must read. Clover writes, "Into such houses unwitting victims wander in film after film, and it is the unconventional task of the genre to register in close detail the victims' dawning understanding, as they survey the visible evidence, of the human crimes and perversions that have transpired there. That perception leads directly to the perception of their own immediate peril."[15] In the case of *Texas Chain Saw*, successful perception-begetting-perception may loosely ally with one's chance of survival; teenager Pam's understanding of her surroundings dawns at a painfully slow rate, allowing her gaze to direct the inventory conducted by the camera, to reproduce for its audience the realization that hers is now (and perhaps always was) a vulnerable animal body in a veritable slaughterhouse. Accordingly, perhaps the film's survivor Sally Hardesty is not simply a lucky hysteric, but a marginally faster reader, able to recognize insidiousness and thus ultimately, against all odds, to escape it.

Yet for the protagonist of domestic horror, such reading proficiency, however hypothetical, is foreclosed. Not by her relative spatial illiteracy, but because the spaces themselves tend to resist the kind of productive perception and interpretive work that Clover ascribes to slasher cinema. It's tempting to read slasher films' compulsive returns to youth-oriented spaces (e.g., summer camps, high schools, sorority houses) as constituting a premise for spatial transgression: the taboo of violence and terror in a relatively innocent milieu. But what if we understand as horror's most potent capacity not transgression, but revelation? In domestic horror, the home's mutation, dissembling, and betrayal of memory are less a stain on a clean surface than a demonstration of what has always been dirty.

Visible Evidence

Repulsion tells the story of a young Belgian esthetician named Carol, who shares an apartment in London with her older sister Helen (Yvonne Furneaux), who is having an affair with a married man called Michael (Ian Hendry), to whom Carol is decidedly allergic. Carol exhibits the affect of a patient on Quaaludes, consistently distant and preoccupied to the point of being asked, while working, if she has fallen asleep. When Michael takes Helen to Italy on holiday, Carol's dreamy condition descends toward a hallucinatory catatonia that's only compounded by her forced leave from work. As Carol spends more and more time alone at home, days and nights bleed together, and the space of the apartment increasingly mutates, manifesting changes both cosmetic and constitutional. *Repulsion* parallels Carol's descent into violence with a formal unraveling of the film itself, as it gradually digresses from conventional treatments of time as well as space, before seeming to snap back into place with Helen and Michael's return to the ruined apartment.

Repulsion's spatial mutations occur over a range, such that some convey as unexpected, producing startle effects for audience and Carol both; for example, when Carol first sees an unknown male figure materialize in the apartment. In Helen's room, Carol fingers the fabrics of her sister's clothes, particularly the feather-trimmed cocktail dress Helen wore to dinner out with Michael. She shuts the wardrobe door and the film score leaps as the figure's dark reflection is caught by the turning mirror. Even to a contemporary audience, the moment retains its suspenseful charge, recalling the infamous bus shot of Jacques Tourneur's *Cat People* (1942).[16] Yet other mutations, both in recurrence and formal quality, work via expectedness, creating a rhythm by which Carol's episodic assaults are organized: Carol goes to sleep, is woken and raped by a dark intruder, and the film fades out and back in on her the next morning in increasing states of disarray. The film further accents a day in–day out temporal rhythm with the sonic rhythm of a ticking clock within these scenes; like a metronome, the clock's ticking neutrally keeps time while Carol struggles in (filmic) silence on the bed.

This rhythm is broken by two retaliatory acts of violence that take place within the apartment and constitute the film's final act: first, Carol bludgeons and kills her irrepressible boyfriend Colin, and second, she uses Michael's razor to slice up her lecherous landlord. Though she suffers— and is seemingly unable to prevent or thwart—nightly attacks by an unknown man, Carol lethally dispatches both real men's attempts at having her. Helen and Michael return from Italy and find the apartment in a literally grave state, with Colin's corpse rotting in the bathroom, the landlord's body in the living room, and an inert Carol lying under Helen's bed.

Visible, dense, communal, porous: Carol's experience of the apartment space attests to the horrific angle inherent to each aspect of apartment living. Such quotidian hassles as unwelcome noise through thin walls and the steady accumulation of objects in shared living spaces are, essentially, horrors of invasion: invasions of privacy, personal space, autonomy, and even bodily integrity. *Repulsion* dramatizes the terror of personal invasion through a depiction of home/home's invasions; not only the invasion of the home by outsiders, as when Carol can't prevent Colin or her landlord from knowing that she's home and entering the space, but also the invasion of the outside by the home. *Repulsion*'s apartment mutates in myriad ways: it divides, when the walls crack open; it distorts, when grasping hands emerge from the hallway walls (fig. 6.1). Toward the end of the film, the space's once superficial instability extends to scale, such that Carol perceives the hallway as extra-long and the living room as enlarged. The hall of hands—an image that repeats within the film—deftly confirms that *Repulsion*'s apartment doesn't simply set the stage for invasion; the apartment itself invades, enacting a penetrative mode of contact through anthropomorphic revelation.

FIG. 6.1. The walls have hands (*Repulsion*, Roman Polanski, 1965).

Where initially she expressed horror at the relatively mundane sight of Michael's personal effects in the bathroom, Carol increasingly perceives structural disturbances in the apartment, nearly all of which have a primary textural component. Even before her time alone, otherwise dopey Carol is acutely attentive to surfaces, running her fingers along the mantelpiece or losing an afternoon to her fixation on cracked concrete. The film demonstrates studiousness toward texture as early as its opening shots, when a close-up of a salon client's clay masked face subverts our sense of what constitutes skin. Though we enter and exit the film through the human eye, the face in *Repulsion* tends to resist readability; repeatedly, we are provoked to consider and to experience conventionally transparent or benign surfaces as disorienting and repellent. At Carol's salon, the face is frequently soiled, as if infected by the apartment's accumulating filth. Her coworker Bridget's cheeks streaked with running makeup, a client's face spattered with milky product mid-rinse: in both instances, the film binds the messy image with the treachery of men. Carol discovers Bridget crying over her boyfriend's behavior, and their client Mrs. Balch lectures the women on male single-mindedness throughout her treatment, such that it's uncertain whether her words or her appearance have caught Carol's attention—and likely, the message of male indecency and the image of facial staining are inextricable. *Repulsion* thus forms a world in which male presence is epidemic, its reach extensive not only to epidermal surfaces but to consumables as well. When Carol is approached on her walk home from work by a city laborer, the camera turns from her, whom we've followed, to linger on his leering expression, before cutting abruptly to Carol's uneaten plate of fish and chips. Close-ups of further unappetizing sights abound: we see potatoes sprouting on the countertop, and return repeatedly to the image of a raw, rotting, and eventually decapitated skinned rabbit, initially meant for Helen to cook for a family dinner, but abandoned when Michael takes her out instead. Rather than simply contributing to a proliferation of repulsive objects, these foods are linked specifically to the impositions of men, from Michael's derailing presence in their apartment to Carol's mysterious home invader.

Both mess and men provoke in Carol a curious ambivalence. On one hand, she seems compelled to clean certain surfaces; after walking in on Michael shaving in her bathroom, she swipes at her nightgown as if sensing an infestation. The film takes care to show her making a similar gesture in the salon basement, when she stares at and brushes off the seat of a neighboring chair. Yet, while Helen is away, Carol doesn't just allow their apartment to fall into disrepair; she actively, if unconsciously, makes messes, as when she overdraws the bath and turns off the faucet but fails to drain the tub. The subsequent image of overflow recalls the macabre televised news item that Helen recounts early in the film, of eels emerging from the prime minister's toilet, an image that reinforces the extensive climate of intrusion, resumed by the bathtub and maintained to varying degrees—from Michael's toothbrush and razor, to the sound of Helen moaning during sex, to Colin's persistent physical advances—all of which constitute panic-inducing violations, penetrations ranging from ambient to increasingly aggressive.

Yet if the apartment penetrates, it also demonstrates permeability. Carol's door may as well be decorative for all the work it does to successfully keep unwanted visitors out; we see Colin and the landlord but also a slew of concerned neighbors pass into the apartment (the latter crowding at the end of the film, ironically calling for a kind of insulation—"Don't touch her"—that Carol, when conscious, was previously denied). Not only are the apartment's boundaries penetrable, but when Carol finds the hallway wall momentarily yielding, clay-like, under her hands, the space itself proves compositionally receptive, proliferating sensational anxiety both affective and textural: nothing here feels as it should.

Arguably, the apartment's most extreme textural transformations are specifically anthropomorphic, from groping hallway hands to the recurrent assailant seemingly native to the domestic space. Three times, we see Carol raped in her bedroom by a shadowy intruder, his face darkened or partially screened yet redolent of the construction worker she encountered on the city street. The intruder is linked to Helen not only through his first appearance (in her bedroom mirror), but also via two shots that manipulate genre convention and offscreen space to tease the spectator with false suspense. First, Carol is sleepless in bed when her doorknob begins to turn slowly—an image that clearly connotes helplessness to prevent pending intrusion—yet it's only Helen, wrapped in a sheet, entering to chide Carol for having thrown away Michael's toiletries. Later, as Carol sleeps, a black-gloved hand enters the top of the frame, and there's a moment of calculated uncertainty before we see that the hand is, again, Helen, come to say good-bye before leaving with Michael for Italy. Traces of both the turning of the bedroom doorknob and the vulnerability of the frame (and by extension, of the room, and of the woman in the room) recur each time Carol is raped, such that the film constructs an associative link between Helen and the violent domestic presence. One might be tempted to interpret the rapist as linked to the apartment in a dispersed manner akin to spatial fission: a major trope by which so-called art-horror multiplies the monster figure in space.[17] Yet the parallel between the intruder and Helen complicates reading Carol's rapist as merely a monstrous extension of the apartment entity.

Helen signifies what Carol is not: unapologetically sexual, romantically receptive, and spatially mobile. Yet, as Carol's sister, Helen may help us see Carol as more than unequivocally averse to contact. For Carol is not purely repulsed by the prospect of physical intimacy—she displays a capacity for closeness in interactions with Helen and also with Bridget (whose short, dark hair recalls Helen visually). In the salon basement, when Bridget attempts to hearten Carol by recounting her recent trip to a Chaplin film, Carol laughs easily and seems comfortable with their proximity, even resting her head briefly on Bridget's chest. Yet when Bridget brings up her boyfriend, Carol lapses back into her near-catatonic state. The sudden tonal shift recalls Carol's petulant reaction to Helen blowing off their family dinner for a night out with Michael; whenever Carol seems ready for homosocial intimacy, men interrupt, such that neither home, nor work, nor even her commute between the two is safe.

If Helen and Bridget serve to demonstrate what "normal" interactivity looks like, Carol seems not wholly oblivious to her difference, even trying to be game for a kiss from Colin in his car, though she ultimately rushes off and wipes her mouth in her building's elevator (interestingly, a gesture that Colin himself repeats after his friend teasingly plants a kiss on him at the pub). Though brief, Carol and Colin's kiss is significant insofar as it informs other moments in which Carol exhibits something in excess of sheer repulsion, something linked to her capacity for and curiosity toward intimacy. We also can't take for granted that Carol is solely disgusted by the nightly intrusions, as the rape scenes are shot without synchronous sound, so the image of Carol's open mouth is displaced from an expected accompanying scream.

The chief primer for reading these scenes' possible ambiguity is a crucial early moment when Carol, seeing Michael's undershirt on the bathroom floor, moves to throw it into the hamper but pauses, briefly lifting it to her face to smell. Carol inhales the shirt and instantly retches; she is clearly physically repulsed, but her impulse to smell the shirt in the first place—like her dead-eyed acquiescence to being kissed by Colin—remains a stubborn complication, a wrinkle in her character that can't be smoothed. More so than abject images and explorations of repulsion alone, then, the film presents a dialectic between repulsion and attraction. The extensive, inevitable momentum of subjects toward one another, for intimacy both erotic and companionate, is precisely what sharpens the sensation of disgust; and as the film produces images and scenes of repulsion, it pairs these with a control variable: some interaction or image that exhibits conformity to social expectation and intimacy standards. When Colin first drops Carol back at work, his disappointment in (and our awareness of) her cool good-bye is compounded by the vision of a woman doubling back to her lover's car to kiss him through the lowered window. *Repulsion* reminds us precisely how a girlfriend—or an apartment—is meant to behave, but it sets up this contrast between normality/convention and pathology precisely to knock it down. For the apartment's mise-en-scène spreads contagiously throughout the film's images, including and beyond nondomestic settings. The long salon hallway, peppered with doors, resembles the apartment's corridor; a cut links Carol's wrinkled bed-sheets to the back of her work uniform. The likeness between sidewalk fracture and wall cracks, or between Carol's bathroom and the mildewed salon basement, demonstrates the apartment's inescapability. The world writ large reminds Carol of her penetrability, and the apartment dwelling exemplifies and disperses the notion of fragile integrity.

Both the apartment's dispersal and Carol's ambivalent inhabitance suggest that the monster from within the home, while perhaps not a monster in the Carrollian sense, is closer to the Freudian uncanny—familiar and yet not, never losing the tinge of the former in the defamiliarization.[18] Home invasion is such a rich and reliable trope for horror because despite all logical and statistical evidence to the contrary, we expect the home to be safe. Domestic horror insists that this mode of horror isn't about transgressing an expectation of safety so much as revealing and emphasizing the futility of that expectation. The home, and the family within the home, is treated not as a safe place, but as a penetrable cell, vulnerable to eels from below, to men from within, to hostile voices on the telephone, and even to ghosts from the past.

Repulsion's horrific symptoms—those aspects that most explicitly gesture toward horror—are consistent with a haunting, wherein the material world is touched by an ostensibly immaterial presence. The apartment's interior appears to both reflect and shape Carol's interiority, not unlike the ways in which cinematic poltergeists might be attributed to a scientifically explicable rather than supernatural cause. Yet there is no possible exorcism, no explanatory flashback to a primal scene, and no late-night expository archival research trip: the film's murderous crescendo affords none of the haunted house film's customary explanation. It's not that the relevant archive is not *not* present, but that it can't be contained, a fact reiterated each time the film apartment's apartmentness is depicted as contagious. Here, the inside/outside boundary-blurring and overall porousness that lead to comedic overhearings and home/office conflations in the typical apartment plot film instead produce the opacity of a nightmare: no space is safe from, let alone possibly antidotal to, the domestic uncanniness Carol experiences everywhere. What we get in place of dawning understanding is a relay between the possible certainty of Carol's mental illness, on one hand, and the ambiguous source of her present trauma, on the other.

A Dark and Roving Eye

At four points in *Repulsion*, we are shown a photograph. First, Carol, left to her own devices after her sister has gone out, absently fingers the surfaces of objects along the mantel. She lifts the ear of a toy pig and sifts through a stack of records, and the camera drifts off to the right, away from the

FIG. 6.2. Carol looks at the photograph, and the apartment reacts
(*Repulsion*, Roman Polanski, 1965).

relative activity of her hands, lighting on a further assembly of objects: paperweights, books, and what appears to be a framed family photo. The photo is black and white and features four older people, two men and two women, seated outdoors in Adirondack chairs, with a young, pigtailed brunette in the foreground with her head on a man's knee, and a stern young blonde girl in the center, standing back, looking toward the man to her left. The camera pushes in, keeping the blonde girl fixed in the frame, and fades out.

Later, having been sent home from the salon, Carol is eating a cracker and regarding the photo in silence when the wall behind the dresser abruptly cracks (fig. 6.2). One might argue that this brief scene depicts a contrast: Carol, placidly looking at the photo in the relative calm of her emptied apartment, is startled by the wall crack as interruption. And what prompts the crack? If the apartment's mutations are in Carol's imagination, her violent imaginings are driven by unresolved, likely traumatic memories triggered by the photograph. This kind of circuit linking mind, memory, and materialization is familiar terrain for horror, particularly in telekinesis narratives; a crystalline example is Brian De Palma's *Carrie* (1976), in which Carrie White endures a meeting in the principal's office after being pelted with tampons in the locker room. As the principal repeatedly misnames her ("Cassie") and Miss Collins attempts to correct him, the film cuts increasingly rapidly between Carrie tightening more deeply into herself and a POV of the ashtray on the principal's desk trembling. We hear a low vibration whenever we see the ashtray, mounting tension until Carrie shouts—"It's Carrie!"—and the ashtray flips off of the desk, shattering against the wall as a light explodes overhead. The editing's climbing tempo thus suggests that Carrie's increasing internal frustration reaches a threshold whereupon it externalizes, acting out on the visible, material world. Specifically, her inability to control her power is what makes the action violent. It's not as if Carrie makes these objects simply float into the air: they break, energy changes. Form transforms.

Similarly, we could read the wall's eruptive rent as an outward expression of whatever Carol is thinking when she looks at the photo (and, more broadly, we might regard all of the apartment's ontological shifts as extensions of Carol's psyche). But this reading produces an "it's all in her head" account that ultimately fails to fully account for the way in which this film rejects closure, specifically by repurposing a conventionally indexical device—the evidentiary photograph—to blur, rather than to clarify.

In its third appearance, the photograph is diegetically acknowledged by Carol's landlord, who enters the apartment (despite her homemade barricades) to collect outstanding rent. In this scene, the landlord moves to spread the living room curtains to "shed a little light on the subject" (the subject being the exact sum of money that Carol has presented), a move that Carol swiftly protests. She plops down on the sofa and rests her hands between her legs, drawing up the hem of her nightgown; the landlord's silhouette frames her in as he ostentatiously removes his glasses to get a better look. Both of his gestures—spreading the curtain, removing his glasses—express detection, a sort of "the better to see you with" that Carol resists. She is monosyllabic to the point that it's surprising when, after the landlord has picked up the family photograph and asked whether it was taken in London, she actually corrects him: "Brussels." He identifies Carol in the middle of the photo before setting it aside, turning his attention entirely from Carol's childhood image to her adult presence. But once the photo is invoked, past and present—like memory, fantasy, and material reality—aren't so easily extricable. Carol struggles away and slices the back of his neck with Michael's razor, this initial slash giving way to a chaos of stabbing. Here again, the photo is a trigger; it's not only the landlord's sexual advance but also his interrogative probing about the photograph that precedes her violent response.

If previously *Repulsion* has couched its spatial disturbances and home invasions in terms of a relatively stable pattern, the second of Carol's killings effectively reroutes the film: her behavior from here on is erratic; time is increasingly elliptical; and the film's form accordingly evolves. In other words, the film assures us that while Colin and the landlord were certainly predatory (to varying degrees), their disposal in no way insulates Carol from the spatialized violence to which she's been subject throughout. It becomes increasingly challenging to map and make sense of her remaining encounters with the apartment: we see her yet again lying awake in her bed, the clock's ticking resumed as she focuses on the ceiling light fixture. The bedside wall cracks open; the film fades to black, and fades in on Carol singing blithely to herself as she mimes ironing with an unplugged appliance. Sugar cubes carpet the kitchen floor; if this is the film's most explicit parody of domesticity, its corresponding take on femininity follows, with Carol applying lipstick in Helen's room. She performs a preparation to go out but the film cuts to her once again in bed, smiling as the camera draws vertiginously close to her face. The church bell sounds and Carol's expression sharpens; she turns back toward the (once cracked) bedside wall to find her assailant figure shirtless beside her. He pushes her facedown, and her freshly applied lipstick smears slowly, in close-up, across the pillowcase.

We next see Carol pantomiming writing with a pin-like instrument on a French door, eyes wide and lips moving. It's unclear whether this is day or night, or how much time has elapsed since the previous rape. When she walks into the living room, the space is as bloodied and disheveled as last she left it, but now at least doubled in size. Back in the hall, grasping arms burst violently from the soft-looking wall until the hall erupts in hands, opening and closing, suggesting whatever difference there was between Carol's man-like intruder and the apartment in which he manifested is now collapsed. The following sequence confirms this, as we see what appears to be a mobile POV of Carol in bed, and the reverse shot depicts the ceiling light fixture in shortened focus drawing threateningly closer to Carol, as if the apartment itself threatens her with assault. This, ultimately, is the last we see of a conscious Carol; the film dissolves the advancing ceiling into the rain-spattered street outside. It's at this point that

Repulsion enacts its status as an apartment film, not only narratively and in terms of its mise-en-scène, but via editing as well, where even divisions between scenes are weakened.

In Polanski's later apartment film *Rosemary's Baby*, the space of the apartment is scary largely because it is penetrable: Rosemary Woodhouse's neighbors possess a secret door, and, more broadly, hostile demonic forces populate her world. Significantly, rape features in both *Repulsion* and *Rosemary's Baby*, but whereas the violation is named in the later film, Carol's rapes remain murky, always evoked; and *Repulsion*'s privileging of the photograph hones this point. In horror, we typically examine photos for evidence, even (or especially) for what eludes the human eye.[19] Such an image is scanned, often enhanced, and, like the Terrible Place, read. The photograph in *Repulsion* is not the site of privileged indexicality, but of further ambiguity. Even if one argues that what's suggested by the photo is so strong as to be argumentative, such a claim fails to account for how we see what's supposedly there: in a close-up so near that it visually abstracts rather than clarifies the image.

At the end of the film, we see the photo a final time: Michael carries Carol out of the disarranged apartment, and the camera again travels away from the action (an assembly of nervous neighbors discouraging Carol's removal) back over the mantel, the television, an upturned basket of yarn, a corner of quilt, the now-creased postcard from Helen in Pisa, and a half-eaten cracker, to land finally on the photograph, now filtered by shadow such that the young blonde girl and the man at whom she's glaring are isolated in the frame (fig. 6.3). The camera pauses and moves in on the girl's eye, a gesture that unmistakably evokes the boomerang nature of proximity: come closer and you see something more clearly, as functions the close-up of Carol's eye in the film's opening shots; come too close, and something once seen clearly will retreat back into abstraction, becoming an indeterminate shape, a quality of darkness.

You can part the curtains, remove your glasses, or lean in close, yet the sheer efforts of scrutiny and proximity do not ensure revelation. Possible explanations abound: one can account for the horror in *Repulsion* by viewing Carol as a woman unspooled by imposed solitude, as in Charlotte Perkins Gilman's "The Yellow Wallpaper," Daphne du Maurier's *Rebecca*, or any number of stories that capitalize on and perpetuate the trope of crazy women.[20] Carol's craziness might be further specified as either

FIG. 6.3. The close-up reveals and withholds (*Repulsion*, Roman Polanski, 1965).

altering her sense of the apartment, such that the apartment itself is actually benign, and it's her perception and subsequent inhabitance of it that make the space look and feel sick. One could also view the apartment as a monstrous, even sentient entity, dispersed figurally in the guise of hands and a man, as well as architecturally, throughout the surrounding city. In this version, the apartment is haunting Carol, and Carol is for whatever reason uniquely sensitive to it, susceptible in a way her sister Helen is not.

But horror here is gaseous: eluding the applicability of a surface/depth model befitting, for example, something like the discovery of a cemetery on which a house is unwisely built. In lieu of an underlying cause, the film shows us the photograph, which seems to show us very little. In domestic horror cinema, the residue of past sexual trauma resists the memory necessary for flashback articulation; what can be, and is, expressed is the made-strangeness of a space we conventionally understand to be safe, and the photograph unlocks a way in which mise-en-scène—inclusive of everything put in front of the camera to be photographed—involves too the oblique expression of what is directly inexpressible.

Epigraph: "Courting Is a Pleasure," also known as "Handsome Molly," is a folk song of unknown date, originating from the British Isles.

1. Lucy Fischer, "Beauty and the Beast: Desire and Its Double in *Repulsion*," in *Cinema of Roman Polanski: Dark Spaces of the World*, ed. John Orr and Elżbieta Ostrowska (London: Wallflower, 2006), 78.

2. Noël Carroll, *The Philosophy of Horror: Or, Paradoxes of the Heart* (New York: Routledge, 1990).

3. For a critical engagement with Carroll's *The Philosophy of Horror*, see Matt Hills, "An Event-Based Definition of Art-Horror," in *Dark Thoughts: Philosophic Reflections on Cinematic Horror*, ed. Steven Jay Schneider and Daniel Shaw (Lanham, MD: Scarecrow, 2003), 138–56.

4. Tony McKibbin, "Polanski and the Horror from Within," in *Cinema of Roman Polanski: Dark Spaces of the World*, ed. John Orr and Elżbieta Ostrowska (London: Wallflower, 2006), 51–61.

5. McKibbin, "Polanski and the Horror from Within," 54–55.

6. Tarja Laine, "Imprisoned in Disgust: Roman Polanski's *Repulsion*," *Film-Philosophy* 15, no. 2 (2011): 37.

7. Laine, "Imprisoned in Disgust," 39.

8. Pamela Wojcik, *The Apartment Plot: Urban Living in American Film and Popular Culture, 1945 to 1975* (Durham, NC: Duke University Press, 2010). By "modern horror," I refer to cinematic works after 1960. See Adam Lowenstein, *Shocking Representation: Historical Trauma, National Cinema, and the Modern Horror Film* (New York: Columbia University Press, 2005), 6.

9. For allegorical interpretations of horror, see Lowenstein, *Shocking Representation*; and Robin Wood, "An Introduction to the American Horror Film," in *Planks of Reason: Essays on the Horror Film*, ed. Barry Keith Grant and Christopher Sharrett (Lanham, MD: Scarecrow, 2004), 107–41.

10. Walter Benjamin, *The Arcades Project*, trans. Howard Eiland and Kevin McLaughlin (Cambridge, MA: Harvard University Press, 1999), 220–21.

11. Laine, "Imprisoned in Disgust," 41.

12. See William Hughes, David Punter, and Andrew Smith, eds., *The Encyclopedia of the Gothic* (Oxford: Wiley-Blackwell, 2013).

13. Carol J. Clover, "Her Body, Himself," *Men, Women, and Chain Saws: Gender in the Modern Horror Film* (Princeton, NJ: Princeton University Press, 1992), 30.

14. The phrase "spatial practice" is from Henri Lefebvre, *The Production of Space*, trans. Donald Nicholson-Smith (Oxford: Blackwell, 1991).

15. Clover, "Her Body, Himself," 30, emphasis added.

16. See Edmund G. Bansak, *Fearing the Dark: The Val Lewton Career* (Jefferson, NC: McFarland, 1995), 133.

17. Carroll, *The Philosophy of Horror*, 47.

18. See Sigmund Freud, *The Uncanny*, trans. David McLintock (London: Penguin, 2003).

19. For contemporary examples of this motif, see *The Omen* (Richard Donner, 1976), *The Sixth Sense* (M. Night Shyamalan, 1999), *Final Destination 3* (James Wong, 2006), *Inside* (Alexandre Bustillo and Julien Maury, 2007), *Insidious* (James Wan, 2010), and *Sinister* (Scott Derrickson, 2012).

20. For a comprehensive feminist discussion of Victorian literature, including the trope of mad/hysterical women in literature and film dating back to Charlotte Perkins Gilman, "The Yellow Wallpaper" (originally "The Yellow Wall-paper. A Story," 1892), see Sandra M. Gilbert and Susan Gubar, *The Madwoman in the Attic: The Woman Writer and the Nineteenth-Century Literary Imagination*, 2nd ed. (New Haven, CT: Yale University Press, 2000).

We think of marriage, or have thought of it, as the entering simultaneously into a new public and a new private connection, the creation
at once of new spaces of communality and of exclusiveness, of a new
outside and inside to a life, spaces expressible by the private ownership
of a house, literally an apartment, a place that is part of and apart within
a larger habitation. —STANLEY CAVELL, *Pursuits of Happiness*

7

REATTACHMENT THEORY

Gay Marriage and the Apartment Plot

LEE WALLACE

Anyone with the least acquaintance with couples counseling can testify to
the strong hold that attachment theory has in the domain of contemporary
relationship therapy, where, whatever the circumstance that brings you
and your partner into the conversational three-way, somewhere along the
line you will be invited to identify as one of three types according to a taxonomy that derives from John Bowlby's classic *Attachment* trilogy: secure,
avoidant, anxious-resistant.[1] Almost miraculously, attachment theory
seems the answer to everything, just as it now flourishes as key to critical
problems in all manner of contexts from evolutionary anthropology to
human-animal studies.[2] There is value, however, in lessening the hold of
a theory that derives from the study of infants and primary caregivers on
the realm of adult attachments, which, though they may have their origins
in infantile pathologies, are nonetheless embedded in the social. As I hope
my title registers, however useful it might be therapeutically, I am analytically detaching from attachment theory in favor of reattachment theory,

a notion I derive from Stanley Cavell's compelling account of marriage as remarriage, an idea he takes from the great Hollywood comedies of divorce and reparation.[3] Although Cavell has been criticized for the sexism inherent in his account of remarriage as "the woman's education by the man," his philosophical musings about modern marriage as the reinvention of sexual and social reciprocities that have a dual basis in exclusivity and communality are strangely fruitful in the contemporary context of gay marriage.[4]

Attaching to gay marriage also prompts me to reattach to the apartment plot, a genre I have previously been drawn to for the way it uses the apartment setting to foreground lesbian stories. I have elsewhere argued that in the post–Production Code era when homosexuality attained new levels of visibility, the apartment chronotope (as Bakhtin might have called it) emerged as the privileged spatial and narrative marker of lesbianism.[5] Whereas earlier lesbian chronotopes—specifically, the schoolroom, college, bar, and prison—had narratively animated the space between sexual privacy and publicity, innocence and corruption, the apartment retained the charge of the sexual underworld while making it consistent with material and professional advancement, hence its capacity to encompass the anxieties and aspirations of post-Stonewall lesbian life in a period when the social acceptance of homosexuality was still something to be won.[6]

Across the opening years of the twenty-first century, however, many of the coordinates by which we plot lesbian and gay stories have changed, the most significant being the legal recognition of same-sex domestic partnerships and the partial absorption of a sexual subculture into the dominant marriage culture from which it had previously derived its outlaw status. The contemporary phenomenon of same-sex marriage and the renewed sanction it gives gay and lesbian parenting pushes apart elements the lesbian apartment plot previously brought together: public and private, respectability and street cred, work and sex. This social shift does not invalidate the apartment plot, but rather reenergizes it along new trajectories, as can be seen to good effect in *Concussion* (Stacie Passon, 2013) and *Weekend* (Andrew Haigh, 2011), two films that derive their timeliness from the contemporary framework of gay marriage and deploy the materiality of apartment space to register the historical passing of an established conception of urban homosexual life. Despite their manifest differences in style and tone and the distinctive metropolitan and provincial imaginaries they engage, the films can be usefully compared to each other and aligned with a broader cycle of films (and television series) that address gay marriage, either directly or obliquely.

Indeed, the gay marriage cycle is now so substantive that it is possible to trace patterns and arcs within it that anticipate or respond to the emergence of gay marriage as a recognized structure of feeling prior to its codification in law. Most obviously, the previously dominant thematic emphasis on the social problem of the nonrecognition of same-sex relationships has receded in favor of an emphasis on the problem of discontent generated within same-sex relationships conceived on a continuum with straight marriages. Films that evidence the former include Ang Lee's *Brokeback Mountain* (2005) and Tom Ford's *A Single Man* (2009), both of which use the retrospectively animated framework of historical melodrama to convey an anachronistic sense of aching injustice around the denial of long-term gay and lesbian partnerships in the here and now.[7] Films that evidence the latter include Stephen Daldry's *The Hours* (2002) and Lisa Cholodenko's *The Kids Are All Right* (2011), plus the many television series that now include disenchanted same-sex couples among their various configurations of modern families.[8] This is not an absolute shift, nor is it strictly chronological. Rather, the cycle retains its appeal and flexibility in being able to reanimate the theme of gay marriage from different perspectives and to different ends, often within the same text. In this sense, the cycle explores the problem of gay marriage that, like the problem of marriage in general, turns on the primary riddle of sexuality and its expression in attachments of more or less durable form.

As Michael DeAngelis reminds us in his introduction to a recent anthology addressing the rise of the bromance in contemporary film and television, in order to maintain audience interest, films that ostensibly celebrate certain thematic content (in the case of bromance, the possibility of nonsexual intimacy between men; in the case of gay marriage films, sexual intimacy between men or between women) necessarily present that content in the form of a problem either in itself (that is, as something that is only attained with difficulty) or in relation to wider social problems that restrict its articulation (such as heteronormative expectations). Though DeAngelis doesn't stress the relation between bromance and gay marriage, he does link the bromance cycle with the "problem marriage" cycle that emerged in the late 1960s and early 1970s, which he typifies as films that exploit "contemporaneous discourses of sexual liberation" but "generally ended up vilifying the same freedoms they set out to celebrate."[9]

This serves as a reminder that popular film has a long history of catalyzing new cycles that de-idealize—and reidealize—marriage in response to changes in its social and legal definition as well as changes in the sexual and emotional expectations people bring to it.

According to Cavell, the greatest of those cycles is the Hollywood comedy of remarriage that arose once marriage was unsanctified by the easy availability and destigmatization of divorce. Emerging in the 1930s and linked to what Cavell describes as the first generation of women who did not have to settle for marriage but might nonetheless choose it, the dialogue-driven comedies of remarriage invariably respond to "the topic of divorce, which raises in a particular form the question of the legitimacy of marriage."[10] Cavell argues that these comedies, which are central to the evolution of the talkie, collectively investigate the terms on which marriage might be ratified anew as both an intimate and a socially utopian form that can meet the contemporary requirements of recognition and reciprocity that radiate out from the heterosexual couple as the first circle of community. Popular attachment to these films, he argues, reflects a complex reattachment to marriage, which in the wake of divorce must necessarily be approached as remarriage, as a revitalized commitment to a form about which no innocence, including sexual innocence, remains. Though the terms of Cavell's engagement with the Hollywood comedy of remarriage are irreducibly idiosyncratic, it is possible to distill from his discussion the simple observation that, at a historical moment in which the institution of marriage has been further unsanctified by the social acceptance of same-sex marriage, whether or not that acceptance is canonized in law, we might expect to see a cycle of gay marriage films emerge that interrogate the terms on which marriage might be reimagined as a viable social and sexual practice or abandoned outright.

If, as Cavell argues, all marriage is remarriage postdivorce, then, postmarriage equality, all marriage is gay marriage, at least for the popular purpose of renegotiating a general attachment to the form. This renegotiation involves some obvious and some unpredictable critiques of marriage and its simultaneous narrative revitalization. However, since marriage continues to couple both its heterosexual and homosexual exponents with sexual and domestic routine, a notable feature of the gay marriage cycle is the consistency with which it utilizes the apartment plot for its established capacity to plot stories and relationships that speak to wider conceptions of fidelity than those normally associated with conjugality, whether straight or gay. In *Concussion* and *Weekend*, this redeployment of the apartment is key to the critique of gay marriage and to its revival as an idealized form for the possibilities of sexual and social happiness across the board.

Concussion and the Lesbian Pied-à-Terre

Stacie Passon's independent film *Concussion* is an exemplary instance of how the lesbian apartment plot is reinflected post–gay marriage. A quirky riff on Luis Buñuel's *Belle de Jour* (1967) and numerous other films in which an apartment facilitates sexual encounters outside the family home, *Concussion* tells the story of a sexually frustrated lesbian suburban mom who, unsettled by a knock on the head, branches into same-sex prostitution from the Manhattan loft she is renovating for capital gain. Although the promotional blurbs that accompany the DVD offer sexual addiction as the framework through which to make sense of this plot, the film is fueled by the more mundane recognition that although marriage is founded in sexual attachment, it cannot guarantee the constancy of mutual attraction or the continued vibrancy of desire in the face of its domestication. At a glance, *Concussion* would seem less interested in engaging the problem of sexual renewal within marriage than imagining a sexual alternative outside it. Beneath the film's awkward occupancy of the codes of prostitution lies the more widespread lesbian wish to claim a symmetry with gay public sex cultures that are thought to assuage the sexual quiescence assumed endemic to long-term relationships in general and to lesbian relationships in particular via the supposed phenomenon of lesbian bed death.[11] Confirmed in both expert and popular discourses as the site for less and less sex across time, long-term lesbian relationships, some of which now take the name marriage, make patent the problem common to all marriage, which is that the institution designed for the social ratification of sexual attachment is also designed to extinguish it. This common problem—that the sexual promise of marriage includes the promise of its disappointment— is also common to common-law marriage, a state defined by habit and repute that many legally single men and women live in whether they want to or not.

Like many straight screen wives before her, *Concussion*'s stay-at-home lesbian wife is trapped in an idyllic New Jersey commuter town, but unlike them, her dilemma has sexual coordinates that cannot be resolved through an appeal to feminism. The film starts crisply with a static title graphic over which a number of female voices can be heard trading the popular piece of advice that after forty a woman has to decide between her ass and her face. When the visuals kick in they reveal a spin class in process, a physical action that places ass and face on the same horizontal plane. The conversation drifts to sex before David Bowie's "Oh! You Pretty Things" starts up, its piano-backed vocals perfectly geared to a midlife meditation on the inevitability of aging. As the soundtrack opens into Bowie's chorus, the camera drifts around the uniformly pretty things, row upon row of fit, slim, forty-something women bent to the task of exercise. Among them is Mrs. Abby Abelman (Robin Weigert), who, as this scene makes graphically clear, takes her place inside a matrimonial order in which lesbians are indistinguishable from the straight women who surround them.

The dreamy opening sequence moves between scenes of women holding yoga poses and static shots of suburban houses and autumnal yards before it abruptly terminates with a rushed cut to an exterior scene in which Mrs. and Mrs. Abelman hustle two children toward a late-model SUV. Running beside her wife Kate (Julie Fain Lawrence), Abby clutches at her bleeding forehead, the result of being hit by a softball thrown at her by her son. Once in the car, the injured mother curses the child before declaring, apropros of everything (the car, the child, the pain), "I don't want this." An impulsive reaction that momentarily betrays the faltering of ordinary attachments (or the ambivalence that drives mother love), this statement sets up the primary conundrum of the film: What do lesbians want, or, more specifically, what do lesbians want from marriage, now that they can have it?

Judging by the evidence the film provides (endorsed by official selection at the 2013 Sundance Film Festival), Abby wants to abandon her suburban domestic routine—the house and yard chores, the school drop-off and pickup run—and tap back into the urban spaces that constituted lesbian life before it boiled down to being married with children. Principally, however, she wants sex, and it is this want that will stretch the bounds of her lesbian marriage back into apartment territory. The film makes clear that stay-at-home lesbian moms cannot rely on their working wives for sexual satisfaction, a situation efficiently scoped out in a scene in which a restless Abby wakes her partner for sex only to have her fall back to sleep midstroke. Abby's solution is to outsource the sex, in the same way we see her outsource the food she and Kate serve at their dinner parties. Without telling her wife, Abby contacts a low-rent call girl who works from a grungy apartment that brings out numerous inhibitions in her, all of which seem to have as much to do with hygiene or health as sex. Abby doesn't want to share drugs or sex toys. Barely seen, the sex takes place on an unmade bed in a cramped room completely unlike any of the other well-lit designer interiors that feature throughout the rest of the film. Afterward, in a scene in which the camera seems newly capable of movement and magnification, Abby has to check her impulse to clean the call girl's bathroom. She will later recall the whole thing as an off-putting encounter with "this very dirty person," something she would go a long way to avoid repeating.

Fortunately, Abby only has to go as far as Manhattan for things to change. The concussion that unsettles her sexually also prompts her to go back to work, a decision her wife encourages. Though she is recognized among her New Jersey friends as a gifted interior designer, Abby's real talent is property speculation, buying up "shit box" apartments in the city and doing them up for quick resale, a project she embarks on with the assistance of a handsome young builder, Justin (Johnathan Tchaikovsky), a semi-intuitive, semisleazy guy who subsequently finds economic opportunity in assisting Abby to find sexual partners through his own network of swingers. Although a series of scenes shows Abby and Justin refurbishing an industrial loft, the work of flipping Manhattan real estate is soon superseded by the work of lesbian sex, as Abby first orders in a high-end escort and then, reversing her role in the sexual commodity supply chain, starts turning tricks herself in the loft apartment.

None of this is presented as a cynical attack on marriage. At worst, Abby might have led herself to believe that she and Kate had tacitly agreed to her having sex outside the relationship. Like many unspoken understandings between intimates, this one hardly bears scrutiny. Early on in the film we see Abby and Kate eating a family dinner. As soon as the kids are excused from the table, the topic turns adult. Abby tells Kate that one of their friends is breaking up with her husband, and Kate, who is a divorce attorney, tells her to put her in touch and she will handle it for free. As the conversation continues, Kate asks a series of matter-of-fact questions ("So, who cheated? Who gets custody? Who gets the house? Is he paying alimony? What about the dog?"), whereas Abby remains preoccupied with the wife's feelings of emotional distress and panic: "She said she couldn't breathe." "That's code for what?" snaps Kate. "She couldn't breathe," Abby repeats, before Kate responds pragmatically, "So she should go breathe. It's sex. Grow up. Go breathe."

With this line and its implications of negotiated nonmonogamy left hanging in the air, a cut takes the action forward away from the suburban dining room to the newly painted apartment shell, an almost blank space in which Abby sits on the corner of the bed waiting for the call girl Justin has set her up with to arrive. The sex scene that follows leads to a conversation in which the call girl (Kate Rogal) tells Abby that she didn't need to make her come. "I liked that," Abby replies, as much to herself as anyone else, a revelation that speaks to a complicated state of play in which the sexual reciprocity and intimacy considered foundational to the institution of marriage is now satisfied outside it in the institution of prostitution. Central to this reversal is the representation of Abby's wife, Kate—who represents divorce as fully as she represents marriage—as someone who never seems to require anything from anyone, sexually or otherwise. The scene in which Kate goes to the apartment and silently confronts a naked Abby would be almost clinically dissociative if it were not entirely consistent with everything else we have come to expect of someone who makes her living coolly navigating other people's marital smash-ups. As emotionally blunted as Abby is raw, Kate only loosens up when talking to a professional peer about her Myers-Briggs Type Indicator, an exchange that occurs in the context of a party in which the rest of their forty-something friends sit around drunkenly recalling the Manhattan sex clubs they used to visit before they married and moved to Montclair.

As much as enjoying giving pleasure to a call girl, it is seeing her wife intensely engaged in conversation with a middle-aged male peer that precipitates Abby's move into prostitution. Across a picaresque series of preliminary interviews and subsequent sexual trysts, Abby gets to display the same ENTP character traits professionally ascribed to her lawyer wife—extroversion, intuition, thinking, perception—all of which make her an adroit escort insofar as this type, one of sixteen in the Myers-Briggs psychological typology, indicates someone who is "Good at reading other people. Bored by routine, will seldom do the same thing the same way, [and] apt to turn to one new interest after another."[12] While each of these encounters is scripted and choreographed to reveal various ostensible truths about female sexuality and its familiar personality types—repressed, masochistic, manipulative—the real story is told by the background detail, the literal walls of the apartment that throw the fore-grounded sexual action into visual and thematic relief.

Abby insists that she will meet her clients only in the architecturally transforming loft, a large, stripped-down, light-flooded space that accrues more furnishings and collectables as the film progresses. In the sex-free suburban house she shares with Kate and the kids, everything is decked out in gray-tone neutrals, those pattern-free, slightly butch surrounds that say lesbian professionals at nest. In the apartment, however, this mildly androgynous style (not too butch, not too femme) is recoded as edgy by dint of association with Abby's art collection (a poster for a Louise Bour-geois exhibition, pieces by the Guerrilla Girls and other feminist artists name-checked in the credit sequence) as much as by the sex-for-money with which it competes for our visual attention.

Ultimately, the apartment provides the conditions for Abby's sexual un-doing in the form of an encounter between her and a client who breaches the code of anonymity that buffers the goings on in the apartment from the goings on of married life. By the time the androgynously named Sam (Maggie Siff) turns up in the apartment, it has already been established not only that the two women share the same New Jersey fitness and par-enting routine but that Abby finds her cute. That is not the problem, how-ever. The problem is that as they begin to have sex in the apartment, Sam questions the suitability of the two-by-six tiles Abby has chosen for the kitchen backsplash. Abby is so deeply rattled by the suggestion that the tiles would have looked better with a paler grout that, when Sam asks to have her hair pulled, Abby complies despite her no-discipline rule. As soon as Sam leaves the apartment Abby is seen, still in her underwear, crouched on the kitchen bench, taking to the tiles with a hammer and chisel (fig. 7.1).

From the start Abby has seemed a lesson in insecure attachment, re-peatedly displaying ambivalence toward the objects, partners, children that surround her in the New Jersey home that she compulsively vacuums and cleans—behaviors that are less inclined to manifest in the child-free space of the minimalist apartment, an adult play-world in which no one eats or shits but every sexual need is met. Now visually apprehended vio-lently detaching tiles from the apartment wall, Abby enacts what seems like a classically suburban neurosis within the urban apartment. The catalyst for this category collapse is Sam, who, unlike Abby, has a marriage setup

FIG. 7.1. Lesbian detachment: Abby expresses ambivalence in apartment space in *Concussion* (Stacie Passon, 2013).

that appears sexually fulfilling but, like Abby, wants to escape the torpid social world stay-at-home wives inhabit when their spouses (male or female) head to the city to work. In getting involved with Sam against her own better judgment, Abby muddies the division she has carefully set up between urban and suburban lifestyles so that it is only a matter of time before her wife figures out what is going on. The film's almost depressive outcome sees Abby returned to an exclusively suburban world, her energies once again directed at major and minor home improvements that have none of the transformative impact observed in the loft apartment conversion (painting the front door, investing in a sprinkler system, adding a wraparound porch). Though she is seemingly reconciled to her sexually disinterested wife and their joint project of lesbian parenting, Abby's continued regret about forfeiting her lesbian apartment life and its ostensibly perfect calibration of intimacy and distance is registered in the final scene, a variation on the opening of the film in which a group of women are assembled in a spin class. The same women are seen exercising away, but now the camera holds on Abby's face and positions Sam over her shoulder just beyond the point of focus. On the basis of nothing more than the visual foreshortening of space and Abby's diegetic intention to take a hot yoga class after the spin class ends, the possibility of an orthodox extramarital affair between the two of them appears on the film's horizon before Brian Eno's "Some of Them Are Old" ushers in the final credits.

Associated with Abby's postconcussion haze, the apartment briefly functions as a reprieve from lesbian marriage, its frustrations and routine. Unlike the earlier apartment plots I identified in post-Code films, which were concerned with lesbian visibility and the difficulty of claiming a sexual story line, the contemporary lesbian apartment plot vents ideological dissatisfaction with suburban marriage in its homosexual iteration. As is made clear in Abby's identification with the divorcing husband to whom she signs over the title deed to the fully renovated apartment, *Concussion* engages the contemporary problem of homosexual conjugality in relation to assumptions about fidelity and infidelity that take their model from straight culture. "Did you leave or did she?" she asks him. "It's hard to say," he replies, and she just nods in agreement. The scene ends there since the film has nothing to add, no alternative imagining of long-term cohabitation or its dissolution that doesn't finally conflate sexual rights with property rights. Abby's decision to transact sex for money in apartment space is less an alternative to this conjugal logic than its feminist desublimation, a critical action that leaves no space for a satisfactory resolution to the narrative either way. Abby can have sex with Sam, or no sex with Kate, and might even get both in a tacit arrangement of the kind hinted at previously, but it really amounts to the same thing: her emotional detachment from attachment. Neither in love with Sam nor not in love with Kate, Abby has no generic plot available to her through which to resolve her lesbian dilemma or even scale the alternatives as anything other than the difference between madness and the battened-down normativity proposed in Eno's lyrics:

> Lucy you're my girl, Lucy you're a star.
> Lucy please be still and put your madness in a jar.
> But do beware, it will follow you, it will follow you.[13]

In this respect the end of *Concussion* resembles the end of Cholodenko's *The Kids Are All Right*, which similarly reinstates the lesbian marriage at any cost, presenting it as a sexually and socially exhausted institution through which women bind themselves to the ongoing unhappiness now understood to be at the heart of middle-class family life in its homosexual as well as heterosexual forms. Although both films conclude by restoring the framework of lesbian marriage, they are the very opposite of the Hollywood comedy of remarriage that Cavell celebrates as reimagining marriage as a sexually and socially utopian "undertaking that concerns, whatever else it concerns, change."[14] In the case of *Concussion*, the change-laden world of the apartment, a place of constant renewal in which sexual encounters never shade into routine or incur other responsibilities, is the thing the lesbian wife must give up in order to return to a marital relationship in which she now understands her needs will continue to go unrecognized beneath the everyday duties of suburban life.[15]

Weekend and the Gay Council Flat

Unlike *Concussion*, which presents same-sex marriage as the ideological and narrative counter to a dreamlike apartment space that has few real-world coordinates outside interior design discourses, *Weekend* uses a socially grounded high-rise apartment block to investigate the possibilities of gay marriage from the perspective of those that have yet to, and might never, enter it. Initially unsuccessful in his bid to secure funding for the script that became *Weekend*, Haigh reset his film in Nottingham in order to access regionally distributed lottery film funds. As a result, *Weekend* was filmed on location in and around the Lenton Flats, a Nottingham housing estate that has its origins in the postwar slum clearances that transformed the urban fabric of both metropolitan and provincial Britain.[16] In 2011, the year *Weekend* was released, the Lenton Flats were slated for redevelopment. Two years later, the five sixteen-story tower blocks were taken down floor by floor in a seven-month demolition process aesthetically compressed into a three-minute time-lapse video commissioned by Nottingham City Homes that concludes with artist impressions of the residential streetscape that is their idealized replacement.[17] Situating *Weekend* in the context of innovations in the provision of public housing reminds us that the rise of same-sex marriage might also be contextualized within a longer history of domestic experimentation in which the boundaries between public and private are actively redescribed in socially utopian or dystopian forms.

Already known to audiences as the bleak setting for Shane Meadows's *This Is England* (2006) and Anton Corbijn's *Control* (2007), the Lenton Flats appear in a different light in *Weekend*. The tower blocks are frequently seen in twilight, and their potentially monolithic scale is typically softened by some natural element in the composition of the frame, just as the potentially drab East Midlands landscape on which they stand, a postindustrial nexus of technology parks and dormitory suburbs connected by congested minor roads and traffic roundabouts, lights up beautifully against a darkening night sky. In the pretitle opening sequence, the apartment tower block is entered through a shot that cuts unexpectedly from an exterior view of medium-density sprawl to autumnal vegetation seen through a high-up apartment window. The camera quickly takes in the tight dimensions of an apartment in which a dark-haired young man silently readies himself to go out. Bathing, dressing, smoking a joint—the things the young man does are less important than the claim they make to ordinariness within a diegetic world dictated by the physical constraints of an actual apartment. In this familiar space, the young man's bodily actions seem habitual, like hitting light switches in the dark. As the scene continues, he sits on his bed and takes a pair of pristine sneakers from their original box before putting them away, a change of mind that takes less than the beat it would be given in a film that marked it out as a significant event. Strung between habit and impulse, the young man's unselfconscious actions confirm that he occupies the space of the everyday, a cinematic convention through which homosexuality can appear as an ordinary thing among other ordinary things.[18]

The everyday feel of the film is maintained as the young man leaves the apartment to go to dinner at his friend's house, then takes a tram into town and drops into a nondescript gay bar. The scenes in the dark and noisy gay bar are as flatly routine as the domestic scenes that precede them. The young man's silent attempt to hook up with a handsome stranger he has followed to the urinal is just as quietly knocked back so that he turns his attention to another, shorter man with whom he dances until the club empties out. The scene then cuts forward to the Lenton Flats, seen in foggy morning light before the camera reenters the apartment to show the young man getting up and making coffee for two. He takes the mugs back to the bedroom, where the man who initially turned him down lies under the duvet. Insofar as it is represented at all, the gay pickup registers as a makeshift arrangement that has its origins in substitutability, not uniqueness, a point underscored by the difficulty of keeping visually separate the various men who move through the club, including the two leads, who share with each other and most of the gay extras in the film a similar on-trend bearded and verging-on-bearish look.

With the initial sexual encounter between the two strangers consigned to a temporal ellipsis, the film goes on to trace the growing intimacy between Russell (Tom Cullen), whose apartment it is, and Glen (Chris New), two men who seem from the start temperamentally at odds though physically at ease with each other in a space in which distance is at a premium. In dramatic terms, the film swivels on the revelation that Glen is due to leave for the States on Sunday afternoon to pursue his art studies, but this plot determinant is of little interest except as the basis for the melancholic condition through which the two men, having just found each other, are already stitched into a bittersweet narrative that, for the spectator (and possibly for them), is all the better for being known from the outset.

On first impressions, Russell is as shy and cautious as Glen is brash and cocky, although this difference is less important than the similarly low-key way that they pass back and forth semi-improvised lines that, like every other element in their diegetic world, aspire to realness. As Dennis Lim points out in a brief essay that accompanies the Criterion Collection DVD released in 2012, "Character-driven dramas are not supposed to make a show of backstory, but in the genre of the blossoming romance—focused on two people for whom the rest of the world has fallen away, and who are hungry to know everything about each other—there is nothing more natural than exposition."[19] Yet exposition is raised to an exponential degree in the morning-after scene, when Glen produces a handheld recorder and asks Russell to recount their night together, explaining that it is part of an art project he is working on. A few hours later in story time, as they sit down to lunch in the apartment kitchen, Glen will elaborate the objective behind the art project, but for the film's purposes it is primarily useful as a device for conveying gay sexual history unspectacularly, including the detail that the two men did not have anal sex the night before.

Although the two men will be seen, and seen to talk, in various other interior and exterior locations across the course of the weekend, the key setting for the developing relationship is the domestic space provided by the apartment, which is nonetheless not a space for the domestication of sex. Full of comfy used furniture and objects salvaged from the local charity shop, the interior of the apartment provides the backdrop for scenes of personal and sexual disclosure that are as likely to be accompanied by the use of drugs and alcohol as they are the drinking of tea and coffee. Sometime on Saturday afternoon Russell will tell Glen that he has no parents to come out to since he grew up in care. This will lead to sex on the couch, followed by the sight of one man assisting the other to wipe semen off his belly as Haigh establishes the council flat as a place for sex, not its exhaustion. As Glen leaves the apartment for the second time, he returns to tell Russell that he is due to leave Nottingham the following day. Transacted in the apartment doorway, this revelation makes clear that the connection between the two men is crucially linked to the apartment's spatial and narrative dimensionalities, which are as naturalistically tight as they are sexually expansive since they include both the sex that is performed as part of the scene and the sexual encounters recounted in dialogue.

As the film proceeds, the wider coordinates of the apartment are revealed in primarily visual terms. The tower block sits inside the larger council estate and its surrounds, a flat spread of grass divided by concrete pathways that appear on the diagonal when seen from above, as they mostly are. Three times between Saturday morning and Sunday afternoon, Russell will look out the window of his fourteenth-floor apartment to watch Glen depart on foot, his yellow or red hoodie standing out brightly in an exterior world otherwise bleached of color. Throughout the film red, yellow, and blue accents emotionally punctuate the various scenes in which the two men come together, separate, text each other, and meet up again across the course of a weekend in which it is hard to keep track of time. In the blue-and-white world of the local indoor baths where Russell works as a lifeguard, for instance, there is an oversized clock that marks out, not the hours or minutes in the day, but only the racing sweep of seconds, the time to be got through before he can see Glen again.

As the seconds-only clock suggests, the temporal logic of the film is durational rather than chronological, just as the actions it represents are often framed as repetitions rather than events in the singular and consequential sense of that term. Glen's pseudo-intellectual art project instantiates this logic, but, in assigning a similar project to the unpretentious Russell, the film perhaps suggests that gay culture in general may have an inclination toward the serial form and its capacity to catch rhythms and intensities missed by more teleological forms, including romantic narratives of the kind that would frame Russell and Glen as star-crossed lovers. Tucked inside the apartment in the early hours of Sunday morning, Russell reveals to Glen that he too records his sexual encounters with other men. The scene cuts forward to the living room, where Russell sits on the floor and reads aloud from his laptop two accounts of casual sex before the task of reading is passed over to Glen. As Glen reads aloud, the camera ratchets focus between his face in the foreground and Russell's face deeper in field, an unusually melodramatic gesture in the context of the rest of the unerringly naturalistic film. The entry recounts Russell's first experience of anal sex with a man who won't exchange numbers with him afterward as he already has a boyfriend, a rejection that makes him feel bad about himself. At the end of the account, Glen closes the laptop, stands, and exits the frame while asking Russell what this guy looked like in order to establish that the man was John, his former boyfriend who lied to him about picking up other men. Though Glen returns to the floor-level shot, the scene abruptly cuts to a close-up of Russell's drugged face in the bathroom mirror as dialogue not synched to the image continues to be heard, another

FIG. 7.2. Gay attachment: Russell and Glen reconcile at the open apartment window in *Weekend* (Andrew Haigh, 2011).

formal innovation out of step with the naturalistic code of the rest of the film.

At the point where the visuals reunite with the sound, the two men are seen sitting on the sofa, but the sense of intimacy between them has dissipated. Pumped up on the lines of cocaine they have taken, they fall into a disinhibited conversation about the pros and cons of gay marriage in which everything one man says arrives as needlessly aggressive to the other. Russell leaves to take a piss, and the image track returns to the close-up on his face in the mirror as it pushes to the brink of tears. A recomposed Russell returns to the living room, where Glen is standing at the open apartment window, and the two men reconcile to the sound of John Grant's "TC and Honeybear," which plays on the stereo (fig. 7.2).

Back in sync with their apartment surroundings and the untroubled night sky onto which both room and lyrics open, the two men smoke marijuana together before a final sexual encounter in which Russell wordlessly invites Glen to fuck him. The most thematically weighted action in the film, this too is a repetition, a serially singular sign of emotional trust that is all the safer for being transacted in the knowledge that the abandonment that will follow is a result of impersonal circumstance—Glen is going to America—rather than personal rejection.

In fucking Russell and then going away, Glen therapeutically reenacts his former boyfriend's role, a point underscored in the morning when he pretends to be Russell's father so that Russell, who has only known serial foster parents, can enact coming out to a figure who does not exist. While these replayable, pseudo-patriarchal dynamics of abandonment and repair are crucial to the emotional satisfactions the film has to offer, they are not all it has to offer. Having established ambivalence and insecurity as the framework within which attachments form, the film releases its gay male protagonists from the apartment into a cinematic ending that can hold them together even as it wrenches them apart. After an interlude that returns everything to a nonreparative present—the tedium of a Sunday morning spent alone in an apartment full of dirty ashtrays and half-empty glasses—the two men meet up in a scene at Nottingham railway station that pays homage to David Lean's *Brief Encounter* (1945), a melodrama that simultaneously de-idealizes and reidealizes marriage from the perspective of an almost-affair. Amid the station crowd of ordinary folk going about their ordinary days, Glen is picked out by his yellow hoodie and red backpack. The two men walk from the station food court to the platform, where the camera positions them at a distance as seen through the wire of a barricade. They stand talking face-to-face, but the dialogue is drowned out by the sound of the train behind them and an announcement over the station public address system. The camera slowly zooms in through the fence to frame them as a couple, and the dialogue is restored in time for us to hear Glen damn Russell for coming to see him off, before he collapses tearfully into the other man's embrace. The two men kiss openly, and when a catcall breaks through the ambient sound of the station, Russell looks defiantly at the camera, having attained his full height for what seems like the first time in the film. Taller and stronger than before, Russell reassures Glen that he will be great in America. Glen gives Russell a crumpled package, saying he couldn't remember his surname, kisses him a final time, then walks out of shot. Russell trembles on the verge of tears as he turns to look after Glen. A cut shows a train departing before the scene shifts forward in time to resettle Russell in the open window of his apartment at twilight. He takes the package from his jacket, reaches in, takes out Glen's recorder, and turns it on. The achingly long take continues over a playback of the morning-after interview between the two men. Russell can be heard to hesitate before Glen instructs him to begin from the start. The image switches to a final exterior vantage point that nestles the gay man in an illuminated window frame, one of several in the darkening hulk of the Lenton Flats, as the opening chords of John Grant's "Marz" sear the otherworldly quality of the visuals into the soundtrack (fig. 7.3). No more than a figural outline suspended in time and light, Russell has become a cipher for our renewed attachment to a world that may not be cut out to meet our needs but remains our best hope for their satisfaction.

But what world is this? In one framing of the story, this world is one in which two men with abandonment issues fall for each other in a relation

FIG. 7.3. Reattachment to the world: Russell is framed in the illuminated window of the apartment block in *Weekend* (Andrew Haigh, 2011).

of growing intimacy, tenderness, and trust that is foreclosed by circumstances and social hostilities beyond their control. But, in another framing of the same story, this world is one in which two men fall for each other in the understanding that their best chance at happiness is supported by spaces outside the apartment that are understood to be continuous with it. Featuring as incidental details in the sexual stories the two men trade between themselves in the process of getting to know each other, these sketchily drawn spaces include bars, saunas, and parks that are the setting for serial encounters with strangers who may or may not become intimates. Always invested with the prospect of gay sex, these spaces— including the space of the apartment itself—are unlike the suburban kitchens, living rooms, pubs, and workplaces featured in the film where straight familiars spend their lives and which, whether gay friendly or potentially hostile, are alike in seeming utterly denuded of cruising possibilities and hence inhospitable to gay life with its practiced sensitivity to strangers.

Throughout the film, the close camera work and careful blocking used inside the apartment are interleaved with distant, zoom-lens shots of an alternative world strongly associated with peripheral noise—the sound of passing traffic or the hubbub of voices and music that drowns out the actors in a pub scene or at the carnival where the two men go, having abandoned Glen's going-away drinks. In the crowded social scenes outside the apartment, the dialogue, when it is heard, is mostly inconsequential. Glen rants against the heterosexual dominance of popular culture and straight people's disgust for gay sex to anyone that will listen, but in the narrative framework of the film Nottingham appears relatively benign, if provincial. Some youths from the Lenton Estate shout "queer" from the anonymity of offscreen space as Glen leaves the apartment building after his first night with Russell, and a group on the bus makes jokes about camp men, but the homophobia seems rote, the sign of a social backwater rather than pointed aggression. Beside a reference to Glen's former boyfriend being beaten up while cruising in a park, the one genuinely aggressive scene, shocking in its ordinariness, occurs at the pool, where Russell sits apart from his male workmates in the break room increasingly discomforted as one of them nastily describes fisting his girlfriend. Outside the apartment, Russell seems detached not only from the straight world of work but also from the warmer domestic world of informal dinners and children's parties presented to him by his childhood friend Jamie. Despite being sutured into this family milieu as godfather to Jamie's child, Russell is most at home in the world when moving through it with his new friend Glen at his side or floating above it in his Lenton Flats apartment.

Although others have read Russell's return to the apartment as a retreat into the fantasy space of "domesticity and marriage," the final frames of the film effortlessly convey his renewed attachment to a socially complex gay world best experienced from the vantage point of apartment space.[20] Framed in the illuminated window of the apartment looking out into the deepening night, Russell might be fantasizing Glen's return, or looking forward to the sexual promise of next weekend, or both. Crucially, these are not presented as exclusive options but framed as mutually supportive ambitions. Neither romantic nor antiromantic, the story's end, like its beginnings in the gay club scene, is geared to affective intensities that may be ephemeral but are also socially sustainable in a community of strangers. Far from presenting the apartment as a space of sexual withdrawal, the film remains resolutely invested in the gay apartment as the place where sexuality and sociality meet. As Cavell points out, traditionally "the joining of the social and the sexual is called marriage,"[21] which is why, in the era of marriage equality, a cycle of films might appear in which the notion of marriage can be expanded to include the possibility of continuous and discontinuous attachments, as well as the spaces in which those serial intimacies might be achieved.

Reattachment Theory

More hopeful than *Concussion*, *Weekend* does not settle for marriage or its negation but holds on to the idea of reattachment, which it understands as both a fragile and a resilient thing. Though a lot of the film's improvised talkiness is given over to debating gay marriage, it is more compelling for the quiet testimony it gives to the capacity for intimacy between strangers, even if that might not stand longer acquaintance. Indeed, acknowledging that sexual attachments and the intimate social worlds we build on them might not persist, or might persist in ways that we can't anticipate at their outset, is the condition under which marriage might now be thought to betoken the uncertainty of happiness as well as its promise. Considered this way, gay marriage remains a rubric for thinking through the social aspects of sexual attachment and the terms on which the social and the sexual might be renegotiated in the face of everything we know about sex and its vicissitudes, including the fact that our attachments, which are often formed on impulse but also subject to rigorous social patterning, are mostly resistant to deliberation and will.

Read together, *Concussion* and *Weekend* reveal that the apartment plot is key to the gay and lesbian narratives of attachment and detachment that now circulate in the wake of marriage equality. Equally, though differently, they repurpose the apartment plot as a complex means of working through some of the anxieties that ghost the socially upbeat accounts of same-sex marriage that have surfaced elsewhere in popular culture. Among other things, these films use the materiality of apartment space to register alternative conceptions of urban homosexual life, whether it is the no-strings contractual sex that occurs in the metropolitan lesbian loft or the chance encounter facilitated by a gay bar on an otherwise dull Friday night in a provincial English town. Working through gay marriage and its discontents, these films newly engage the apartment plot as the means by which marriage might be expanded beyond the neoliberal version of privatized domesticity that its queer critics often take it to be.[22] Whether or not this still-unfolding cycle can reconcile any of us to the idea of marriage as a social answer to the riddle of sexual attachment remains to be seen.

NOTES

1. John Bowlby, *Attachment and Loss*, vol. 1: *Attachment* (New York: Basic Books, 1969); John Bowlby, *Attachment and Loss*, vol. 2: *Separation, Anxiety and Anger* (New York: Basic Books, 1973); and John Bowlby, *Attachment and Loss*, vol. 3: *Loss, Sadness and Depression* (New York: Basic Books, 1980).

2. See, for example, Hiltrud Otto and Heidi Keller, eds., *Different Faces of Attachment: Cultural Variations on a Universal Human Need* (Cambridge: Cambridge

University Press, 2014); and Ben Rockett and Sam Carr, "Animals and Attachment Theory," *Society and Animals* 22, no. 4 (2014): 415–33.

3. Stanley Cavell, *Pursuits of Happiness: The Hollywood Comedy of Remarriage* (Cambridge, MA: Harvard University Press, 1981).

4. Cavell, *Pursuits of Happiness*, 5. For an interesting retake on the issue of female reeducation via marriage, see Áine Mahon, "Marriage and Moral Perfectionism in Siri Hustvedt and Stanley Cavell," *Textual Practice* 29, no. 4 (2015): 631–51.

5. Lee Wallace, *Lesbianism, Cinema, Space: The Sexual Life of Apartments* (New York: Routledge, 2009).

6. For a fuller account of these chronotopes that variously and interconnectedly support narratives of pre-Stonewall lesbian life, see Wallace, *Lesbianism, Cinema, Space*, 5–12.

7. In a typically incisive critique of *Brokeback Mountain*, D. A. Miller links the film's success to liberal self-congratulation in the area of marriage equality. D. A. Miller, "On the Universality of *Brokeback Mountain*," *Film Quarterly* 60, no. 3 (2007): 50–60. I discuss the way *A Single Man* makes an affective case for gay marriage in Lee Wallace, "Tom Ford and His Kind," *Criticism: A Quarterly for Literature and the Arts* 56, no. 1 (2014): 21–44.

8. For a discussion of Daldry's film in the context of queer handlings of marriage, see Julianne Pidduck, "The Times of *The Hours*: Queer Melodrama and the Dilemma of Marriage," *Camera Obscura* 28, no. 1, 82 (2013): 36–67. Cholodenko's film and the predictable critiques of homonormativity it engendered are discussed by Jodi Brooks in "*The Kids Are All Right*, the Pursuits of Happiness, and the Spaces Between," *Camera Obscura* 29, no. 1, 85 (2014): 111–35. As Dana Heller elaborates in a brilliant reading of Showtime's *The L Word* (2004–9) and its unscripted reality spin-off *The Real L Word* (2010–11), the gay marriage cycle has now extended itself into nonfiction franchises. Dana Heller, "Wrecked: Programming Celesbian Reality," in *Reality Gendervision: Sexuality and Gender on Transatlantic Reality Television*, ed. Brenda R. Weber (Durham, NC: Duke University Press, 2014), 123–46.

9. Michael DeAngelis, "Introduction," in *Reading the Bromance: Homosocial Relationships in Film and Television*, ed. Michael DeAngelis (Detroit: Wayne State University Press, 2014), 15. DeAngelis first explores the marriage-as-problem cycle of films in "Mispronouncing 'Man and Wife': The Fate of Marriage in Hollywood's Sexual Revolution," in *Hetero: Queering Representations of Straightness*, ed. Sean Griffin (Albany: SUNY Press, 2009), 129–49.

10. Cavell, *Pursuits of Happiness*, 20.

11. In *American Couples: Money, Work, Sex* (New York: William Morrow, 1983), Philip Blumstein and Pepper Schwartz applied the term "lesbian bed death" to the diminishment of sexual activity reported between women in long-term relationships. Although this research has been contested in the field, lesbian bed death continues to command popular airtime within lesbian-friendly contexts such as Alison Bechdel's syndicated comic strip *Dykes to Watch Out For*.

12. For more information on the Myers-Briggs Type Indicator, see the Myers and Briggs Foundation (http://www.myersbriggs.org). Although her services are never advertised as such, Abby appears to offer her clients two things: sex and talk or, more correctly, sex or talk, since the sex stops once the talk kicks in. Returning clients, such as the overweight women's studies undergraduate in need of alternative mothering or the complicated older woman who seems to identify with Abby as a more successful version of herself, are not shown in sexual clinches but lie around talking, even reading, as if they too had succumbed to lesbian bed death.

13. Brian Eno, "Some of Them Are Old," on *Here Come the Warm Jets* (Island Records, 1974), accessed December 29, 2017, https://www.lyrics.com/lyric/821125.

14. Cavell, *Pursuits of Happiness*, 257.

15. This dull restoration of married life after infidelity recalls the post-adultery scenario imagined in the work of Laura Kipnis, which posits marriage as a training ground for broader forms of social resignation. Laura Kipnis, "Adultery," *Critical Inquiry* 24, no. 2 (winter 1998): 289–327.

16. Part of a nationwide experiment in social housing, the Lenton Flats are a brutalist corollary to the aspirant middle-class suburban housing estates seen under construction at the end of another Nottingham-based film, Karel Reisz's *Saturday Night and Sunday Morning* (1960).

17. The demolition video shows a mechanical crane eating into a building like a crudely animated dinosaur ("Total Reclaim brings down Lenton Court in Nottingham, UK," posted February 14, 2017, https://www.youtube.com/watch?v=ZoFyYWX3V9A). The effect is beautiful, although Nottingham City Council is keen to dissociate itself from the derelict flat that features in the video, which was the creation of the set design team associated with Anton Corbijn's *Control* and not the result of municipal neglect.

18. While many reviewers have noted *Weekend*'s dual affiliation to British social realism and American independent cinema (the latter reflected in its premiering at the sxsw Film Festival), the film also conforms to broader conventions for representing everyday life. For an account of those conventions, see Andrew Klevan, *Disclosure of the Everyday: Undramatic Achievement in Narrative Film* (Trowbridge, U.K.: Flicks, 2000).

19. Dennis Lim, "*Weekend*: The Space between Two People," Criterion Collection, August 21, 2012, https://www.criterion.com/current/posts/2426-weekend-the-space-between-two-people.

20. Stephanie Deborah Clare, "(Homo)Normativity's Romance: Happiness and Indigestion in Andrew Haigh's *Weekend*," *Continuum: Journal of Media and Cultural Studies* 27, no. 6 (2013): 786. Alternatively, Shannon Weber has used Russell's defense of gay marriage to dispute the queer critique of the same-sex marriage movement as necessarily homonormative and assimilationist. Shannon Weber, "Daring to Marry: Marriage Equality Activism after Proposition 8 as Challenge to the Assimilationist/Radical Binary in Queer Studies," *Journal of Homosexuality* 62 (2015): 1147–73. For a sensitive account of how the film uses the parallel traps of assimilationism and queer radicalism to point to the ongoing difficulty of being gay in the "radioactive

half-life" of homophobia, see Paul Brunick, "Reach Out and Touch Someone," *Film Comment* 47, no. 3 (2011): 63.

21. Cavell, *Pursuits of Happiness*, 31.

22. The queer critique of marriage has generated a vast literature since the appearance of Michael Warner's *The Trouble with Normal: Sex, Politics, and the Ethics of Queer Life* (New York: Free Press, 1999). Maggie Nelson has more recently mined this literature to produce an account of a nuptial as an "infinite conversation," a phrase that echoes Cavell's original conceptualization of the comedies of remarriage as the "conversation" America engaged as soon as Hollywood learned to talk. Maggie Nelson, *The Argonauts* (Minneapolis: Graywolf, 2015), 146.

The Wire isn't interested in a dream. This is America, man.
—C. W. MARSHALL AND TIFFANY POTTER, "'I Am the American Dream'"

The Baltimore of *The Wire* is an imagined totality, which is intended to
symbolize desires and anxieties around the meanings of nationhood,
citizenship, urbanity, and justice in the United States. —LIAM KENNEDY
AND STEPHEN SHAPIRO, "Tales of the Neoliberal City"

8

"WE DON'T NEED TO DREAM
NO MORE. WE GOT REAL ESTATE"

The Wire, Urban Development, and the Racial
Boundaries of the American Dream

PAULA J. MASSOOD

Near the end of *The Wire*'s third season, Stringer Bell (Idris Elba), one
of the show's main characters (at least in that he was a regular presence
throughout the first three years), is gunned down while inspecting a downtown Baltimore property. At this point in time, Stringer is functioning as
one half of B&B Enterprises, a development company in the process of
renovating previously undervalued buildings into upscale residential and
commercial properties. But, as anybody familiar with the show knows,
Stringer is also the brains behind the Barksdale and Bell drug empire, and
his murder is the result of both his and his partner's bad decisions related
to a very different type of real estate, the control and possession of local
drug corners. As viewed by the cops investigating them and the crooked
politicians bribing them, B&B Enterprises is either a money-laundering front
or a source of easy money. But for Stringer, the company also is a legiti-
mizing project, a means of social and economic mobility that will enable
him and his partner, Avon Barksdale (Wood Harris), to leave the criminal

life. His death is tragic, not only because it's ordered by his partner and lifelong friend, but also because it occurs at the moment when Stringer appears to have succeeded in acquiring his version of the American Dream: property. For viewers, his death also concludes a fascinating narrative trajectory that draws from a number of familiar generic conventions.

Since its premiere in 2002, *The Wire* has been studied through a multitude of rubrics, ranging from the political to the aesthetic. On its most basic generic level, the show, which aired on HBO for five seasons, is a police procedural that details the experiences of an unconventional crime unit made up of misfits drawn from different Baltimore police squads. But *The Wire* is also a whole lot more. It began its first season, for example, as a seemingly simple narrative focusing on small-scale drug dealing in West Baltimore's public housing projects and morphed over five seasons into an exploration of union corruption, neoliberal economics, sex trafficking, political fraud, the failures of public education, and the dissolution of the mainstream press. By its final episode, *The Wire* had shifted from asking micro questions related to urban poverty, drug abuse, and crime in Baltimore's impoverished African American neighborhoods to macro questions surrounding ethics and morality in a rapidly globalizing world. In effect, it went from crime narrative to a tragedy of epic proportions.

As this suggests, *The Wire* has always been much more than a police procedural or a crime drama, despite the fact that the major law enforcement characters, such as Detectives McNulty, Bunk, Freamon, and Greggs and Lieutenant Daniels, bind the seasons together (and unlike most other characters, they survive to the end). Because of its serial format, the show had the space and time to develop a number of generic and plot motifs—its writers borrowed freely from the mystery, the thriller, the crime drama, the tragedy, the melodrama—and much scholarship has analyzed its coherence and break from these generic conventions.[1] But what has heretofore been overlooked are the ways in which *The Wire* also draws from two seemingly incompatible, and yet interconnected, cinematic influences, the gangster film and the apartment plot. In order to understand how these genres function in the series, it is important that we shift our focus from the police figures so central to *The Wire* and concentrate on Stringer Bell and Avon Barksdale, the show's major drug figures. It is in their narrative trajectory that *The Wire* borrows heavily from the gangster genre, particularly the African American gangster and gangsta film.[2] Moreover, Stringer's stress on property ownership, particularly residential property, as a means of social and economic mobility suggests a link to the apartment plot, where an apartment "motivates and shapes the narrative in some key way."[3] In what follows, therefore, I discuss the ways in which apartment spaces motivate *The Wire*'s narrative in crucial, and ultimately deadly, ways. I identify the interactions between the gangster genre and the apartment plot in the series, with a focus on the importance of urban space and place in its narratives of "mobility, impermanence, and porousness."[4] If the gangster genre is as much about acquiring the American Dream (in the form of social and economic belonging) as it is about criminality, then what happens when that dream is directly connected to real estate? *The Wire*'s generic interconnections show us the deadly stakes faced by young black men trying to assimilate into American society. In the end, this is what makes Avon and Stringer's story stand out from the show's other generic explorations.

The Wire focuses on a number of African American gangsters/gangstas, including Avon Barksdale and Stringer Bell, and to a lesser extent Proposition Joe (Robert F. Chew), Marlo Stanfield (Jamie Hector), and an assortment of underlings and street soldiers. At first glance the characters are no more than common drug dealers earning money by selling addiction and misery in different Baltimore neighborhoods (Avon and Stringer on the West Side, Prop Joe on the East Side, and Marlo as an interloper in their territories). And yet their stories, principally Stringer's, explore themes of economic and spatial mobility, key elements of the gangster film. Avon and Stringer's business success is only partially based on their ability to instill fear and/or loyalty in their subordinates and drug customers. Their greater achievement is in becoming involved in Baltimore's expanding property market. Their immediate goal is to launder drug profits. The long-term intention, fueled by Stringer's application of Keynsian economic theories to their business model, is to become legit. That their business holdings include property is no coincidence: Stringer's plan is based on a desire to diversify into legal businesses as a path away from drugs. It's also based on necessity, as the property narrative is played out against a backdrop of the increasingly contested spaces of their old territory, the result of the state's demolition of the housing projects that functioned as the main location for their drug business. Like the mostly white politicians and businessmen behind the urban renewal on Baltimore's West Side, Stringer and Avon have moved into areas (downtown Baltimore) that were previously closed to them in their former lives as drug dealers.

Indeed, in this narrative scenario, they have become the actants of gentrification rather than its victims.

There's no doubt that Stringer's story in particular adapts the conventions of the classic gangster film. From its very first appearance in early cinema, the genre focused on stories of ethnic and (eventually) racial outsiders attempting to succeed through alternative economies, thereby functioning as a means of exploring national identity and the mythology of the American Dream through the tropes of economic and social mobility. In dealing with the nation's burgeoning city spaces, fueled by European immigration and African American migration, gangster films had a twofold function: for reformers and politicians, the genre's cautionary tales and moral endings often "defus[ed] the unsettling forces of immigration, industrialization, and consumerism" by offering morality tales of the city's unsavory temptations.[5] For audiences, particularly new immigrants and migrants moving into the nation's urban spaces, the genre's focus on outsider heroes provided popular stories of striving and material success, even if they often ended tragically. Gangster films often melodramatically suggested that everyone, regardless of origins, had equal access to capital (money, cars, apartments, clothing); there was merely a correct or incorrect path to the acquisition of these material possessions.

In my opinion, the gangster genre's contradictions—its cautions and its celebrations—are particularly complex in the African American gangster film, and much of my research has been focused on tracing the politics and aesthetics of the form. Black gangster films, particularly race films from the 1930s and '40s, "used many familiar elements of the genre, including urban locations, plots charting the rise and fall of a criminal protagonist, and narratives of economic and social mobility."[6] And yet they adapted the genre's conventions to present "narratives geared toward their black urban audiences, who themselves were looking for stories featuring African American characters and plots that reflected their everyday reality."[7] As everyday reality changed—from urbanization and industrialization to deindustrialization, globalization, and gentrification—the black gangster film developed different aesthetics and political strategies to address the shifting African American cityscape.

Independent film companies began producing gangster films with African American protagonists in the 1930s. The films, like *Dark Manhattan* (Harry L. Fraser, 1937) for example, were much like those featuring Italian and Irish gangsters in that they presented organized crime as businesses

and gangsters as businessmen. Where they differed was in their representation of black gangsters, who were often race men who gave back to their
community through employment opportunities and philanthropy.[8] The
narratives offered the possibility of economic mobility through hard, albeit illegal, work. By the 1970s, however, the black gangster morphed into
a gang leader, drug dealer, or pimp—especially in those films borrowing
from blaxploitation conventions—and the possibility for mobility outside
of the strictly defined parameters of the ghetto decreased. Moreover, the
criminal protagonist of the 1970s was less community focused, with his
rebellion often serving individuals goals over larger gains. More recent
urban-based gangsta/hood narratives, such as *Menace II Society* (Hughes
Brothers, 1993), continued this exploration of gangster (now gangsta) life
and its protagonists' desire for social and economic mobility, while simultaneously underscoring the physical, psychological, and social boundaries
determining the lives of young African American men in urban areas.[9]
By this point in the genre's development, criminal activities lacked the
organizational structure of earlier organizations. The emphasis was on the
present over the past or future.

Just as *The Wire* encompasses a variety of generic traits, it also captures
the elements of different moments in the history of the black gangster film,
from its classical mode through its most recent, gangsta-rap-inflected iteration as hood films. Stringer's character, for example, falls within the
tradition of the black gangster of the 1930s. Not only does he view what
he does as a business, but he also, unlike many of his associates, looks beyond the boundaries of the neighborhood. Mark Anthony Neal describes
Stringer as a character with a "cosmopolitan worldview," who is a "citizen of
the world . . . rather than a tightly-knit hood."[10] Stringer thinks outside of
the box both spatially (by buying properties outside West Baltimore) and
economically (through diversification). Like the gangsters from the 1930s,
he transforms drug dealing into a business based on corporate models
and insists that B&B's legitimate enterprises, like his copy shop, function
as true businesses.

A scene from season 1 illustrates both Stringer's business acumen and
his personal ethos. While in the copy shop that serves as his de facto office, Stringer notices that his young staff members (drawn from the street)
haven't been completing customers' orders, thereby jeopardizing the op-
eration. In an attempt to transform them from corner boys into counter
staff, he tries to teach the young men the difference between "elastic" and

"inelastic" product, and warns them "not to bring that [corner] bullshit up in here." Instead, he wants the copy shop to "run like a true fucking business. Not no front. Not no bullshit." In later seasons his desire to be a gentleman businessman is signified through his insistence that co-op members comply with Robert's Rules of Order during meetings. Stringer's crucial difference from earlier gangsters, however, is that he expresses no concern for his immediate community. His lessons to the younger generation are geared toward his own economic interests and not, according to Linda Williams, "to preserve a community or provide work beyond paying lieutenants and corner boys."[11]

Stringer's business approach is influenced by models learned in classes taken at a local community college and defined by a long view: cooperation with competitors for the profit of all, a cognizance of changing business climates (whether it be the drug trade or urban renewal), and an ability to adapt to the situation. To the first goal, he organizes competing drug families into the New Day Co-op, a business association that allows each group access to quality product at reduced prices (fig. 8.1). The last two goals are evident in Stringer's establishment of B&B Enterprises, his and Avon's property company. Unfortunately, his approach, which, Neal argues, "is clearly beyond the realm of the corners," runs counter to Avon's, who is interested in neither working with other dealers nor property development. Unlike Stringer's more traditional gangster mentality, therefore, Avon holds to his gangsta roots. Indeed, he's so focused on the minutiae of local drug territories (real estate with a lowercase *r* and *e*) that he continues a destructive turf war with Marlo Stanfield, against his partner's advice.

So how does the apartment operate in this narrative of African American drug dealers in West Baltimore, a territory almost solely defined by public housing towers and abandoned row houses? In *The Apartment Plot*, Pamela Wojcik argues that, among other things, the apartment plot "conveys ideologies of urbanism," particularly focusing on white, middle-class city spaces in the postwar era.[12] She juxtaposes this concept to the African American apartment and suggests that "black urban life . . . exists outside the usual area of the apartment plot," primarily because the tenement (or the housing project) figured more prominently in films focusing on African American city life. In short, the mid-twentieth-century apartment plot was aesthetically and ideologically concerned with white urban space, whereas black urban space was marked as impoverished and problematic. In such a scenario, "the apartment plot enacts a form of containment, maintaining and

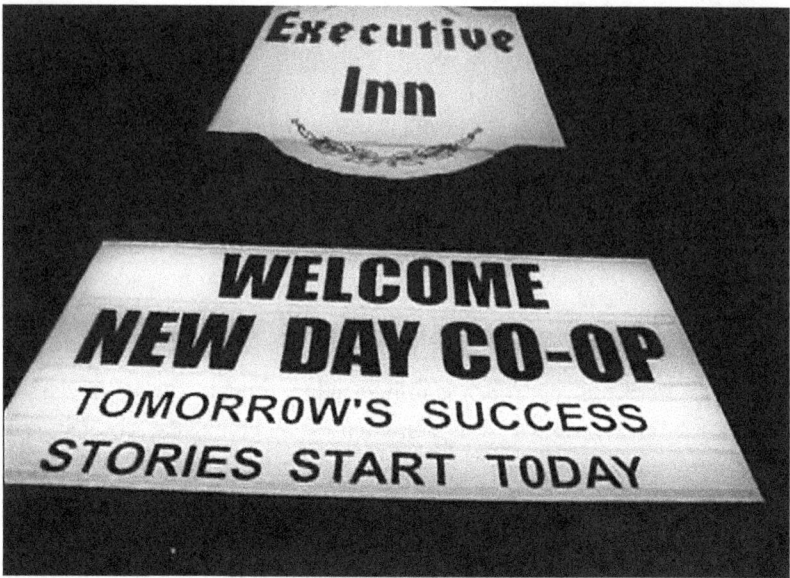

FIG. 8.1. The New Day Co-op: where "Tomorrow's Success Stories Start Today" (*The Wire*, season 3).

strengthening residential segregation *at the level of representation* to present a fantasy of the urban as exclusively a white middle-class space."[13] African American apartments were rarities, and if they appeared they were used to "signify a character's class rise and escape from the ghetto."[14] Moreover, whether located outside the white status quo or marked as a distinctive and rare status shift, the African American apartment underscores the importance of place—either maintaining one's position or "moving on up"—in their characters' lives. The apartment, therefore, functions as more than setting or backdrop; it is a discourse on the delimitation or acquisition of space. In this way it's linked to the gangster narrative's focus on mobility within strictly defined spatial and economic parameters. Indeed, it's these connections between the gangster film and the apartment plot that make *The Wire* so interesting.

While examples of apartments occupied by both black and white characters abound in *The Wire*, the apartment plot operates mostly metaphorically in the series. In fact, most characters give neither a first nor a second glance to apartment spaces, which are nothing more than shelter or background to larger narrative concerns.[15] Despite this absence of real spaces, there are two central ways in which the apartment plot functions, and both are linked to the discourses of mobility that run throughout *The Wire*. The first example is located in Stringer's desire to shift from drug dealing into property development. To the uninitiated, it may seem as though B&B's activities form one of the show's major story lines. In fact, they are a subplot that emerges gradually over the first three seasons as the police start tracing and surveilling Avon's activities (in the beginning of the series he, not Stringer, is the focus of the police investigation).[16] In season 1, B&B first appears as an unnamed aside as Freamon (Clarke Peters), one of the officers investigating Avon, begins to follow the drug money. His observation that when "you follow drugs you get drug addicts and dealers. But you start to follow the money, and you don't know where the fuck it's going to take you" already suggests that Avon and Stringer are in a different class from common street dealers. The subplot then develops in season 2 after Avon is imprisoned and Stringer manages the business on his own. At this point, Stringer begins to implement the business models he's learned in classes: join with other dealers to ensure better product and to reduce territorial conflict, run money laundering fronts as legitimate establishments, and acquire undervalued properties in soon-to-be-developed neighborhoods. The B&B subplot receives its most concentrated airtime in season 3, as Stringer readies for the development of the company's first building in downtown Baltimore. For Stringer, the building is the culmination of years of work transforming himself from street delinquent to respectable Baltimore businessman. As he soon learns, however, it is also his entry into white-collar crime, an entirely different but no less treacherous territory. As he pays bribes to crooked politicians and developers who have no intention of helping B&B, he realizes that there's little difference between drug crime and the business world.[17]

As David Lerner argues, "Location is a central theme of [*The Wire*'s] Season Three, especially as it applies to business and the separation between real and imagined space," and B&B's downtown properties often operate as signifiers of a different sort of life for Stringer, rather than an actual lifestyle.[18] It's not until the end of the season, when Stringer is murdered, for example, that an actual B&B property appears on-screen. This stands in contrast to the drug corners, housing projects, and abandoned row houses that are ubiquitous across the entirety of *The Wire*'s five seasons. Until the building is shown on-screen, B&B's holdings have been

FIG. 8.2. Imagined spaces: Tracking B&B Enterprises' real estate holdings (*The Wire*, season 3).

only verbally referenced in discussions between detectives, displayed as photos on crime boards, or marked as points on a map in the squad's offices (fig. 8.2). In other words, they are imagined spaces, existing in the minds of the police and, by extension, the audience. And yet, they are mapped and exist as a simulacra of a real estate empire.

The properties also represent a very particular form of twenty-first-century real estate acquisition, one that goes hand in hand with urban renewal projects and contemporary gentrification processes. In such a scenario, urban renewal fuels speculation in abandoned or rundown properties in formerly unattractive (read: black and/or Latino) urban neighborhoods with little or no concern for the real residents of such spaces. Through the process of renewal, here code for removal, renovation, and/or construction, such properties realize a massive return on a developer's initial investment. Additionally, their transformation into luxury apartments—the new crack for the wealthy and white—suggests a form of territorial creep not dissimilar from turf wars over drug corners. Indeed, this focus on speculation—where apartments are more likely to appear as floor plans (imaginary aeries) rather than real spaces—suggests a twenty-first-century iteration of the apartment plot. In this scenario, the draw resides in what may be, not what is, an appeal directly related to Stringer's desire to be something other than a drug dealer.[19]

As the above suggests, one of the key elements of the African American apartment plot is urban renewal, and *The Wire* offers two variations on the theme, one that creates something new and one that draws on the not so new. The new is offered in the show's narrative of the development of Baltimore's downtown district, the location of B&B's investments. This subplot runs throughout the series's five seasons and makes appearances in a variety of situations, from B&B's aforementioned investments to the wheeling and dealing of a string of mayors, city council members, and union leaders in the Port of Baltimore, all of whom promise some version of a new city.[20] While Stringer's death ends the B&B story, the development narrative continues in the series, most directly when the same politicians and businessmen who worked with (and stole from) Stringer attempt to entice another West Side dealer, Marlo Stanfield, to invest in building projects located either adjacent to the port or on the site of a former housing project. Unlike Stringer, who saw such investments as paths to legitimacy, Marlo, like Avon, is far less interested in this route, and it's unclear whether he accepts their deal or returns to the streets. Since he's modeled after a different sort of gangster than Stringer—a gangsta who is "young, black, and doesn't give a fuck"—the latter scenario makes the most sense.[21] This interpretation is supported in the show's final episode, in which Marlo abandons a downtown cocktail party filled with politicians and wealthy businessmen and returns to the streets of West Baltimore.

The Wire also examines a more traditional, or not so new, form of urban renewal in its references to Baltimore's history of urban planning and the larger effects of state-sanctioned housing policies on impoverished city neighborhoods. The same season that ends with Stringer's death, for example, begins with the razing of the Franklin Terrace Towers (fig. 8.3). Since *The Wire*'s pilot episode the towers, along with the low-rises that stood in their shadow, functioned as the headquarters for Avon and Stringer's drug business. Their destruction at the beginning of season 3 precipitates the turf war that eventually leads to the end of the pair's control of the drug trade in the area, as Marlo is able to make inroads into West Baltimore's corners. As the buildings are readied for implosion, Mayor Royce (Glynn Turman) explains to the gathered crowd of residents and local politicians that urban renewal is more than "a word," it's a "philosophy." In this context, his philosophy is nothing more than the use of eminent domain as thinly veiled property grab intended to replace the terrace structures with mixed-income housing that may or may not be home to the terrace's displaced residents.

FIG. 8.3. The demolition of the Franklin Terrace Towers changes the game in West Baltimore (*The Wire*, season 3).

Royce's speech is intercut with a discussion that takes place among three of Avon and Stringer's midlevel corner men, Bodie (J. D. Williams), Poot (Tray Chaney), and Fruit (Brandon Fobbs), who provide a different analysis of events. While Poot and Fruit's observations tend toward nostalgia for a lost past, Bodie's interpretation of the situation is both more caustic and more insightful. According to the young dealer, "Downtown suit-wearing ass bitches done snatched up the best territory in the city from y'all." Bodie's assertion is most immediately about the loss of the group's guaranteed drug depot in the terrace, but it unintentionally makes a larger point: in the drug trade, as with property, location matters, and those with the best real estate make the highest profit. While attempting to make inroads elsewhere, Avon and Stringer lose their corners and blocks to "downtown suit-wearing ass bitches," upon whose goodwill they rely for their new endeavor's success. The destruction of the towers also means that they will eventually lose more territory to Marlo.

The demolition of the towers reflects a more extended history of urban renewal over the past three to four decades, one that witnessed the failure of modernist high-density public housing in places such as Baltimore and Chicago and the movement to clear such developments to make room for lower-rise housing that, according to policy makers, would spark community feeling and decrease criminality. In the early 1990s, Baltimore's high-rise stock, which had replaced many of the city's original row houses in the 1950s, began to be torn down and replaced with mixed-population developments, much like the row houses that were originally displaced by the projects. Lexington Terrace, one of the locations that inspired *The Wire*'s Franklin Terrace Towers, is one such example. Razed in 1996, the site now houses the Terraces, an eighteen-acre mixed-use, mixed-income complex that combines market-rate and low-income row houses with office space and an apartment building housing seniors. The scene and the mayor's speech imply a similar future for the fictional terraces. What this suggests is that while B&B Enterprises was setting its sights on new territory, a combination of "suit-wearing ass bitches" representing public and private interests were taking over West Baltimore, promising reform and a new Baltimore. That the show's creators reference Baltimore's urban development as "historically characterized by boom-and-bust sequences" suggests, according to David M. Alff, the ways in which *The Wire* highlights the "disjunctive relationship between the transformation of landscape and [the] transformative rhetoric" used to excuse its real effects.[22] While it does not specifically focus on a particular apartment space, the show's attention to "the physical spaces that Baltimore's people inhabit" suggests the indirect ways in which apartments motivate the story.[23]

The second way the apartment plot functions is more intimate, and is located in Stringer's desire to live in an apartment leased in his own name. The topic first appears near the beginning of season 3 when Avon returns home after serving prison time for possession of drugs. Stringer interrupts his friend's welcome-home party to provide him with a tour of the luxurious waterfront apartment he's arranged for Avon. As he shows his friend his new home, Stringer provides details of the investments he's made while Avon was in jail, the results of which have enabled the apartment and an expensive SUV to be leased, as Stringer proudly stresses, "in your name." As suggested earlier, African American apartments outside of housing projects and tenements "generally signify" a positive economic and spatial shift.[24] That the apartment is leased in Avon's name indicates just such a shift in economic and spatial circumstances, one that makes Stringer proud because he views the space as reflecting his and his partner's success. Avon, whose business interests have always focused on drug corners, is more interested in the women at his party, suggesting that the links between social and spatial mobility and legitimacy are much more important for Stringer than for Avon.

Avon's apartment reappears a few episodes later when he and Stringer meet up again in the penultimate show before the latter's death. The relations between the two friends have become increasingly strained over their differences of opinion on strategies for dealing with Marlo Stanfield's incursions into their territory, among other tensions. Avon and Stringer's discussion, which takes place on a balcony overlooking Baltimore's redeveloped waterfront, is melancholy, touching upon the men's childhoods and their desires for the future.[25] In the present, the men's luxurious surroundings represent their success at moving from the corners, the world of their youth, to something they only dreamed about as children. As they reminisce about the past and strategize for the future, their philosophical and ideological differences—which were already shown to be widening over the seasons—are given historical context: Avon, who was and continues to see himself as a gangsta, wants to maintain control of the drug blocks on the West Side even if this means starting a war with Marlo, whereas Stringer wants to leave such behavior, and crime, behind. In Avon's world, such thinking—and therefore surroundings—is incompatible with his chosen identity, one where he "bleeds red" and Stringer "bleeds green." To further signify their differences spatially, Avon keeps another apartment (not in his name) for his more nefarious activities. This latter location, which was both acquired and occupied against Stringer's advice, is an unfinished warehouse space in an unidentified part of the city. It houses Avon's arsenal, and eventually serves as the site of final arrest (based on Stringer's tip about the location) in the series.[26]

Stringer, whom Avon remembers in an earlier discussion as "being all into that Black pride shit, talking about two grocery stores and making mother fuckers proud," views business and property ownership as a path out of the ghetto, "his own form of the American Dream's aspiration to middle class status."[27] Unlike Avon, who self-identifies as "just a gangsta," Stringer is a "suit-wearing businessman" (in Avon's words). He is an old-school striver who believes that economic success is the key to full citizenship. For Stringer, property and belonging serve as an economic-political linkage that is underscored in his observation to Avon, "We don't have to dream anymore. We got real estate." But real estate isn't enough to protect him from the violence of the streets, which proves to be a resilient border crosser. In the end, Omar Little (Michael Kenneth Williams) and Brother Mouzone (Michael Potts), two figures from his drug operations, gun him down for reasons ultimately unrelated to downtown property.

Much has been made, and written, of Stringer's untimely death, and most analyses tend to focus on three general (and connected) areas. The first echoes Avon's observations about his partner and suggests that Stringer was not hard enough, or gangsta enough, to survive the mean streets of West Baltimore. Most notably, Linda Williams suggests that "the business-minded, forward-looking, goal-oriented, and strategic Stringer Bell proves to be naïve; his ghetto ass is not 'smart enough or hard enough.'"[28] The second interpretation focuses on Stringer's economic models and suggests that they are incompatible with either—or both—the drug or property businesses. Peter Clanfield, for example, argues that Stringer's naïveté and his "undoing plays partly as the result of a capitalist utopianism."[29] In short, Stringer believes too much in the transformative nature of capitalism, a weakness of many gangster protagonists. The third, and related, interpretation argues that Stringer's reliance on the writings of economists such as Adam Smith fails to equip him for a world in which "a certain quality of life is [already] commodified for the already wealthy . . . while everyone else's options shrink."[30] In this reading, Stringer tragically never realizes that the narrative of the American Dream, and its capitalist promise of economic and social mobility, is gone.

While each of these interpretations holds true to some extent—and *The Wire* is certainly sprawling enough to accommodate multiple, often-contradictory readings—I suggest that we return to Stringer's demise through the related frames of the gangster genre and the apartment plot. As I've been stressing throughout this discussion, Stringer is modeled after a classic gangster who acts out the myths of the American success story. Like the classic gangster, Stringer is flawed: blinded by his own hubris and desire for the accumulation of wealth, he orders the murder of Avon's nephew for the sake of business. He also shows little respect for or interest in his community, whether for the young, expendable corner men and boys he and Avon employ, or when he breaks a long-standing agreement with members of rival drug crews by ordering a hit on Omar Little on a Sunday. In his seminal essay "The Gangster as Tragic Hero," Robert Warshow observes that the "gangster's whole life is an effort to assert himself as an individual, to draw himself out of the crowd, and he always dies because he is an individual."[31] Like Warshow's gangster, Stringer oversteps his position by wanting too much and forgetting his place. That as an African American gangster he overlooks the community makes his trespasses even more serious. In the end, Stringer is done in by his dreams of real estate. Indeed, he dies because he doesn't know, or forgets, his place.

FIG. 8.4. In the end, Stringer Bell is done in by his dreams of real estate. He dies because he doesn't know his place (*The Wire*, season 3).

Stringer is assassinated in the penultimate episode of season 3, while inspecting one of B&B's properties. The murder scene ends with two static long takes. The first is a close-up of a B&B Enterprises billboard taken from the interior of the room where Stringer is murdered. The final image of the episode consists of a long shot with his prone body on the floor, with the same billboard visible through a window in the background (fig. 8.4). The combination of shots underscores the tragedy of the moment. Stringer may have real estate—and Detective Bunk (Wendell Pierce) will later refer to him as a "well-propertied man"—but it's not enough to insulate him from the street and its legacy of the violent maintenance of boundaries. Indeed, that he's shot in his own building, in the shadow of the sign declaring his success, suggests the dangers inherent in a drug dealer trying to go straight. For Warshow, such an ending is apt, because, "at the bottom, the gangster is doomed because he is under the obligation to succeed, not because the means he employs are unlawful. In the deeper layers of the modern consciousness, all means are unlawful, every attempt to succeed is an act of aggression, leaving one alone and guilty and defenseless among enemies: one is punished for success."[32]

What is to be made of the apartment plot with Stringer dead, and B&B Enterprises deceased along with him? The next episode provides a clue.

It opens where the previous one ends: at the murder scene. We first see another close-up of the B&B billboard—this time from outside, where the police investigation is being staged—before a cut to the crime scene (we follow Detective Bunk via a tracking shot into the space). Once again there is a long shot of Stringer's prone body, with the B&B sign in the background. I want to return momentarily—and as the beginnings of a conclusion—to the earlier discussion of the African American apartment. The cinematic absence of African American apartment spaces, and the focus on upscale/white apartments, according to Pamela Wojcik, "enacts a process of urban renewal at the level of representation."[33] In other words, "racialized spaces [such as apartments or cities] give whites access to social inclusion and upward mobility while imposing unjust forms of exploitation and exclusion on communities of color."[34] With Stringer's death we apprehend the manifold ironies related to the African American apartment plot, because in the moment that we finally see one of B&B's buildings, we witness the violent elimination of the man who helped to make it possible. Like the projects, row houses, and other unwanted entities torn down or eliminated to make way for a new Baltimore, Stringer is, by being removed from the frame, removed at the level of representation.

There is one final example of *The Wire*'s ironic and ultimately tragic relationship to the apartment. Soon after they investigate the crime scene, Detectives McNulty (Dominic West) and Bunk enter Stringer's waterfront apartment and are surprised at its understated elegance and cosmopolitan tastes. McNulty, who's spent three seasons in pursuit of Stringer and Avon, is baffled by what seems like a disconnect between the drug dealer he thought he knew and the man reflected in Stringer's home. This is the first and only time that audiences see Stringer's actual living space—a "deluxe apartment in the sky" that he inhabited legitimately and, importantly, in his own name. The apartment is located in a downtown luxury building and boasts waterfront views, well-appointed furnishings, and a library reflecting Stringer's interests, most notably, a copy of Adam Smith's *The Wealth of Nations*. In shock, McNulty asks himself (and perhaps the audience), "This is Stringer's? Who in fuck was I chasing?" Indeed, who in fuck was Stringer Bell? The second in command of a West Baltimore drug ring? The partner in B&B Enterprises, a development company with key holdings in Baltimore's gentrifying downtown area? Or was he an intelligent striver who managed to achieve his version of the American Dream:

an apartment in his own name? Unfortunately, elements of the gangster genre and the apartment plot prevent us from ever knowing Stringer Bell. This is the ultimate, yet generically fitting, tragedy.

NOTES

1. One common avenue of discussion has been the show's links to either tragedy, melodrama, or both, with the former frequently suggested by David Simon, *The Wire*'s creator. Simon has consistently connected the series to classic tragedy, for example: "We've basically taken the idea of Greek tragedy, and applied it to the modern city-state. . . . What we were trying to do was take the notion of the Greek tragedy, of fated and doomed people, and instead of these Olympian gods, indifferent, venal, selfish, hurling lightning bolts and hitting people in the ass for no good reason—instead of those guys whipping it on Oedipus or Achilles, it's the postmodern institutions. . . . Those are the indifferent gods." From Margaret Talbot, "Stealing Life: The Crusader behind *The Wire*," *New Yorker*, October 22, 2007. See also Liam Kennedy and Stephen Shapiro's discussion of the series's relationship to the Greek tragedy in "Tales of the Neoliberal City: *The Wire*'s Boundary Lines," in *The Wire: Race, Class, and Genre*, ed. Liam Kennedy and Stephen Shapiro (Ann Arbor: University of Michigan Press, 2012); and Linda Williams's rejection of the series as tragedy in *On "The Wire"* (Durham, NC: Duke University Press, 2014). Williams, like Amanda Ann Klein, in "'The Dickensian Aspect': Melodrama, Viewer Engagement, and the Socially Conscious Text," in *"The Wire": Urban Decay and American Television*, ed. Tiffany Potter and C. W. Marshall, 177–89 (New York: Bloomsbury, 2009), views the series as melodrama.

2. Note that while the gangster film and the gangsta or hood film share commonalities, they are not the same thing. The former refers to films featuring African American gangsters made during the 1930s and '40s (with some additions, such as *Black Caesar* [Larry Cohen, 1973], in the 1970s); the latter refers to films made in the 1990s and beyond. For more on this, see Paula J. Massood, *Making a Promised Land: Harlem in Twentieth-Century African American Photography and Film* (New Brunswick, NJ: Rutgers University Press, 2012).

3. Pamela Robertson Wojcik, *The Apartment Plot: Urban Living in American Film and Popular Culture, 1945 to 1975* (Durham, NC: Duke University Press, 2010), 3.

4. Wojcik, *The Apartment Plot*, 5.

5. Jonathan Munby, *Public Enemies, Public Heroes: Screening the Gangster Film from "Little Caesar" to "Touch of Evil"* (Chicago: University of Chicago Press, 1999), 5.

6. For more on the race film industry and genre filmmaking, see Paula J. Massood, "Harlem Is Heaven: City Motifs in Race Films from the Early Sound Era," in *Black City Cinema: African American Urban Experiences in Film* (Philadelphia: Temple University Press, 2001).

7. Massood, *Making a Promised Land*, 13.

8. There were actual models of the African American gangster-philanthropist, particularly Casper Holstein and Ellsworth "Bumpy" Johnson. Holstein, who con-

trolled the Harlem numbers racket during the 1920s (the Harlem Renaissance years), was known for his generosity and support of the arts, including funding a number of prizes awarded by *Opportunity* magazine. Johnson, involved in Harlem's numbers during the 1930s and '40s, often provided needy Harlemites with food and money. See Massood, *Making a Promised Land*, 78–79 and 174–75, respectively.

9. This latter concern is especially connected to *The Wire*'s youngest characters (such as Wallace, Dukie, Mikey, and Namond), whose visions of the future are circumscribed by the drugs, crime, and poverty in their midst. Of the younger characters listed, only Namond escapes his fate, by leaving the neighborhood and being taken in by retired police officer Howard Colvin. Wallace is executed in the first season at Stringer's request; Dukie ends up addicted to drugs; and Mikey, after a stint with the Barksdales, goes rogue, much like Omar Little, a series regular until he's unceremoniously dispatched by a neighborhood boy near the end of the final season.

10. Mark Anthony Neal, "'A Man without a Country': The Boundaries of Legibility, Social Capital, and Cosmopolitan Masculinity," *Criticism* 52, no. 3–4 (summer and fall 2010): 399.

11. Williams, *On "The Wire,"* 100.

12. Wojcik, *The Apartment Plot*, 7.

13. Wojcik, *The Apartment Plot*, 227, emphasis added.

14. Wojcik, *The Apartment Plot*, 235. While Wojcik cites *The Jeffersons* as one example of the African American apartment plot from the 1970s, the blaxploitation-gangster hybrid *Black Caesar* offers another example of the apartment functioning as both a signifier of segregated urban space and class mobility. After he succeeds in taking over Harlem's drug trade, gangster Tommy Gibbs (Fred Williamson) decides to acquire the high-rise Manhattan apartment where his mother works as a maid for its white inhabitants. A subsequent discussion between mother and son reveals that the building is restricted, and black and Jewish residents are not allowed. This does not stop Gibbs, however, from purchasing the apartment for his mother.

15. Row houses, on the other hand, play a significant role in season 4, as they become the location for Marlo Stanfield's soldiers, Snoop and Chris, to deposit the bodies of rival dealers. In effect, they not only signal decay and abandonment, they enable it.

16. During the first season the investigation is dedicated to identifying Avon Barksdale, whose appearance is a mystery to police.

17. Marsha Kinder argues that Stringer's faith in business is his ultimate failure: "Despite Stringer's intelligence and driving ambition, he is still too naïve to understand the power dynamics that drive the so-called legitimate worlds of business, law, and politics"; "Re-Wiring Baltimore: The Emotive Power of Systemics, Seriality, and the City," *Film Quarterly* 62, no. 2 (winter 2008): 52.

18. David Lerner, "Way Down in the Hole: Baltimore as Location and Representation in *The Wire*," *Quarterly Review of Film and Video* 29, no. 3 (2012): 219.

19. A quick glance at either the *New York Times Sunday Magazine* or its weekend real estate section on any given week provides multiple examples of the floor plans of yet-to-be-realized luxury developments in the city and elsewhere.

20. The majority of season 2, for example, is focused on the efforts of the port workers' unions to secure a future for Baltimore's working waterfront. These efforts fail, and portions of the port reappear in season 5 as an investment property, called New Westport, offered to Marlo Stanfield.

21. This description is taken from one of the opening monologues in the Hughes Brothers' *Menace II Society*. It is used to describe one of the main characters, O-Dog, just as he is about to murder a shop owner over a perceived insult to his mother.

22. David M. Alff, "Yesterday's Tomorrow Today: Baltimore and the Promise of Reform," in *"The Wire": Urban Decay and American Television*, ed. Tiffany Potter and C. W. Marshall (New York: Bloomsbury, 2009), 25.

23. Peter Clanfield, "'We Ain't Got No Yard': Crime, Development, and Urban Environment," in *"The Wire": Urban Decay and American Television*, ed. Tiffany Potter and C. W. Marshall (New York: Bloomsbury, 2009), 40.

24. Wojcik, *The Apartment Plot*, 235.

25. The apartment looks over the city's Inner Harbor area, a section of Baltimore's waterfront district that was redeveloped in the 1970s and '80s as an effort by the city to reinvent the former sites of abandoned and rotting warehouses and piers.

26. While tensions between the partners had been growing all season, and were caused by a variety of factors, it seems fitting that Stringer divulged the location of Avon's alternate apartment to the police. In using the space, Avon rejected all that Stringer had built. Likewise, Stringer will be murdered in one of B&B's apartments, based on a tip of Avon's regarding his partner's whereabouts.

27. Williams, *On "The Wire,"* 95.

28. Williams, *On "The Wire,"* 97.

29. Clanfield, "'We Ain't Got No Yard,'" 44.

30. Williams, *On "The Wire,"* 101.

31. Robert Warshow, "The Gangster as Tragic Hero," in *The Gangster Film Reader*, ed. Alain Silver and James Ursini (New York: Limelight, 2007), 15.

32. Warshow, "The Gangster as Tragic Hero," 15.

33. Wojcik, *The Apartment Plot*, 227.

34. Williams, *On "The Wire,"* 174. Williams here is specifically engaging with George Lipsitz's interpretation/criticism of *The Wire*, which appeared in *How Racism Takes Place* (Philadelphia: Temple University Press, 2011).

BIBLIOGRAPHY

Agnew, Vanessa. "Introduction: What Is Reenactment?" *Criticism* 46, no. 3 (2004): 327–39.

Akerman, Chantal. Interview. Supplementary material. *Jeanne Dielman, 23 Quai du Commerce, 1080 Bruxelles.* Criterion, 2009. DVD.

Albrecht, Donald. *Designing Dreams: Modern Architecture in the Movies.* New York: Harper and Row, 1986.

Alff, David M. "Yesterday's Tomorrow Today: Baltimore and the Promise of Reform." In *"The Wire": Urban Decay and American Television,* edited by Tiffany Potter and C. W. Marshall, 23–36. New York: Bloomsbury, 2009.

Alpern, Andrew. *Luxury Apartment Houses of Manhattan: An Illustrated History.* New York: Dover, 1993.

Alpern, Andrew. *The New York Apartments of Rosario Candela and James Carpenter.* New York: Acanthus, 2002.

Altman, Rick. *The American Film Musical.* Bloomington: Indiana University Press, 1987.

Babington, Bruce, and Peter William Evans. *Affairs to Remember: The Hollywood Comedy of the Sexes.* Manchester: Manchester University Press, 1989.

Bansak, Edmund G. *Fearing the Dark: The Val Lewton Career.* Jefferson, NC: McFarland, 1995.

Benjamin, Walter. *The Arcades Project.* Translated by Howard Eiland and Kevin McLaughlin. Cambridge, MA: Harvard University Press, 1999.

Bergstrom, Janet. "*Jeanne Dielman, 23 Quai du Commerce, 1080 Bruxelles* by Chantal Akerman." *Camera Obscura* 1, no. 2 (1977): 114–23.

Blumstein, Philip, and Pepper Schwartz. *American Couples: Money, Work, Sex.* New York: William Morrow, 1983.

Bowlby, John. *Attachment and Loss,* vol. 1: *Attachment.* New York: Basic Books, 1969.

Bowlby, John. *Attachment and Loss,* vol. 2: *Separation, Anxiety and Anger.* New York: Basic Books, 1973.

Bowlby, John. *Attachment and Loss,* vol. 3: *Loss, Sadness and Depression.* New York: Basic Books, 1980.

Bristow, Gwen, and Bruce Manning. *The Invisible Host.* New York: Mystery League, 1930.

Brookes, Ian. "The Eye of Power: Postwar Fordism and the Panoptic Corporation in *The Apartment*." *Journal of Popular Film and Television* 37, no. 4 (November 2009): 150–60.

Brooks, Jodi. "*The Kids Are All Right*, the Pursuits of Happiness, and the Spaces Between." *Camera Obscura* 29, no. 1, 85 (2014): 111–35.

Brunick, Paul. "Reach Out and Touch Someone." *Film Comment* 47, no. 3 (2011): 63.

Bruno, Giuliana. *Atlas of Emotion: Journeys in Art, Architecture, and Film*. New York: Verso, 2002.

"Bull Market Architecture." *New Republic*, July 8, 1931, 192.

Canby, Vincent. "Jeanne Dielman." *New York Times*, March 23, 1983.

Carroll, Noël. *The Philosophy of Horror: Or, Paradoxes of the Heart*. New York: Routledge, 1990.

Casey, Edward S. *Getting Back into Place: Toward a Renewed Understanding of the Place-World*. Bloomington: Indiana University Press, 1993.

"Castles in the Air." *New Yorker*, June 4, 1927, 37.

Cavell, Stanley. *Pursuits of Happiness: The Hollywood Comedy of Remarriage*. Cambridge, MA: Harvard University Press, 1981.

Chase, Arthur M. *The Party at the Penthouse*. New York: Dodd, Mead, 1932.

Chudacoff, Howard P. *The Age of the Bachelor: Creating an American Subculture*. Princeton, NJ: Princeton University Press, 1999.

Citron, Michelle, Julia Lesage, Judith Mayne, B. Ruby Rich, and Anna Marie Taylor. "Women and Film: A Discussion of Feminist Aesthetics." *New German Critique* 13 (winter 1978): 82–107.

Clanfield, Peter. "'We Ain't Got No Yard': Crime, Development, and Urban Environment." In *"The Wire": Urban Decay and American Television*, edited by Tiffany Potter and C. W. Marshall, 37–49. New York: Bloomsbury, 2009.

Clare, Stephanie Deborah. "(Homo)Normativity's Romance: Happiness and Indigestion in Andrew Haigh's *Weekend*." *Continuum: Journal of Media and Cultural Studies* 27, no. 6 (2013): 785–98.

Clover, Carol J. *Men, Women, and Chain Saws: Gender in the Modern Horror Film*. Princeton, NJ: Princeton University Press, 1992.

Cohan, Steven. *Masked Men: Masculinity and the Movies in the Fifties*. Bloomington: Indiana University Press, 1997.

Corbin, Amy Lynn. *Cinematic Geographies and Multicultural Spectatorship in America*. New York: Palgrave Macmillan, 2015.

"Costly Club Raided as Gambling Place." *New York Times*, January 22, 1932, 10.

Curtis, Barry. *Dark Places: The Haunted House in Film*. London: Reaktion, 2008.

Davenport, Marcia. "New Apartments." *New Yorker*, August 11, 1928, 60.

DeAngelis, Michael. "Introduction." In *Reading the Bromance: Homosocial Relationships in Film and Television*, edited by Michael DeAngelis, 1–26. Detroit: Wayne State University Press, 2014.

DeAngelis, Michael. "Mispronouncing 'Man and Wife': The Fate of Marriage in Hollywood's Sexual Revolution." In *Hetero: Queering Representations of Straightness*, edited by Sean Griffin, 129–49. Albany: SUNY Press, 2009.

de Certeau, Michel. *The Practice of Everyday Life*. Translated by Steven F. Rendall. Berkeley: University of California Press, 2011.

de Lauretis, Teresa. *Technologies of Gender: Essays on Theory, Film, and Fiction*. Bloomington: Indiana University Press, 1987.

De Wolfe, Elsie. *The House in Good Taste*. New York: Century, 1913.

Dimendberg, Edward. *Film Noir and the Spaces of Modernity*. Cambridge, MA: Harvard University Press, 2004.

Doane, Mary Ann. "Women's Stake: Filming the Female Body." *October* 17 (summer 1981): 22–36.

Elsaesser, Thomas. *Fassbinder's Germany: History, Identity, Subject*. Amsterdam: Amsterdam University Press, 1996.

Felski, Rita. "The Invention of Everyday Life." *New Formations* 39 (1999–2000): 13–31.

Ferriss, Hugh. *The Metropolis of Tomorrow*. New York: Ives Washburn, 1929.

Feuer, Jane. *The Hollywood Musical*, 2nd ed. Bloomington: Indiana University Press, 1993.

Feuer, Jane. "The Self-Reflective Musical and the Myth of Entertainment." In *Genre: The Musical*, edited by Rick Altman, 159–74. New York: Routledge and Kegan Paul, 1981.

Fischer, Lucy. "Beauty and the Beast: Desire and Its Double in *Repulsion*." In *Cinema of Roman Polanski: Dark Spaces of the World*, edited by John Orr and Elżbieta Ostrowska, 76–91. London: Wallflower, 2006.

Fowler, Catherine. "*Jeanne Dielman 23 Quai du Commerce 1080 Bruxelles / Jeanne Dielman*." In *The Cinema of the Low Countries*, edited by Ernest Mathijs, 131–40. London: Wallflower, 2004.

Fraterrigo, Elizabeth. *Playboy and the Making of the Good Life in Modern America*. New York: Oxford University Press, 2008.

Freud, Sigmund. *The Uncanny*. Translated by David McLintock. London: Penguin, 2003.

Frey, Sami. "Autour de *Jeanne Dielman*." Supplementary material. *Jeanne Dielman, 23 Quai du Commerce, 1080 Bruxelles*. Criterion, 2009. DVD.

Garber, Marjorie. *Sex and Real Estate: Why We Love Houses*. New York: Pantheon, 2000.

"Gardens and Roof-Gardens in the Heart of New York." *Vogue*, July 15, 1926, 55.

Gilbert, Sandra M., and Susan Gubar. *The Madwoman in the Attic: The Woman Writer and the Nineteenth-Century Literary Imagination*. New Haven, CT: Yale University Press, 1979.

Gnam, Hugo, Jr. "Penthouse Acres." *Arts and Decoration* 47 (September 1937): 16–18, 47.

Hawes, Elizabeth. *How the Apartment House Transformed the Life of the City, 1869–1930*. New York: Alfred A. Knopf, 1993.

Hein, Carola. *The Capital of Europe: Architecture and Urban Planning for the European Union*. Westport, CT: Praeger, 2004.

Heller, Dana. "Wrecked: Programming Celesbian Reality." In *Reality Gendervision: Sexuality and Gender on Transatlantic Reality Television*, edited by Brenda R. Weber, 123–46. Durham, NC: Duke University Press, 2014.

Herzog, Amy. *Dreams of Difference, Songs of the Same: The Musical Moment in Film*. Minneapolis: University of Minnesota Press, 2010.

Highmore, Ben. *Everyday Life and Cultural Theory: An Introduction*. London: Routledge, 2002.

Hills, Matt. "An Event-Based Definition of Art-Horror." In *Dark Thoughts: Philosophic Reflections on Cinematic Horror*, edited by Steven Jay Schneider and Daniel Shaw, 138–56. Lanham, MD: Scarecrow, 2003.

Hughes, William, David Punter, and Andrew Smith, eds. *The Encyclopedia of the Gothic*. Oxford: Wiley-Blackwell, 2013.

Jacobs, Jane. *The Death and Life of Great American Cities*. New York: Random House, 1961.

Jacobs, Lea. *The Wages of Sin: Censorship and the Fallen Woman Film*. Madison: University of Wisconsin Press, 1991.

Jagose, Annamarie. *Orgasmology*. Durham, NC: Duke University Press, 2013.

Jagose, Annamarie. "Thinkiest." *PMLA* 125, no. 2 (2010): 378–81.

Johnston, Claire. "Towards a Feminist Film Practice: Some Theses." In *Movies and Methods*, vol. 2, edited by Bill Nichols, 315–26. Berkeley: University of California Press, 1985.

Kennedy, Liam, and Stephen Shapiro. "Tales of the Neoliberal City: *The Wire*'s Boundary Lines." In *The Wire: Race, Class, and Genre*, edited by Liam Kennedy and Stephen Shapiro, 147–69. Ann Arbor: University of Michigan Press, 2012.

Kinder, Marsha. "Reflections on *Jeanne Dielman*." *Film Quarterly* 30, no. 4 (summer 1977): 2–8.

Kinder, Marsha. "Re-wiring Baltimore: The Emotive Power of Systemics, Seriality, and the City." *Film Quarterly* 62, no. 2 (winter 2008): 50–57.

Kipnis, Laura. "Adultery." *Critical Inquiry* 24, no. 2 (winter 1998): 289–327.

Klein, Amanda Ann. *American Film Cycles: Reframing Genres, Screening Social Problems, and Defining Subcultures*. Austin: University of Texas Press, 2011.

Klein, Amanda Ann. "'The Dickensian Aspect': Melodrama, Viewer Engagement, and the Socially Conscious Text." In *"The Wire": Urban Decay and American Television*, edited by Tiffany Potter and C. W. Marshall, 177–89. New York: Bloomsbury, 2009.

Klevan, Andrew. *Disclosure of the Everyday: Undramatic Achievement in Narrative Film*. Trowbridge, U.K.: Flicks, 2000.

Kuhn, Annette. *Women's Pictures: Feminism and Cinema*. London: Routledge and Kegan Paul, 1982.

Lagrou, Evert. "Brussels: Five Capitals in Search of a Place—the Citizens, the Planners and the Functions." *GeoJournal* 51, no. 1/2 (2000): 99–112.

Laine, Tarja. "Imprisoned in Disgust: Roman Polanski's *Repulsion*." *Film-Philosophy* 15, no. 2 (2011): 36–50.

Lakeland, Mary Jo. "The Color of *Jeanne Dielman*." *Camera Obscura* 3–4 (1979): 216–18.

Lasner, Matthew Gordon. *High Life: Condo Living in the Suburban Century*. New Haven, CT: Yale University Press, 2012.

Lefebvre, Henri. *The Production of Space*. Translated by Donald Nicholson-Smith. Oxford: Blackwell, 1991.

Lefebvre, Henri. "The Right to the City." In *Writings on Cities*, translated and edited by Eleonore Kofman and Elizabeth Lebas, 63–181. 1968. Oxford: Blackwell, 2003.

Lerner, David. "Way Down in the Hole: Baltimore as Location and Representation in *The Wire*." *Quarterly Review of Film and Video* 29, no. 3 (2012): 213–24.

Lim, Dennis. "*Weekend*: The Space between Two People." Criterion Collection, August 21, 2012. https://www.criterion.com/current/posts/2426-weekend-the-space -between-two-people.

Lipsitz, George. *How Racism Takes Place*. Philadelphia: Temple University Press, 2011.

Loader, Jayne. "*Jeanne Dielman*: Death in Installments." In *Movies and Methods*, vol. 2, edited by Bill Nichols, 327–39. Berkeley: University of California Press, 1985.

Lowenstein, Adam. *Shocking Representation: Historical Trauma, National Cinema, and the Modern Horror Film*. New York: Columbia University Press, 2005.

Mahon, Áine. "Marriage and Moral Perfectionism in Siri Hustvedt and Stanley Cavell." *Textual Practice* 29, no. 4 (2015): 631–51.

Mangolte, Babette. Interview. Supplementary material. *Jeanne Dielman, 23 Quai du Commerce, 1080 Bruxelles*. Criterion, 2009. DVD.

Marchand, Roland. *Advertising the American Dream*. Berkeley: University of California Press, 1985.

Marcus, Sharon. *Apartment Stories: City and Home in Nineteenth-Century Paris and London*. Berkeley: University of California Press, 1999.

Margulies, Ivone. *Nothing Happens: Chantal Akerman's Hyperrealist Everyday*. Durham, NC: Duke University Press, 1996.

Marshall, C. W., and Tiffany Potter. "'I Am the American Dream': Modern Urban Tragedy and the Borders of Fiction." In *"The Wire": Urban Decay and American Television*, edited by Tiffany Potter and C. W. Marshall, 1–14. New York: Bloomsbury, 2009.

Massood, Paula J. *Black City Cinema: African American Urban Experiences in Film*. Philadelphia: Temple University Press, 2001.

Massood, Paula J. *Making a Promised Land: Harlem in Twentieth-Century African American Photography and Film*. New Brunswick, NJ: Rutgers University Press, 2012.

Mayne, Judith. *The Woman at the Keyhole: Feminism and Women's Cinema*. Bloomington: Indiana University Press, 1990.

McGuire, John Thomas. "Exploring the Urban Milieu: Billy Wilder, Four Films, and Two Cities in the United States." *Quarterly Review of Film and Video* 30, no. 5 (2013): 435–48.

McKibbin, Tony. "Polanski and the Horror from Within." In *Cinema of Roman Polanski: Dark Spaces of the World*, edited by John Orr and Elżbieta Ostrowska, 51–61. London: Wallflower, 2006.

McRobbie, Angela. "Passionate Uncertainty." *Sight and Sound* 2, no. 5 (1992): 28–29.

Meares, Holly. "The James Oviatt Building: The Bespoke Brilliance and Pretension behind an Art Deco Masterpiece." KCET, September 6, 2013. https://www.kcet.org /history-society/the-james-oviatt-building-the-bespoke-brilliance-and-pretension -behind-an-art-deco.

Miller, D. A. "On the Universality of *Brokeback Mountain*." *Film Quarterly* 60, no. 3 (2007): 50–60.

Miller, Donald L. *Supreme City: How Jazz Age Manhattan Gave Birth to Modern America*. New York: Simon and Schuster, 2014.

Mulvey, Laura. "Visual Pleasure and Narrative Cinema." In *Movies and Methods*, vol. 2, edited by Bill Nichols, 303–14. Berkeley: University of California Press, 1985.

Mumford, Lewis. "Towers." *American Mercury*, February 1925, 193–96.

Munby, Jonathan. *Public Enemies, Public Heroes: Screening the Gangster Film from "Little Caesar" to "Touch of Evil."* Chicago: University of Chicago Press, 1999.

Naficy, Hamid. *An Accented Cinema: Exilic and Diasporic Filmmaking*. Princeton, NJ: Princeton University Press, 2001.

Neal, Mark Anthony. "'A Man without a Country': The Boundaries of Legibility, Social Capital, and Cosmopolitan Masculinity." *Criticism* 52, no. 3–4 (summer and fall 2010): 399–411.

Nelson, Maggie. *The Argonauts*. Minneapolis: Graywolf, 2015.

"The New York Apartment of Conde Nast, Esq." *Vogue*, August 1, 1928, 44–47.

Orbasli, Aylin. *Tourists in Historic Towns: Urban Conservation and Heritage Management*. London: Taylor and Francis, 2002.

Osgerby, Bill. "The Bachelor Pad as Cultural Icon: Masculinity, Consumption and Interior Design in American Men's Magazines, 1930–65." *Journal of Design History* 18 (spring 2005): 99–112.

Osgerby, Bill. *Playboys in Paradise: Masculinity, Youth and Leisure Style in Modern America*. New York: Berg, 2001.

Otto, Hiltrud, and Heidi Keller, eds. *Different Faces of Attachment: Cultural Variations on a Universal Human Need*. Cambridge: Cambridge University Press, 2014.

Patterson, Patricia, and Manny Farber. "Kitchen without Kitsch." *Film Comment* 13, no. 6 (1977): 47–50.

"Penthouse at London Terrace." *New Yorker*, July 19, 1930, 61.

"Penthouse Gardens to Be Open to Public." *New York Times*, May 14, 1933, N5.

"Penthouse Is Raided as Gambling Club." *New York Times*, January 21, 1932, 2.

"Penthouse Raided as Gaming Resort." *New York Times*, June 2, 1932, 10.

"Penthouse Raided; Liquor Confiscated." *New York Times*, September 14, 1931, 2.

"Penthouses Bloom for Garden Tour." *New York Times*, May 5, 1939, 24.

Perlmutter, Ruth. "Feminine Absence: A Political Aesthetic in Chantal Akerman's *Jeanne Dielman, 23 Quai de Commerce, 1080 Bruxelles*." *Quarterly Review of Film Studies* 4, no. 2 (1979): 125–33.

Pidduck, Julianne. "The Times of *The Hours*: Queer Melodrama and the Dilemma of Marriage." *Camera Obscura* 28, no. 1, 82 (2013): 36–67.

Pope, Virginia. "Now the Penthouse Palace Is Evolving." *New York Times*, March 23, 1930, SM5.

Queen, Ellery. *Penthouse Mystery*. New York: Grosset and Dunlap, 1941.

Rasmussen, Cecilia. "L.A. Then and Now; an Art Deco Jewel with a Glittery History." *Los Angeles Times*, September 10, 2000. http://www.stanthony.ws/archive/oviatt_building_history.pdf.

Relph, Edward. *Place and Placelessness*. London: Pion, 1976.

Rich, B. Ruby. *Chick Flicks: Theories and Memories of the Feminist Film Movement*. Durham, NC: Duke University Press, 1998.

Roberts, Mary Fanton. "A Garden Apartment That Overlooks New York." *Arts and Decoration* 23 (September 1925): 46.

Roche, Arthur Somers. *Penthouse*. New York: Dodd, Mead, 1935.

Rockett, Ben, and Sam Carr. "Animals and Attachment Theory." *Society and Animals* 22 (2014): 415–33.

Rogerson, Ben. "Wilder's Mensch: United Artists and the Critique of Fordism." *Arizona Quarterly* 70, no. 1 (spring 2014): 53–80.

Romanczyk, Katarzyna M. "Transforming Brussels into an International City: Reflections on 'Brusselization.'" *Cities* 29, no. 2 (2012): 126–32.

Rosenbaum, Jonathan. "Edinburgh Encounters: A Consumers/Producers Guide-in-Progress to Four Recent Avant-Garde Films." *Sight and Sound* 45, no. 1 (1976): 18–23.

"Roundup Nets Two in Penthouse Home." *New York Times*, June 13, 1933, 40.

Ruppert, Peter. "Fassbinder, Spectatorship, and Utopian Desire." *Cinema Journal* 28, no. 2 (winter 1989): 28–47.

Ruttenbaum, Steven. *Mansions in the Clouds: The Skyscraper Palazzi of Emery Roth*. New York: Balsam, 1986.

Schama, Simon. *The Embarrassment of Riches: An Interpretation of Dutch Culture in the Golden Age*. New York: Vintage, 1997.

Schechner, Richard. *Between Theater and Anthropology*. Philadelphia: University of Pennsylvania Press, 1985.

Schleier, Merrill. *Skyscraper Cinema: Architecture and Gender in American Film*. Minneapolis: University of Minnesota Press, 2009.

Schleier, Merrill. *The Skyscraper in American Art: 1890–1931*. New York: Da Capo, 1990.

Schmid, Marion. *Chantal Akerman*. Manchester: Manchester University Press, 2010.

Seebohm, Caroline. *The Man Who Was Vogue: The Life and Times of Condé Nast*. New York: Viking, 1982.

Sikov, Ed. *Laughing Hysterically: American Screen Comedy of the 1950s*. New York: Columbia University Press, 1994.

Silverman, Kaja. "Fassbinder and Lacan: A Reconsideration of Gaze, Look, and Image." *Camera Obscura* 7, no. 1 (1989): 57–59.

Silverman, Kaja. *Male Subjectivity at the Margins*. New York: Routledge, 1992.

Slater, Avery. "*Jus Sanguinis, Jus Soli*: West German Citizenship Law and the Melodrama of the Guest Worker in Fassbinder's *Angst Essen Seele Auf*." *Cultural Critique* 86 (winter 2014): 92–118.

Solnit, Rebecca. *Inside Outside*. San Francisco: Artspace, 2006.

Sprackling, Helen. "An Apartment in the Twentieth-Century Manner." *House Beautiful*, November 1930, 484–86.

Talbot, Margaret. "Stealing Life: The Crusader behind *The Wire*." *New Yorker*, October 22, 2007. http://www.newyorker.com/magazine/2007/10/22/stealing-life.

"Three Seized in Raid on Park Ave. Penthouse." *New York Times*, September 3, 1932, 4.

"Trap Policy Gang in Penthouse Raid." *New York Times*, February 20, 1934, 44.

Wagner, George. "The Lair of the Bachelor." In *Architecture and Feminism*, edited by Debra L. Coleman, Elizabeth Ann Danze, and Carol Jane Henderson, 193–220. Princeton, NJ: Princeton Architectural Press, 1996.

Wallace, Lee. *Lesbianism, Cinema, Space: The Sexual Life of Apartments*. London: Routledge, 2009.

Wallace, Lee. "Tom Ford and His Kind." *Criticism: A Quarterly for Literature and the Arts* 56, no. 1 (2014): 21–44.

Walsh, David. "An Interview with Tsai Ming-liang, Director of *The Hole*." World Socialist Web Site, October 7, 1998. https://www.wsws.org/en/articles/1998/10/tsai -007.html.

Warner, Michael. *The Trouble with Normal: Sex, Politics, and the Ethics of Queer Life*. New York: Free Press, 1999.

Warshow, Robert. "The Gangster as Tragic Hero." In *The Gangster Film Reader*, edited by Alain Silver and James Ursini, 11–18. New York: Limelight, 2007.

Weber, Shannon. "Daring to Marry: Marriage Equality Activism after Proposition 8 as Challenge to the Assimilationist/Radical Binary in Queer Studies." *Journal of Homosexuality* 62 (2015): 1147–73.

Weinraub, Judith. "She Looked Good Being Passive, But . . ." *New York Times*, July 31, 1976, 31.

White, R. P. "What! Penthouses Here? First One Was Built Twenty Years Ago to Perpetuate Real Living." *Los Angeles Times*, April 23, 1933.

"Why We Like This Place." Here Comes the Guide. Accessed October 19, 2017. http://www.herecomestheguide.com/southern-california/wedding-venues/oviatt -penthouse.

Wigoder, Meyer. "The 'Solar Eye of Vision': Emergence of the Skyscraper Viewer in the Discourse on Heights in New York City, 1890–1920." *Journal of the Society of Architectural Historians* 61 (June 2002): 152–69.

Williams, Linda. *On "The Wire."* Durham, NC: Duke University Press, 2014.

Wilson, Emma. *Alain Resnais*. Manchester: Manchester University Press, 2006.

Wojcik, Pamela Robertson. *The Apartment Plot: Urban Living in American Film and Popular Culture, 1945 to 1975*. Durham, NC: Duke University Press, 2010.

Wood, Robin. "*The Hole*." *Cineaction* 48 (1998): 54–57.

Wood, Robin. "An Introduction to the American Horror Film." In *Planks of Reason: Essays on the Horror Film*, edited by Barry Keith Grant and Christopher Sharrett, 107–41. Lanham, MD: Scarecrow, 2004.

Wright, Gwendolyn. *Building the American Dream: A Social History of Housing in America*. Cambridge, MA: MIT Press, 1981.

CONTRIBUTORS

STEVEN COHAN is Dean's Distinguished Professor Emeritus, Syracuse University, and past president of the Society for Cinema and Media Studies. His books include *Masked Men: Masculinity and the Movies in the Fifties* (1997), *Incongruous Entertainment: Camp, Cultural Value, and the MGM Musical* (2005), and the forthcoming *Hollywood by Hollywood: The Backstudio Picture and the Mystique of Making Movies*.

MICHAEL DEANGELIS is associate professor of media and cinema studies at DePaul University. He is the author of *Gay Fandom and Crossover Stardom: James Dean, Mel Gibson, and Keanu Reeves* (2001) and *Rx Hollywood: Cinema and Therapy in the 1960s* (2018). He also edited the anthology *Reading the Bromance: Homosocial Relationships in Film and Television* (2014).

VERONICA FITZPATRICK is a writer and PhD candidate in English and film studies at the University of Pittsburgh. Her work has appeared in *cléo: a journal of film and feminism*, *Ploughshares*, *Safundi*, *Thresholds*, *World Picture*, and elsewhere.

ANNAMARIE JAGOSE is the dean of the Faculty of Arts and Social Sciences at the University of Sydney. She is internationally known as a scholar in feminist studies, lesbian/gay studies, and queer theory. She is the author of four monographs, most recently *Orgasmology* (2012), and also an award-winning novelist and short story writer.

PAULA J. MASSOOD is professor of film studies at Brooklyn College, CUNY, and is on the doctoral faculty in the Program in Theatre at the Graduate Center, CUNY. She is the author of *Black City Cinema: African American Urban Experiences in Film* (2003) and *Making a Promised Land: Harlem in Twentieth-Century Photography and Film* (2013), and editor of *The Spike Lee Reader* (2007).

JOE MCELHANEY is professor in the Department of Film and Media Studies at Hunter College and in the Program in Theatre at the Graduate Center, CUNY. His books include *The Death of Classical Cinema: Hitchcock, Lang, Minnelli* (2006); *Vincente Minnelli: The Art of Entertainment* (2006); *Albert Maysles* (2009); and *A Companion to Fritz Lang* (2015). His essays have appeared in numerous collections and journals.

MERRILL SCHLEIER is professor emeritus of art and architectural history and film studies at the University of the Pacific. Her books include *Skyscraper Cinema: Architecture and Gender in American Film* (2009) and *The Skyscraper in American Art, 1890–1931* (1990). She has published numerous book chapters and articles on the relationship of architecture and cinema in such venues as the *Journal of the Society of Architectural Historians, Film Studies, Mosaic, Journal of Architecture, Cinema Journal, Journal of Theory and Criticism*, and *Quarterly Review of Film and Video*. Her recent chapters include "Postwar Hollywood, 1947–1967," in Lucy Fischer, ed., *Art Direction and Production Design* (2015) and "*No Down Payment* (1957): Whiteness, Japanese American Masculinity, and Architectural Space in the Cinematic Suburbs," in Stefano Baschiera and Miriam De Rosa, eds., *Film and Domestic Space* (forthcoming 2018).

LEE WALLACE is an associate professor in gender and cultural studies at the University of Sydney. She is the author of *Sexual Encounters: Pacific Texts, Modern Sexualities* (2003) and *Lesbianism, Cinema, Space: The Sexual Life of Apartments* (2009). The essay that appears here is part of a larger project on gay and lesbian domesticity that was funded by the Australian government through an Australian Research Council Future Fellowship. She is currently completing a book-length manuscript that considers cinematic and theoretical accounts of gay marriage from the perspective of remarriage.

PAMELA ROBERTSON WOJCIK is professor in the Department of Film, TV and Theater at the University of Notre Dame and president of the Society for Cinema and Media Studies. She is author of *Fantasies of Neglect: Imagining the Urban Child* (2016), *The Apartment Plot: Urban Living in American Film and Popular Culture, 1945 to 1975* (2010), and *Guilty Pleasures: Feminist Camp from Mae West to Madonna* (1996). She is series editor of *Screening Spaces* and editor of *New Constellations: Movie Stars of the 1960s* (2011), *Movie Acting: The Film Reader* (2004), and, with Arthur Knight, *Soundtrack Available: Essays on Film and Popular Music* (2001).

INDEX